Celebrity Sells

Hamish Pringle

John Wiley & Sons, Ltd

Other Wiley Editorial Offices

John Wiley & Sons Inc., 111 River Street, Hoboken, NJ 07030, USA

Jossey-Bass, 989 Market Street, San Francisco, CA 94103-1741, USA

Wiley-VCH Verlag GmbH, Boschstr. 12, D-69469 Weinheim, Germany

John Wiley & Sons Australia Ltd, 33 Park Road, Milton, Queensland 4064, Australia

John Wiley & Sons (Asia) Pte Ltd, 2 Clementi Loop #02-01, Jin Xing Distripark, Singapore 129809

John Wiley & Sons Canada Ltd, 22 Worcester Road, Etobicoke, Ontario, Canada M9W 1L1

Wiley also publishes its books in a variety of electronic formats. Some content that appears in print may not be available in electronic books.

Library of Congress Cataloging-in-Publication Data

Pringle, Hamish.
  Celebrity sells / by Hamish Pringle.
     p. cm.
Includes bibliographical references and index.
  ISBN 0-470-86850-3 (Paper : alk. paper)
  1. Brand name products--Marketing. 2. Celebrities. 3.
Selling--Psychological aspects. I. Title.
HD69.B7 .P75 2004
659.13--dc22
                            2003023256

British Library Cataloguing in Publication Data

A catalogue record for this book is available from the British Library

ISBN 0-470-86850-3

Typeset in 11/14pt Goudy by Laserwords Private Limited, Chennai, India

This book is printed on acid-free paper responsibly manufactured from sustainable forestry in which at least two trees are planted for each one used for paper production.

'With celebrity seemingly the new religion, Hamish explains how to harness the zeal of the worshippers in pursuit of the brand.'

Lorna Tilbian – Media Analyst at Numis Securities

'Celebrity is a phenomenon of the new age. I am not certain I like it, but I am sure like everyone else in both society and this industry I need to understand it and deal with it. Hamish Pringle offers a rare insight into the new power of celebrity and how we can engage with it.'

Clive Jones – Director, ITV Plc

'When advertising a brand, using a celebrity is easy, getting it right is not. Hamish Pringle's book is an essential road map, which shows you how to avoid the potential landmines, while capitalizing on the (usually) sizable investment, with its corresponding risks.'

Rupert Brendon – President and CEO of Institute of Communications & Advertising, Canada

'*Vogue* has always photographed famous people because it understands the interest its readers have in the notion of being famous and being beautiful. Top photographers of the day, whether it is Cecil Beaton or Lord Snowdon or Mario Testino, enhance the appeal of the portrait and add to the celebrity status of the photograph. *Celebrity Sells* is a timely book on this fascinating subject.'

Stephen Quinn – Publishing Director of Vogue

'Had a celebrity endorsed this fascinating book, it probably would have been more effective. However, you've just got me.'

John Hegarty – Creative Director of Bartle Bogle Hegarty Ltd

'A must read not only for anybody fascinated by the way in which the worlds of commercialism and the celebrity feed off each other, but any agency account person anxious to avoid the pratfalls when signing up a star name.'

John Tylee – Associate Editor of Campaign magazine

'As an account director, I once persuaded Sir Robert Mark to say, "I am convinced that the Goodyear Grand Prix S is a major contribution to road safety". Now as Chief Executive of the Marketing Society I am convinced that Hamish Pringle's *Celebrity Sells* will be a major contribution to any advertiser's understanding of this topic.'

Hugh Burkitt – Chief Executive of The Marketing Society

'Lineker seemed like a good idea at the time – Hamish tells us why.'

John Webster – Executive Creative Director of BMP DDB

'All marketers want their brands to be famous. Hamish Pringle reveals how some brands have achieved instant fame through a link with the already famous. His book is an entertaining read and shows how celebrity endorsement can be incredibly effective – when the fit is right.'

Lesley Brydon – Executive Director of the Advertising Federation of Australia

'Clearly the use of celebrities in marketing is an important area for attention because so much of it goes on. So there is a real need for a book like this that explores the phenomenon. It is not quite as simple as it looks. It would be a mistake to assume that the use of celebrities is a false use of value. There are many layers of advertising value from attention through to retention, from general aura to specific properties, etc. This book explores in a thorough way this important and growing area.'

Edward de Bono – author of WHY SO STUPID?: How the Human Race has Never Really Learned to Think *(available from Blackhall Publishers, Blackrock, Dublin, Ireland)*

' "Celebrity is as celebrity does" as J K Rowling's Professor Lockhart is on record as declaring. And look what happened to him. In another lively critique of conventional wisdom in marketing, the IPA's Hamish Pringle provides a one-stop shop for those considering celebrities to promote their brands and demonstrates where the best practice – and the worst – is to be found.'

Dr Jonathan Reynolds – Director, Oxford Institute of Retail Management. Fellow of Templeton College & Lecturer in Management Studies, Saïd Business School University of Oxford

'Celebrity is good for you! In business, politics or simply to reinforce your ego – I look, I act and I feel like somebody famous – celebrity has the most dramatic influence on modern life. Why? Hamish Pringle makes a remarkable in-depth analysis of this new and fascinating subject, which is all but superficial; a wonderful book pre-destined to its own celebrity!'

Stéphane Garelli – Professor at the University of Lausanne and Professor at IMD Business School, Lausanne, Switzerland

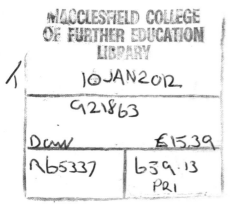

To Sebastian, Benedict, Tristan and Arabella: all stars in my eyes.

Contents

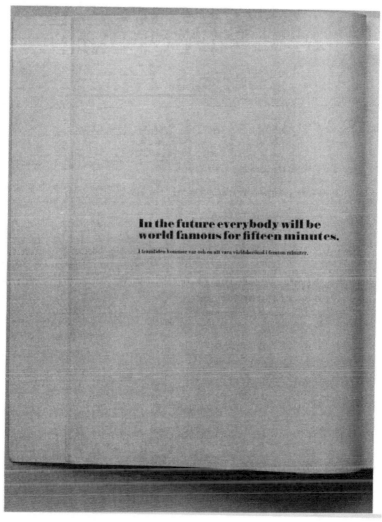

In the future everybody will be world famous for fifteen minutes.

I framtiden kommer var och en att vara världsberömd i femton minuter.

Source: Moderna Museet, Stockholm

This is a reproduction of the frontispiece of the catalogue for the Andy Warhol exhibition held at the Moderna Museet in Stockholm, Sweden, 10 February–17 March in 1968. Andy Warhol attended the opening with Viva Hoffman and 24,633 people came to see the show. This is the earliest known reference for this most famous quote on fame, which has been misquoted almost ever since! As the media and the phenomenon of celebrity globalize, maybe Warhol was right in his original?

Acknowledgements

First and most importantly, I must acknowledge the contribution that my primary researcher, Wendy Tanner, has made to this book. She has drafted the summary case histories, conducted all the interviews and has worked tirelessly over an intense four-month period providing me with valuable information. Wendy has also marshalled the resources of the three graduates whose work experience turned out to be sourcing images and information. Of these Roz Kyle ended up working on the project for several months and has done a great job. In short, *Celebrity Sells* could not have been produced without Wendy and I am most grateful to her for all her efforts on my behalf and that of the IPA.

This book has been written as a part of my job, so all the royalties will go the IPA. Given the support the organization and its membership has provided this is only right and proper and many of my IPA colleagues and members have given input to the work, either by taking soundings from our members on particular points, contributing ideas themselves or reading sections of the manuscript and giving helpful feedback. Others have provided technical support or helped in liaising with the publisher, endorsers and agencies to ensure the best possible accuracy and, of course, in proof reading. Specifically I must acknowledge John Drakopoulos, Jill Bentley and Tessa Gooding, who read the manuscript, Chris Hackford, Ketta Murphy, Marina Palomba and Roger Ingam who prepared the Appendix, Geoffrey Russell and Otto Stanton.

There has also been a lot of support and help given by key individuals in the agency membership of the IPA. Thanks are due to Bruce Haines and Stephen Woodford who both gave their support to the project as Presidents of the IPA and Tim Broadbent, Chairman of the IPA Value of Advertising Committee, who also read the manuscript. I am especially grateful to one of the industry's leading figures, Jeremy Bullmore, for providing the Foreword. Simon Bolton, Matthew Bull, Paul Costanoura, Judith Frame, Mark Hanrahan, Paul Jackson, Jim Kelly, David Kershaw, Nick Kendall, Nick Lockett, Romilly Martin, Sarah Martin, Scott Paton, Simon Sole, Simon Sherwood, Angela Walker and Antony Young have all been very helpful.

Special thanks must be given to our interviewees, who have given their time and valuable expertise. David Abbott, Bridget Angear, Paul Angus, Chris Cowpe, Malcolm Green, Ted Heath, John Hegarty, Kenny Hill, Alun Howell, Russ Lidstone, Frances Royle, Peter Souter, Richard Storey, John Webster and Michael Winner have added fascinating extra dimensions to the specific celebrity campaigns that they talk about. As they talked they brought the creative process to life and so I've chosen to reproduce their contributions in their own words.

And, of course, I must applaud the authors of the prize-winning IPA Effectiveness Awards case histories which have told us so much about how celebrity advertising and marketing communications work and from which the ten summaries featured in the book are drawn. There are so many authors' names that I've acknowledged them at the beginning of each case and the full details on all the published 'celebrity' papers are in the appendix. We owe it to them, and to ourselves, to read their papers in the original, as this is the accumulated 'case law' of our business and we all need to know it.

I've had invaluable input from some key market research companies and they have been most generous in allowing the use of their findings: David Iddiols and Clive Ellis, HPI Dominic Twose, Millward Brown; Jim Law, mruk Research; Chris Williamson, NTC Research. Having quantitative data of this nature is of great benefit to the industry as it contributes to best practice, increased understanding and professionalism, which enhances the ability of agencies to deliver the return on marcoms investment their client partners require.

Other leading industry figures have given me the benefit of their expertise and these include: Alan Cluer, Jackie Cooper, Niall Fitzgerald, Martin Glenn, Ron Mowlam and Keith Weed, plus John Tylee and Peter Wallis who both read the manuscript. Many people in marketing, media or other organizations have provided images and advice and they are: Ben Crawley, Dominic Good, Anthony Greaves, Francis Halewood, Beverley Hall, John Horner, Barry Howells, Giles Keeble, Martin Loat, Greg Marsh, Valerie Moar, Zoe Potter, Stephen Quinn, Richard Tidmarsh, Margaret Rose and Sarah Vidler. Matthew Coombs of WARC.com and Tim Goodfellow of Butterworth-Heinemann, the two other main IPA publishers, have also been most cooperative.

A third of the manuscript was produced while on holiday at Cap Negre in the Lavandou, in the south of France. By a wonderful coincidence we took a house belonging to Pat Icke, whose late husband Norman was a creative director at Leo Burnett for many years, so it is a small world! Vivienne, our children and a changing cast of house guests were very tolerant of my stints at the laptop and of the sound of me dictating using my Dragon voice-recognition software. I must also mention the management of 'Le Club de Cavaliere' and thank them for use of their internet connection when my own developed a fault. Finally, I must thank Claire Plimmer, my editor at Wiley, for her immediate commitment to the idea of the book and for seeing it through to fruition.

Foreword

Personally, I blame Publius Syrus. Two thousand and forty-four years ago he said (and I translate): 'You need not hang up the ivy branch over the wine that will sell.'

Rather later, William Shakespeare, always one to make good use of existing sources, wrote 'Good wine needs no bush.' (*As You Like It*.)

And later still (or so it is alleged) Ralph Waldo Emerson (1803–1882) proclaimed: 'If a man write a better book, preach a better sermon, or make a better mouse-trap than his neighbour, tho' he build his house in the woods, the world will make a beaten path to his door.'

The question I intend to put to Publius Syrus when I bump into him in a later life is this: 'After a two-day march, you arrive exhausted in a strange village. How will you find good wine if there is no ivy branch to guide you?'

And the challenge I shall put to Ralph Waldo Emerson is this: 'Go into deep woods. Make a better mousetrap. And wait. I will gladly pay you a golden sovereign for every citizen who, prompted entirely by extra-sensory perception, beats a path to your door.'

Before a product can be bought by anyone, it has first to find a place on a scale of fame. At the very lowest end of this scale is simple awareness. At the highest end of this scale is global celebrity. Today, many brands are more famous than the most famous of people – a fact the young Victoria Beckham acknowledged in her autobiography when she wrote: 'Right from the beginning, I said I want to be more famous than Persil Automatic.'

As a generalization, famous brands have greater value to their consumers than obscure brands. Just as famous actors command higher fees, famous brands find it easier to maintain both distribution and margins. The commercial value of brand celebrity is now enthusiastically recognized.

Like all enthusiasms, however, it can be carried to extremes. It is often said of the media that they like nothing better than to build up the fame of politicians or entertainers through excessive publicity and adulation only to knock them down again at least as energetically. But, in fairness to the media, the first stage of this familiar process seldom takes place without the happy collaboration of the individuals themselves. In essence, they willingly collude in the construction of a reputation for themselves which increasingly exceeds their delivery.

The same danger faces brand owners, who, so converted are they to the value of celebrity, forget that celebrity without intrinsic worth is a fragile and deluding commodity.

To be successful, mousetraps need to be known to exist. All other things being equal, a famous mousetrap will make more money than an obscure mousetrap. But a mousetrap that relies entirely on its celebrity and forgets to make sure that it remains at least as efficient at trapping mice as its competitors is doomed to a decline of fearful and unforgiving velocity.

It will have committed that terminal commercial sin. It will have been caught marketing.

There may be other books about brands and celebrities and their close relationship but I'm not aware of them. Hamish Pringle here charts increasingly important waters.

Jeremy Bullmore
Non-Executive Director, WPP plc

Introduction

Celebrity in advertising defined

If you search on Amazon for books that contain the word 'celebrity' in their title, nearly 500 items come up, but none of them is primarily about the proven effectiveness of the use of celebrities in advertising.

So this book is intended for two main audiences. First, people who are involved in marketing, advertising, media and all sorts of commercial communications who want to understand how best to use celebrities in support of their brands and, second, the general reader who is fascinated by celebrity and wants to gain additional insights into a phenomenon that seems to have no bounds.

Three things in particular spurred me into writing *Celebrity Sells*.

First, the unprecedented publicity that the IPA Effectiveness Awards received in the national press in December 2002, which was almost entirely focused on the Sainsbury's campaign starring Jamie Oliver.

Second, the sense that 'celebrity' is becoming all pervasive with the media dominated by editorial featuring celebrities, fronted by celebrities and about celebrities.

Third, the unavoidable buzz that I get when I see someone famous. A glimpse of Bridget Bardot at Club 55 in St Tropez in 2002 created a frisson of excitement that simply had to be shared with other people.

Writing this book has enabled me to think more deeply about these things and to set a context in which the specific role of celebrity in building and promoting brands can be assessed and some of the outstanding work by the agencies that create these asset-building ideas can be showcased.

So the media are awash with commentary on celebrity and while there is obviously a simple entertainment factor at work, which makes it so pleasurable to read about famous people, it seems likely that this fascination with famous people is also purposeful. Celebrity endorsement acts as a signpost to quality and can significantly enhance the reputation of a brand. In using products which have a celebrity association, consumers get a little bit extra in terms of imagery, aspiration and entertainment and this is often just enough to tip the balance in favour of one brand instead of its competitors on the supermarket shelf or in an internet search engine return.

But I do not think that these relatively straightforward and functional utilities of celebrity are enough of an explanation for this extraordinary phenomenon. One of the most powerful drivers of human behaviour is the desire to reproduce and to reproduce 'successfully'. In pursuing this end I believe that, whether consciously or not, many men and women seek to mate with the most successful, desirable or powerful person they can within their peer group and ideally beyond it. They do this in self-reaffirmation and also to endow their children with the benefits of a gene pool that can take them further up the social and economic ladder.

'Successful' is a highly subjective measure when applied to members of the opposite sex and opinions change as fashions change in what is deemed to be beautiful or desirable in terms of personal appearance, behaviour or chosen lifestyle. If beauty is in the eye of the beholder it is clear that the lens through which we look at the world is heavily conditioned by what is deemed by opinion leaders, and thus eventually the general populace, to be desirable.

Therefore my own belief is that the role celebrities play in people's lives goes beyond a voyeuristic form of entertainment, but actually fulfils an extremely important research and development function for them as individuals and for society at large. People use celebrities as role models and guides. Our informal survey of IPA members revealed that 84% of them had, at some time or other, been told that they resemble someone famous. It seems highly likely that people empathize with particular sorts of celebrities, perhaps ones who do look a bit like them or whom they aspire to resemble. As these celebrities change their hairstyle, their mode of dress, their partners, their houses and have their children, they are in a sense acting out a parallel life to which people can relate, aspire and imitate.

Celebrity as 'personal R&D' also gives an explanation for the inexorable process by which the media build up people and then knock them down. The 'Wheel of Fortune' most certainly turns for celebrities and there are very few which survive in the long run. On the way up the media lionize them, discover everything about them and present it to the public for their scrutiny and approbation. On the way down the same relentless process is at work, but this time all the foibles, weaknesses, indiscretions and even illegal acts are produced on a plate and spotlighted for the same public to devour.

However, while there is some philosophizing, the main purpose of this work is a practical one: to help practitioners when they are developing a celebrity campaign for the brand of which they are the custodians. It's worth saying at the outset that throughout this book the word 'advertising' has the sense that the general public gives it, that is 'anything that has a name on it is advertising'. This consumer definition is from extensive qualitative research conducted in the year 2002 by the Advertising Standards Authority (ASA), the UK advertising self-regulatory body. Its simplicity and directness reminds us that, while the industry sees itself promoting brands in a whole host of different ways, it's all 'advertising' from the customer's point of view.

Within the marcoms industry, practitioners tend to segment these activities into particular niches and refer to the agencies that specialize in them as being in the creative, media, direct marketing, self-promotion, public relations, sponsorship, digital, new media and outdoor sectors, to name just a few. It would be very longwinded to list all these specialisms every time and so the word 'advertising' will be used instead. Occasionally, and for variety, the words 'marcoms', 'marketing communications' or 'commercial communications' are employed instead of 'advertising'. These terms are used interchangeably to signify all the means by which brands are promoted by agencies on behalf of their client companies and, in this book in particular, by using celebrities.

It's also important to be clear at the outset what is meant by 'celebrities' because there are many famously successful brand campaigns, which feature people (real or created), animals, cartoons, animatronics and puppets who start off as anonymous characters, but through media exposure and their likeability become extremely well-known brand ambassadors and even quasi-celebrities in their own right.

The Jolly Green Giant who personifies Green Giant foods, Howard, the staff member who became a singing star in the Halifax campaign, the adorable Labrador puppy in the Andrex commercials and the red telephone on wheels sounding off for Direct Line insurance are all examples of successful brand representatives which have become famous. Indeed, there are a large number of case histories in the IPA Effectiveness Awards Databank that feature these sorts of brand character or icon and demonstrate how powerful they can be in building brands.

But their celebrity is entirely a function of what they do for their particular brand and they have no values beyond those bestowed on them by the advertising and marketing communications in which they feature. With relatively few exceptions these brand characters or icons rarely move on beyond the world of the brand that created them and thus, unlike true celebrities, they do not have a life of their own. Despite the rather exceptional case of Rowan Atkinson's character from the Barclaycard ads reappearing as the star of the *Johnny English* movie, we don't generally see the Dulux dog winning Crufts or Ask Jeeves' butler appearing in period dramas by Merchant Ivory!

Contrariwise a genuine celebrity has a clearly defined personality and reputation: he or she is known to be extremely good at something beyond appearing in advertising and it is their outstanding skill in their chosen field of endeavour which has brought them into the public eye and made them an object of veneration and respect. Even the ersatz stars of reality TV shows who have a talent for 'surviving' or 'It Girls' who are simply famous for being famous can acquire a temporary notoriety which can be harnessed for a brand in a celebrity campaign if the timing is right. Thus for the purposes of this book, a 'celebrity' is anyone who is familiar enough to the people a brand wishes to communicate with to add values to that communication by association with their image and reputation.

As we watch movie stars on the screen or great sportsmen on the pitch we are in awe of them but we also get to know them. We learn about their capabilities and their characters and it is this appreciation of them that leads people to be somewhere on the spectrum of involvement with a particular celebrity, which ranges from 'mildly interested', to 'genuine fan', to 'groupie' and, in extreme cases, to 'stalker'.

In choosing a star to be associated with, the advertiser is attempting to gain instant fame, for some of the glitz and glamour to rub off on their brand and to acquire by association some of the characteristics and values of the celebrity with whom they're partnered.

This book sets out to show how best to do this and is divided into six main parts.

The first of these looks at the impact of celebrities on everyday life. The purpose here is to set out the social context in which brands are operating and to remind the reader, as if it were necessary, how all pervasive the phenomenon of celebrity is nowadays.

The second part looks at the media and marketing environment in which celebrity campaigns appear and discusses how they work in the context of some current theories of branding.

Part III examines how advertisers and their agencies should go about the process of choosing the right celebrity for their brand. It also puts forward some ideas on how people relate to celebrities in advertising and how market research can be used to analyze their effectiveness.

Part IV deals with the many ways in which celebrities can be used to promote brands and is intended to open up the whole range of possibilities that advertisers and their agencies should consider.

Part V is concerned with the practicalities of managing the relationship with celebrities and discusses approaches to negotiation, contracts and costs and also sets out the pitfalls awaiting the unwary agency or advertiser.

Part VI looks at ten examples, drawn from the IPA Effectiveness Awards Databank, on how celebrities have helped build brands. Accompanying these summary cases there are interviews with some of the key people involved in the creation of the campaigns. Among others, leading figures such as David Abbott, John Hegarty and John Webster have given their insights.

The proven results in these papers are truly impressive: for example, between 1995 and 2002, Walkers' market share rose 6% in grocery and 3% in impulse purchase outlets, while that of their competitors' actually declined. Their ROI was £1.70 per £1 spent. The advertising-generated income delivered by the Bob Hoskins campaign for BT was £297 million, representing an ROI of 6:1 over the period. The Jamie Oliver campaign for Sainsbury's added an incremental £1.12 billion in revenue and achieved an ROI of £27.25 for every advertising pound spent.

The final part of the book looks ahead at the future of celebrity and how it might evolve, thus giving brand custodians some new ideas on how to engage with the stars.

PART I

The Impact of Celebrities on Everyday Life

Introduction

The title of this book assumes that everybody naturally believes that celebrities do sell. However, while we are surrounded by personal evidence of the prevalence of celebrities in everyday life, it's worth considering the extent to which we are all influenced by famous people in the way that we live our lives. Celebrity is so all pervasive nowadays but we probably don't pause to give it much thought and perhaps we only really think that celebrities sell in the most overt sense of when they are promoting a brand.

There are also some who believe that there should be legislation preventing the use of celebrities in advertising or marketing communications as endorsers of companies, products or services. To do this would be a significant infringement of the commercial freedom of speech, but, more importantly, it would challenge the very concept of celebrity in society. As we shall see this would be impossible without an absolutely fundamental change to human nature, the way we think and behave and indeed the way society evolves. It might also cause one or two problems with our governmental process, because, after all, politicians are celebrities too!

So this opening section of the book looks at the many and various ways in which celebrity affects us, starting with a fairly broad-ranging review of how the media, including movies, TV, newspapers, radio and magazines, feed off the cult of celebrity and no doubt reinforce it in the process. Then, in a sequence which becomes progressively more personal, we will see how celebrities influence how we look, how we dress, where we live and, ultimately, our body shape.

1

Celebrity's impact on the media

As we shall see, celebrity impacts on so many aspects of everyday life it's hardly surprising that it has the same sort of effect on the media. Hollywood and the movie industry is based entirely on the creation of stars and the leading icons of the silver screen have had a very significant influence on generations of cinemagoers. Hollywood is a market in celebrities that represents the pinnacle of a global phenomenon. In an inexorable process the public votes with its wallet for actors and actresses whom they favour and as they climb over each other in the popularity stakes some of them eventually arrive as contemporary gods at the top of the fame mountain.

Public fascination with celebrities has a long history, however the increased opportunities to glimpse into their private lives via intrusive media, means that people can get ever closer to their idols and spend considerable sums of money doing so. If celebrity were not so important to millions of people in human society then it would be absolutely impossible for stars to enlist the legions of fans who follow them and thus to command the fees they do. No doubt the film studios, the talent scouts, the agents and the journalists who make, break and feed off celebrities have a part to play, but in the end there is a deep need in human society to generate these iconic figures, worship them and then very often pull them back down to earth.

Market research can help establish the value of celebrities. 'Q Scores' have been established in the USA for over 40 years and these are a product of a Long Island USA research company called Marketing Evaluations. Q Scores are drawn from their consumer panel measuring the familiarity and appeal of performers, characters, sports and sports personalities, broadcast and cable programmes, as well as company and brand names. The data

Figure 1 *Celeb 'Celebdaq'.*
Source: Private Eye/Ligger.
© Pressdram Limited 2002. Reproduced by permission.

analysis summarizes the various perceptions and feelings that consumers have, into a single, 'likeability' measurement. Tom Hanks has topped their chart as the most likeable actor since 1995 and his Q Score has consistently been at least double the score for the average actor.

There are also many lists that attempt to establish the monetary value of movie stars, and there's even the 'Celebdaq' online index that enables players to buy and sell shares in stars on a virtual stock exchange (Figure 1).

But perhaps the clearest indication is what they get paid per picture nowadays. No doubt each of these celebrities also has accumulated wealth, but in a sense that isn't a measure of their current market value derived from their popularity today.

These rankings are a snapshot in time and represent the hierarchy of fame that to a large degree orientates a significant section of global society, who take their social, behavioural and presentational lead from these Hollywood stars. These movie celebrities represent the pinnacle of the social Darwinist peak, but they are being challenged increasingly by the stars that television and other media generate.

Forbes Magazine ranks celebrities in terms of their earnings over the past 12 months and while movie people do still make up nine places in the list, the rest are taken by stars from the worlds of TV, music and sport. Top of the Forbes Global Celebrity 100 is Jennifer Aniston, the 'Friends' star who reportedly earned £21 million in 2002, including £600,000 per episode of the hit comedy show. Part of Aniston's appeal in her role as 'Rachel' in 'Friends', which has made her a megastar, is her distinctive hairstyle and no doubt this is why L'Oréal has struck a sponsorship deal with her to endorse their hair products. It seems that many major advertisers want to get close to the 'Friends' effect and it's forecast that the demand for airtime in the final episode scheduled for May 2004 will force the price up to $2 million per 30-second spot or roughly £66,000 a second!

Forbes Global Celebrity 100

1 Jennifer Aniston
2 Eminem and Dr Dre
3 Tiger Woods
4 Steven Spielberg
5 Jennifer Lopez
6 Sir Paul McCartney
7 Ben Affleck
8 Oprah Winfrey
9 Tom Hanks
10 The Rolling Stones
11 Will Smith
12 The Osbournes
13 Michael Jordan
14 Mike Myers
15 JK Rowling
16 Nicole Kidman
17 George Lucas
18 Eddie Murphy
19 Michael Schumacher
20 Jim Carrey

Source: Forbes Magazine.
Reprinted by permission of Forbes Magazine © 2003 Forbes inc.

The *Hollywood Reporter* at the end of 2002 also gave top ten rankings for male and female stars, with, perhaps unsurprisingly, Tom Hanks and Tom Cruise as equal first. The top ten female rankings see the likes of Sandra Bullock overtaking long-time actresses Meg Ryan and Jodie Foster but it is Julia Roberts who takes the top spot.

Over the last decade we have moved into a new era in which the voracious appetite of the consuming public for all things celebrity has generated entire segments of the magazine market, transformed the contents of the broadsheet newspapers and given birth to a whole new genre of TV programme. Soap operas have always been generators of huge numbers of celebrities on both sides of the Atlantic, in Europe and indeed around the world. The day-to-day sagas that reflect, albeit in a slightly heightened fashion, everyday life, have been hugely successful. In the UK 'Coronation Street', whose first episode appeared in December 1960, is still one of the most watched programmes in the country and younger pretender 'EastEnders' born in 1985, commands an audience just as big and has recently been extended to four new episodes per week, plus a fifth weekend 'omnibus' edition.

The phenomenon of reality TV, which makes celebrities out of ordinary people and also gives faded celebrities the opportunity to redeem themselves, is a global one. John de Mol one of the former owners of Endemol and creator of the 'Big Brother' format has already amassed a fortune estimated at $1 billion. 'Big Brother' has now become a programme seen in 30 countries around the world and has spawned a host of imitators. It's also a show which has created some of the highest ever levels of audience participation through its voting dimension and on average 2 million people vote for the expulsion of a house member using either an SMS text message, email, or a telephone call. 'Big Brother' has also created big business for other media. Tabloid newspapers such as the *Sun*, which have picked up strongly on the programme and championed particular inhabitants of the house, have seen very significant sales impacts. Jade Goody has also done extremely well for *Heat* magazine. Their cover featuring a Jade makeover in August 2002 was their best selling of all time, achieving sales of 655,000 compared to the previous year's average of 554,000. Because of the relentless exposure that participants in the Big Brother house receive, the audience feels they get to know them with a degree of intimacy which may well exceed that which they share with their own partners and friends and thus they have a very keen desire to follow their fortunes, their highs and their lows. In addition, because these instant celebrities are in fact 'someone just like me' they can live out social scenarios, ways of being and ways of talking, vicariously through another person and without risk. Hence the appeal of the makeover story about Jade Goody (Figure 2).

'Pop Idol' in the UK is another 'everyday celebrity' show that has created huge audiences and competitors such as 'Pop Stars' and 'Fame Academy'. In the USA the final of 'American Idol' generated record ratings of 23 million viewers for Fox, the US broadcaster, which was their biggest audience for a non-sports programme in over ten years. Six months later even that record was trounced by the 40 million viewers who tuned into the final of Fox TV's reality show 'Joe Millionaire' to see Evan Marriott, a construction worker pretending to be the heir to a fortune, pick the winner from 20 women who had travelled to a French chateau to win his heart. In the context of the Academy Awards ceremony on ABC the previous year achieving a viewership of 41.8 million, this is an astonishing achievement and confirmation of the degree to which 'everyday celebrity' has pervaded society.

The impact of celebrity can also be seen in one-off TV documentaries as well as in programme series and in a way these individual shows, which

Figure 2 *Cover of* Heat *magazine.*
Source: Heat magazine.
Reproduced by permission of EMAP PLC.

have to build an audience for one night only, demonstrate the power and fascination of famous people for the public even more strongly. In November 1995 Martin Bashir's notorious confessional interview with Diana, Princess of Wales was watched by more than 21 million viewers. Eight years later on Monday 3 February 2003 Bashir's extraordinary documentary about Michael Jackson gripped 14 million UK viewers, with 1.7 million viewers recording the programme to watch it later on. This represents an audience share of

54% and means that the Jackson documentary is likely to be among the most watched programmes of that year. The impact was also huge in the USA with 27 million people watching the documentary on ABC.

The celebrity phenomenon has largely been created by the movies and television, but there is no doubt that other media have played a significant part. Indeed a whole new sector has grown up that promotes and feeds off celebrity culture. Magazines such as *Hello!*, *OK!*, *Heat* and *Now!* sell an enormous number of copies per issue and it's estimated that in 2002 the total sale of celebrity-related magazines approached 100 million in the UK, with sales of the four main celebrity magazines alone selling over 2.5 million per week by the beginning of 2003. Further, even the most highbrow of broadsheet newspapers such as *The Times* or the *Daily Telegraph* are increasingly celebrity driven and it's hard to find an issue that does not feature a 'personality' on its front cover. Not such a long time ago these newspapers would have primarily dealt in newsmakers from the worlds of politics, business or finance. Nowadays they are as likely to feature Sven-Goran Eriksson as Ericsson in their main news item.

All media have become suffused with celebrity. The newsreaders on TV, the magazine editors and the lead journalists have become celebrities too. TV commercials or print advertisements that feature stars and appear in this media environment fit in naturally with it, so it's hardly surprising that up to 20% of all advertising employs celebrities. All the evidence suggests that these campaigns are very effective in promoting the corporate, product and service brands with which they are aligned.

2

Celebrity's impact on hair and makeup

Our media are saturated with celebrity and there's no doubt that entertainment value is an enormous part of the appeal of programming and editorial about famous stars. But there is also a practical benefit in all this. Very large numbers of people use stars as role models and nowhere is this more evident than in the area of personal appearance. Despite the enormous diversity of human beings, how often do we see someone whom we feel strongly resembles someone else we know? Indeed, at the macro level there seem to be a relatively limited number of physical types. In the case of hair colour, for example, L'Oréal's Professionelle Artec Colorist Collection features just 12 specific colours to cover the complete spectrum of women's hair.

Celebrities are aspirational examples and at any given time there will be a star archetype for a particular hair colour, which can offer more ordinary people a useful role model. It's no accident that there is always a position for top Hollywood or TV stars with blonde (Diaz, Stone, Monroe), brunette (Cruz, Berry, Leigh), black (Jolie, Zeta-Jones, Taylor) and auburn (Kidman, Roberts, Rogers) hair as these represent the major groupings in society. And within each of these hair colour types there is the opportunity for segmentation in terms of hair type (straight, wavy, curly etc.) and cut (long, short, natural, styled etc.).

An informal survey conducted via the IPA website revealed that 84% of the respondents had at one time or another been told that they look like a famous person. Figure 3 shows pictures of three of them: perhaps you can guess which celebrities other people had told them they look like. (The answers can be found upside down at the foot of the figure.)

Much of human behaviour, and specifically purchasing, can be attributed to the desire to improve presentation and desirability. When someone identifies with a celebrity from a physical point of view, they may see an

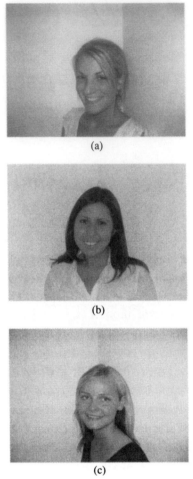

(a)

(b)

(c)

Jenna = Britney Spears; Alex = Minnie Driver; Clare = Cameron Diaz

Figure 3 *(a) Jenna. (b) Alex. (c) Clare.*
Source: IPA.

enhanced fantasy reflection of themselves in the media and imitate the things the star has done to make the most of their appearance in their own case (Figure 4). This is a relentless process with famous people under constant scrutiny as they rise in the bloom of youth and then inevitably succumb to the ageing process. Then their position as an archetype and role model in the pantheon of stars is usurped by a younger model who has stolen their fickle public. From this we can see the way in which the hair, makeup and, indeed, fashion industries operate in relation to the celebrities they constantly generate and which customers support through emulation and the purchasing that this entails (Figure 5).

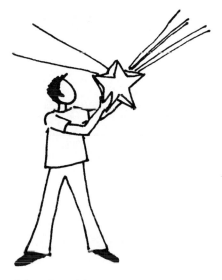

Figure 4 *Our lives refracted through a celebrity's.*

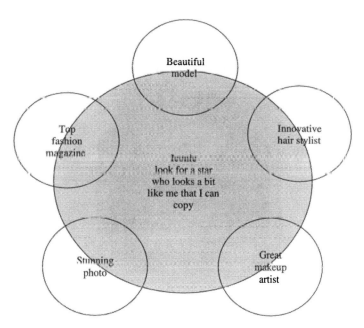

Figure 5 *Model for relationship between beauty and fashion industries and celebrities.*

And of course photography is crucial and has generated celebrities of its own, with the cameramen who helped make the models famous becoming famous themselves. The work of star photographer of celebrities, Mario Testino, who produced iconic photographs of Diana, Princess of Wales,

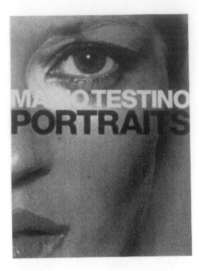

Figure 6 *Testino Exhibition.*
Source: National Portrait Gallery.
Reproduced by permission of Robert-Carr Archer.

Figure 7 Vogue *December 1991 cover of Diana, Princess of Wales.*
Source: Vogue/Conde Nast.
Reproduced by permission of Conde Nast.

was sufficiently well regarded to be celebrated at an exhibition at London's
National Portrait Gallery in 2003 (Figures 6 and 7).

This mass preoccupation with personal appearance has generated enormous industries. The global market for hair care products is estimated to be

worth \$35.2 billion a year, while in Europe it amounts to some €12.72 billion and in the UK alone customers spend £1061 million on making the best of what they have got on top. In addition, the hairdressing and salon business is worth \$3110 million in the USA and £59.4 million in the UK, where in Central London alone there are over 1000 hair salons! These are truly astonishing sums of money and it means that on average each individual in the UK is spending £55 per year on shampoos, conditioners and other hair treatments.

Today there is hardly a hair care or cosmetics company that does not have a celebrity 'face' to represent its brand in the marketplace and the usage of hair products and cosmetics by women continues to grow. For example, according to the Target Group Index (TGI), one of the largest research databases in the UK, based on an annual survey of some 26,000 people, the percentage of UK women using hair styling mousses has risen from 37% in 1987 to 49% in the 2003.

The role of celebrity in the hair care market is very powerful, not only in terms of the stars who set trends but also the hairdressers who create them and become celebrities themselves in the process. Perhaps the first global celebrity hairdresser was Vidal Sassoon (Figure 8), whose top models were Grace Coddington, now an editor at *Vogue*, Jean Shrimpton and Peggy Moffitt. All of these were the basis of a business that was eventually sold to Procter & Gamble as part of its buyout of Richardson-Vicks in 1985.

Another celebrity hairdresser, Leonard, started life with Rose Evanski and then became a Vidal Sassoon stylist. He broke away from the strictures of

Figure 8 *Vidal Sassoon.*
Source: Vidal Sassoon.

Figure 9 *Twiggy.*
Source: John Wiley & Sons.
Reproduced by permission of Barry Lategan.

the Vidal Academy to form his own salon to pursue his more individualistic approach focused more on the particular needs of each client. In 1966 he created the famous geometric cuts for models including Twiggy, photographed by Barry Lategan in the mid-1960s, and he continued to style Twiggy's hair until the mid-1970s (Figure 9).

In turn, John Frieda, a protégé of Leonard, became a star as a result of the sleek blonde bob 'Purdey cut' that he created for Joanna Lumley in 1976 for her role in 'The New Avengers'. Frieda, whose unique Frizz-Ease range is used by Kerry Warn, International Creative Consultant at John Frieda's, to create Nicole Kidman's stunning appearance both at Oscar™ ceremonies and in everyday life, sold his company in September 2002 for $450 million. The company's success is largely based on the John Frieda Frizz-Ease brand launched in 1990 but his Sheer Blond brand is equally successful. Both of

Figure 10 John Frieda.
Source. John Frieda.

these product ranges targeted women with particular hair types and gave them the potential to make the most of themselves (Figure 10).

Today, one of the most successful celebrity hairdressers is Nicky Clarke, who charges £300 for an appointment or £500 for a fast track appointment. He too has a range of hair care products, 'Hairomatherapy', based on a combination of natural ingredients and essential oils launched in 1993 and was bought by Wella, the world's second largest hair care brand in 2001.

One of the many reasons why David Beckham is such a powerful celebrity is that he has experimented most publicly with his hairstyles and has therefore given permission to millions of men to do likewise. He has shown blonde men in particular all sorts of different looks that can enhance their appearance which they might not have previously considered possible for themselves. Beckham's endorsement of Brylcreem has been part of a widespread young

Figure 11 *Dennis Compton Brylcreem advertisement.*
Source: History of Advertising Trust/Brylcreem.

male trend back to the use of gels, waxes and other hair finishes that were last fashionable in the 1950s before long hippy locks came in (Figure 11).

The manner in which people style their hair is full of cultural references and symbolism. When David Beckham changes his hairstyle (and he does it quite frequently) it makes the national press each time. His startling 'Mohican' haircut, reminiscent of a Kings Road punk's, caused a sensation and was widely imitated around the country. Then he resurrected the 'mullet', a style which had become a laughing stock but which he managed to make look good. Then he adopted a girl's 'Alice band' and managed to make that most girlish of accessories work for a male. Continuing his love affair with black music he adopted a braided 'cornrow' style and wore it to his meeting with Nelson Mandela. In between times he has adopted the more traditional boy-next-door centre parting and fringe and a short crop gelled into fashionable spikes. He has even appeared with a razor-cut eyebrow to complement his asymmetrical 'tramline' haircut (Figure 12).

The great thing about all Beckham's innovations is that they are relatively inexpensive and therefore the style is such that ordinary kids around the world can imitate and experiment with it for themselves. In the same way women take their lead in terms of hairstyles from celebrities too and have done for centuries. In a passage from her book *Georgiana, Duchess of Devonshire*, Amanda Foreman describes how her hairstyle was a key factor in creating her celebrity in the 1770s:

> Women's hair was already arranged high above the head, but Georgiana took the fashion a step further by creating the three-foot hair tower. She stuck pads of horse hair to her own hair using scented pomade and decorated the top with miniature ornaments. Sometimes she carried a ship in full sail, or an exotic arrangement of stuffed birds and waxed fruit, or even a pastoral tableau with little wooden trees and sheep. Even though the towers required the help of at least two hairdressers and took several hours to arrange, Georgiana's designs inspired others to imitate her. 'The Duchess of Devonshire is the most envied woman of the day in the Ton,' the newspapers reported. In less than a year Georgiana had become a celebrity. Newspaper editors noticed that any report on the Duchess of Devonshire increased their sales. She brought glamour and style to a paper. A three-ring circus soon developed between newspapers who saw commercial value in her fame, ordinary readers who were fascinated by her, and Georgiana herself, who enjoyed the attention. The more editors printed stories about her, the more she obliged by playing up to them.
>
> (*Georgiana Duchess of Devonshire*, Amanda Foreman, Harper Collins (1998))

Over 200 years later celebrities are still using their hair as one of their most distinctive characteristics and a key aspect of their own 'brand' iconography. Jennifer Aniston of 'Friends' is rated as one of the most powerful stars in the world and her hairstyle has been one of the most imitated globally. It is said that Hillary Clinton's career didn't really take off until she transformed her hair from a dark unkempt student look to the altogether sleeker blond that we know her as now.

Some critics say that the widespread use of cosmetics is something that has been forced on modern women by voracious capitalist consumer goods

Figure 12 GQ cover featuring Beckham with his St George's Cross haircut.
Source: GQ/Conde Nast.
Reproduced by permission of Conde Nast.

companies aided and abetted by their creatures in the media. However, the phenomenon of human beings painting their faces and adorning themselves dates well back into prehistory and pre-media, giving the lie to this simplistic analysis. What is believed to be the first example of lipstick was found in the Sumerian region of Ur, some 200 miles south of Babylon and estimated to be over 5000 years old. A round copper alloy box, measuring 6 cm in diameter by 5 cm in height, buried almost 2000 years ago in Roman London was found in July 2003 and opened to reveal what archaeologists believe is face cream – and the finger marks of the woman who used it (Figure 13).

Guerlin is credited with the introduction of liprouge in a stick form, but the first modern lipstick in a metal case was produced in 1915 by Maurice Levy of the Scovil Manufacturing Company of Waterbury, Connecticut.

One of the criticisms of the advertising industry is that it creates idealized stereotypes that in some way it forces ordinary women to live up to. It is alleged that by doing this advertising makes women dissatisfied with the way they are and leads them to spend an unnecessary amount of money attempting to conform with an impossible image of beauty. Leaving aside for the moment whether or not people have free will and control over their own purses, it's worth looking at a well-documented example of an advertising campaign that deliberately attempted to wean a brand off a long-term diet of celebrity endorsement in favour of relatively unknown models presenting a more 'accessible' notion of beauty.

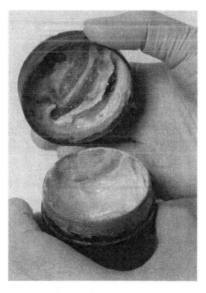

Figure 13 *2000-year-old makeup on display at the Museum of London.*
Source: Museum of London.

In 2000 Revlon Inc. hired a new outside advertising agency, Kirshenbaum Bond & Partners, to modernize its image and parted company with celebrity supermodel Cindy Crawford, its prime 'face' for 11 years. Apparently their market research had revealed that their customers were tired of celebrity and wanted a more normal or everyday version of beauty portrayed in Revlon advertising. Responding to this, KB&P developed a new campaign featuring relatively unknown 'girl-next-door' models and a new slogan 'It's fabulous being a woman'. Some $90 million was allocated to the campaign, a 30% increase on 2000. However, it was not a success. Sales from continuing operations fell 3.1% to $972.6 million in the nine months ended the 30 of September compared with $1 billion in the corresponding year before. Revlon's share of the cosmetics market fell 10.6% in the 52 weeks ended December 2000 to 15.1%, according to Information Resources Inc., a market research company that tracks sales in the sector. Faced with this disastrous foray into 'more ordinary' female imagery Revlon did an abrupt about turn and went straight back to celebrity endorsement using actresses such as Halle Berry, Julianne Moore and James King, star of the cult movie *Blow*. This strategy seems to have paid off. In July 2003, the company published figures showing that market share for Revlon had grown to 17% from 16.4% a year earlier, while overall sales were up 5%.

Nearly all the major cosmetics brands have known for decades what Revlon had to relearn, which is that celebrities sell cosmetics. The list of just some of the famous stars and models who have been enlisted to their causes reads like a mini-who's who:

Elizabeth Arden: Elizabeth Taylor, Catherine Zeta-Jones
Estee Lauder: Elizabeth Hurley, Liya Kebede, Carolyn Murphy
Lancome: Juliette Binoche, Marie Gillain, Elizabeth Jagger, Christiana Reali, Isabella Rossellini, Ines Sastre, Mena Suvari, Uma Thurman
L'Oréal: Jennifer Aniston, Laetitia Casta, Natalie Imbruglia, Milla Jovovich, Natassja Kinski, Beyoncé Knowles, Jennifer Lopez, Andie MacDowell, Sarah Jessica Parker
Maybelline: Sarah Michelle Geller
Max Factor: Marlene Dietrich, Greta Garbo, Madonna
Revlon: Halle Berry, Cindy Crawford, Salma Hayek, Melanie Griffiths, James King, Lucy Liu, Julianne Moore, Claudia Schiffer, Rachel Weisz
Rimmel: Kate Moss

Watching movies and TV shows featuring celebrities, reading about them in magazines and newspapers and logging onto their websites all provide great entertainment for millions of people. But celebrities also fulfil a very valuable function as role models. In a sense, they are a very public form of human research and development, which people can use to make the best of their own appearance. They can follow successful experiments in hair and makeup carried out by some of the most glamorous people in the world, some of whom friends say look just a little bit like them.

3

Celebrity's impact on fashion

For many centuries human beings have lived in cultures where appearance is largely dominated by garments and where our relative attractiveness or perceived status is signified by what we choose or are entitled to wear, by way of rank or wealth.

Tribal leaders, pharaohs, emperors, kings and queens have all been fundamental to setting the clothing fashions of their times, but nowadays the influence of political leaders has waned significantly in this respect. President Kennedy's wife Jackie was the last political figure to have had a major influence on global fashion and her iconic sunglasses, immortalized in photographs and by Andy Warhol, continue to be a fashion look that gets recycled. Diana, Princess of Wales is the only contemporary royal figure to have had any influence on the way people dress in recent times and so it seems that we have turned elsewhere for our inspiration in what to wear.

For the last century it has been increasingly celebrities who have had the most enormous impact in co-creating fashion and thus eventually what most people wear. In April 2003 a list of the top 100 women who 'defined a century' was published by *Harpers & Queen* magazine. With the help of the Getty Images Gallery they put together the associated 'Style Queens of the 20th Century' exhibition. The list contained the following names:

Lady Violet Astor socialite **Lauren Bacall** actress **Anne Bancroft** actress **Tallulah Bankhead** actress **Brigitte Bardot** actress **Ingrid Bergman** actress **Jane Birkin** actress **Jacqueline Bisset** actress **Honor Blackman** actress **Patti Boyd** model **Louise Brooks** actress **Maria Callas** diva **Fiona Campbell-Walter** socialite **Lady Daphne Cameron** socialite **Capucine** actress **Leslie Caron** actress **Betty Carloux** model **Coco Chanel** designer **Cyd Charisse** actress **Claudette Colbert** actress **Joan Collins** actress **Lady Diana Cooper** socialite **Sophie Dahl**

model **Bette Davis** actress **Marion Davies** actress **Dame Judi Dench** actress **Catherine Deneuve** actress **Marlene Dietrich** actress **Dolores Del Rio** actress **Diana, Princess of Wales Dovima** model **Doris Duke** millionairess **Faye Dunaway** actress **Shirley Eaton** actress **Britt Ekland** actress **Marianne Faithfull** singer **Loulou de la Falaise** model **Jane Fonda** actress **Greta Garbo** actress **Ava Gardner** actress **Paulette Goddard** actress **Cee Zee Guest** socialite **Celia Hammond** model **Françoise Hardy** singer **Rita Hayworth** actress **Edith Head** fashion designer **Audrey Hepburn** actress **Katharine Hepburn** actress **Baby Jane Holzer** model **Anjelica Huston** actress **Lauren Hutton** actress **Frida Kahlo** artist **Christine Keeler** socialite **Grace Kelly** actress/princess **Jacqueline Kennedy** former 1st lady **Eartha Kitt** singer **Veronica Lake** actress **Vivien Leigh** actress **Gina Lollobrigida** actress **Sophia Loren** actress **Joanna Lumley** actress **Ida Lupino** actress **Ali MacGraw** actress **Madonna** singer **Jayne Mansfield** actress **Princess Margaret Elsa Martinelli** actress **Daphne du Maurier** writer **Melina Mercouri** actress **Unity, Diana & Nancy Mitford** socialite/fascist leader's wife/writer **Marilyn Monroe** actress **Jeanne Moreau** actress **Tina Onassis** heiress **Barbara 'Babe' Paley** socialite **Anita Pallenberg** actress **Gwyneth Paltrow** actress **Suzy Parker** model **Patsy Pulitzer** socialite **Mary Quant** designer **Lee Radziwill** socialite **Indrani Rahman** beauty queen **Charlotte Rampling** actress **Diana Rigg** actress **Jane Russell** actress **Jean Seberg** actress **Cybill Shepherd** actress **Jean Shrimpton** model **Carly Simon** singer **Kay Spreckles** Mrs Gary Cooper **Barbra Streisand** singer **Elizabeth Taylor** actress **Gene Tierney** actress **Penelope Tree** model **Twiggy** model **Veruschka** model **Diana Vreeland** fashion designer **Anna May Wong** actress **Natalie Wood** actress

The name of each of these women resonates with memories and associations and a feeling that, yes, they did make an impact, they did change for the better what their fans felt about life and, further, that in their behaviours they were positive role models for the looks of a large number of people.

In creating these iconic figures, there is very often a complex interrelationship between the famous designers, supermodels and celebrity customers who feature in the leading glossy magazines such as *Vogue*, which chronicle this extraordinary process.

Through this incestuous mechanism fashion is developed and showcased and it is this hothouse world in which the 'research and development' is carried out for what ultimately arrives on the world's high streets and shopping malls. When we see the photographs from the Paris haute couture shows with impossibly beautiful models wearing clothes that could not exist outside a salon, what we are actually witnessing is creativity at the leading edge of fashion which is exploring new ideas in clothing expressed in an extreme way to make a powerful visual statement. The catwalks are a rarified form of theatre, where the audience adds almost as much cachet to the brand as the designers and supermodels. Indeed, rumour has it that, depending on status, stars are paid from £10,000 up to £60,000 in 'appearance fees' on top of first-class travel and accommodation to take a seat in the front row, get photographed and generate payback in terms of increased media coverage.

A relatively small number of extremely wealthy women do in fact buy modified versions of these clothes, but it is generally accepted that this process is not profitable in itself. Its function is to create an aura of exclusivity around a brand that has great appeal to wealthy people, many of whom are celebrities. However, the real revenues are generated by the sales of ready-to-wear derivations, other related products and in particular by the fragrances that are linked to these fashion houses. Another way in which the haute couture shows act as the engine room of the fashion economy is to create a context in which mass market clothing can be produced which picks up on the fashion leads exemplified by the catwalk, but translated into more usable and wearable items. And, of course, many other fashion retailers feed off the ideas that the great designers produce. The fashion shows in Paris, Milan, New York and London are besieged by buyers and merchandisers from the chain stores who plagiarize the looks and styles that they see and rush them back to base for them to be adapted, pattern cut, sampled and delivered to store as quickly as possible. It is said that the Spanish chain Zara can achieve this in just three weeks on its mile-long production line!

In the 1950s models, while beautiful, were not famous in their own right and were paid to show off the clothes rather than themselves. Jean Shrimpton was perhaps the first UK model to become a true household name in the 1960s and it was the incestuous relationship with photographers, particularly David Bailey, and designers such as Mary Quant which crystallized the Mod look that epitomized the Swinging Sixties. Bailey became such a star in his own right that he was contracted to give celebrity endorsement to Olympus cameras in a long-running series of press ads and TV commercials. These capitalized on his professional photographic credentials while debunking them humorously to make the ordinary snapshot photographer feel more confident in using an Olympus. In several of these TV spots he co-starred with George Cole, cast as the bumbling pro, and there were also cameo appearances by James Hunt and Lord Lichfield (Figure 14).

The advent of the 'supermodels' in the 1980s and 90s created a new phenomenon where the likes of Naomi Campbell, Elle MacPherson and Claudia Schiffer became famous for 'Not getting out of bed for less than

Figure 14 *David Bailey and George Cole.*
Source: David Bailey.

£10,000 a day'. These models were seen wearing the kind of clothes that they modelled on the catwalk in their private lives and were photographed by the paparazzi socializing with rock stars, movie stars, politicians, motor racing drivers and all sorts of other celebrities who themselves were wearing elements of the fashions which these supermodels had helped create. More recently there's been a trend towards using celebrities as models, with actresses such as *Lord of the Rings* star Cate Blanchett working for Donna Karan, chart toppers J Lo and Christina Aguilera appearing for Louis Vuitton and Versace respectively, Missy Elliott and Madonna as a duo for Gap, Victoria Beckham for Rocawear and the emerging Jagger dynasty turning out for H&M in the shape of Mick's daughter Jade and granddaughter Amber.

Although the top two earners in fashion positions in *The Sunday Times* Pay List for 2002 were occupied by the men behind Monsoon and French Connection, seven out of the top ten were fashion models confirming the value to customers of their key role in crystallizing 'looks that I can copy' for women. Today supermodel Erin O'Connor reportedly rules the roost in financial terms (Figure 15), while, in a reflection of the fickle and competitive nature of the fashion business, Naomi Campbell has dropped out of the list. So too have previous incumbents, designers Alexander McQueen and Stella McCartney.

Figure 15 Tatler *September 2003 cover of Erin O'Connor.*
Source: Tatler/Conde Nast.
Reproduced by permission of Conde Nast.

The stars of pop, rock and rap music are great customers of the top fashion labels but in another example of the reciprocal relationship between creator and customer, the top fashion designers plunder street fashion, often closely associated with particular genres of music for their inspiration. The 1960s saw the lead coming from London's Carnaby Street, Kings Road and Portobello Market, where young kids picked up second-hand military uniforms from such shops such as 'I Was Lord Kitchener's Valet' and turned them into another look that came to typify the era. This has been immortalized in the most famous album cover of all time, British pop artist Peter Blake's artwork for 'Sgt Pepper's Lonely Hearts Club Band', featuring the Fab Four in a psychedelic take on military regalia.

In 1969 Mick Jagger, fronting the Rolling Stones, and previously most closely associated with blue jeans and leather jackets, stunned the fans gathered for the now legendary Hyde Park concert by appearing in what many people thought was a girl's dress. In fact, it was a smock belonging to Marianne Faithfull worn over white jeans. This outrageous getup, combined with his theatrical reading of *Adonis*, Shelley's elegy to John Keats, in memory of the departed Brian Jones and the releasing of white cabbage butterflies into the sky launched a whole new kind of dandyfied rock star who fused masculine and feminine in a new androgynous look. The 1970 cult movie *Performance* starring Jagger pushed the idea of bisexuality even further.

Many people would attribute the origins of 1970s' 'Glam Rock' to David Bowie and his 'Aladdin Sane' look and acts ranging from Slade to Sweet to T. Rex and Swedish group Abba, whose use of silvery shiny satiny fabrics, allied to platform boots, created a look that was emulated by many others, with Queen's Freddy Mercury taking it to the heights of theatrical glamour. It spilled over into the high street at the start of the decade and dominated its early years (Figure 16).

In a classic example of action begetting reaction, Malcolm McLaren and Vivienne Westwood single-handedly created the punk rock look with its safety pins, bondage straps and sadomasochistic rips and tears, launching from their legendary shop 'Sex' at the end of London's Kings Road. But without the astonishing impact of the Sex Pistols it is unlikely that this iconic style would have dominated the late 1980s and gone on to be recycled periodically ever since. The early 1980s also saw the emergence of the slogan T-shirt originated by band Frankie Goes to Hollywood with their enormous hit 'Relax' and Katharine Hamnett's 1983 'Choose Life' T-shirt collection, which featured her famous soapbox slogan 'Stop Acid Rain', 'Preserve the Rainforests' and other protest messages.

Hollywood has long had a huge influence on fashion as in so many other areas of life. When Clark Gable appeared with a bare chest in the 1934 film *It Happened One Night* sales of vests fell off dramatically. James Dean in the 1955 movie *Rebel Without a Cause* was one of the earliest exponents of the biker look comprising black leather jacket and jeans often teamed with a white T-shirt. Over the decades a succession of stars has perpetuated it, including Marlon Brando, Bruce Springsteen, George Michael and, of course, Elvis Presley in his early years.

Figure 16 Vogue *May 2003 cover of Kate Moss.*
Source: Vogue/Conde Nast.
Reproduced by permission of Conde Nast.

This inspiration from celebrity rock stars feeding through into mainstream fashion applies not only to complete looks but also to specific items. One of the biggest selling girl groups of all time, TLC, single-handedly put combats and cargo pants on the map and one of Britney Spears' enduring claims to fame has been to turn the midriff into a surprisingly erogenous zone by combining crop tops with low-rise jeans. The penchant of 'Gangsta' rap stars such as Tupac Shakur, Biggie Smalls and Puff Daddy for wearing outrageously ostentatious gold jewellery has spawned another whole look and indeed a new entry into the dictionaries, namely the expression 'Bling bling' or to wear your gold on show in a vulgar display of wealth.

The public's voracious desire for new looks and styles is such that a single photo of the right dress on the right body can launch not only a new look but also a whole career. Liz Hurley stole the show at the premiere of *Four Weddings and a Funeral* despite the fact that she was competing with the actual stars of the movie. She did this through adroit planning and a mutually beneficial deal with the Gianni Versace who lent her that extraordinary 'safety pin' dress. Top designers make these kinds of arrangement all the time and providing a dress for the right person on the right occasion can create acres of free publicity. The high point of this activity, of course, is the annual Hollywood Oscars™ where intense activity goes on behind the scenes with the top stylists manoeuvring for position and vying with each other to secure the most photogenic dress for their client to wear while making that crucially important walk from the stretch to the door. Accessorized with fabulous jewellery from Harry Winston and shoes from Manolo Blahnik, the total look can do wonders for the actress, the designer and the label while, of course, flattering the male escort too.

Accessing that fantasy is easy if you can afford shoes that retail at anything from £250 to £750 a pair and, indeed, many customers use these brands and their logos as a conspicuous consumption to assert their status and wealth. But there are many much less expensive ways of plugging into a star's fairy-tale lifestyle. How many people have we seen imitating John Travolta in his iconic white suit from *Saturday Night Fever* and what fun have we had at their expense while they thought they were doing it so well! Perhaps the star who is most adroit at this is Madonna, having invented so many new identities for herself to promote a new musical style.

Rock bands have always made very significant sums of money by selling the tour T-shirt or jacket, but in a more recent development music and catwalk stars have crossed over into the world of fashion. Kylie and Elle MacPherson both have their own lines in underwear. All these celebrity brand extensions enable people to access the stars' fashions and accessories at affordable prices. At the other end of the scale cars can be fashion accessories and supermodels can enhance the perception. Claudia Schiffer draped her scarcely clothed self over the Citroën Xanthia in an ironic echo of the 1960s' motor show cliché and Ford has recently signed Jodie Kidd to promote their latest Focus (Figure 17).

Another great source of fashion inspiration comes from the world of sport. As with the many genres and tribes within music there are multiple sources of ideas in sports with polo, snowboarding, skiing, golf, tennis, motorsport

Figure 17 *Jodie Kidd.*
Source: Ford.
Reproduced by permission of piranhakid.

and even mountaineering all generating looks and styles that range in their impact from niche to mainstream. It would be hard to find a beach anywhere in the world on which people aren't seen wearing derivatives of Californian surfing gear as produced by brands such as O'Neill and Quiksilver. In the same way there can't be many streets anywhere without kids wearing the baggy trousers and shoes which originated from in-line skaters who wore them for functional reasons: the trouser legs had to be wide enough to fit over the boots. The shoe brands associated with this sport such as Airwalk, DCs and Vans have gone global on the strength of it. And, of course, many of these brands use famous sporting celebrities to endorse their clothing and footwear. They are used to showcase new looks and styles that are closely associated with outstanding sporting performance as well as fashionability.

This ever shifting kaleidoscope of stars and fashions provides ordinary mortals with many things. First, great entertainment as we see beautiful people looking wonderful and, occasionally, plain daft. Second, we can identify particular looks and styles that might work for us. Third, when we see a new fashion in a shop we can see the reference point back to the stars and the catwalks that validates what might otherwise be a scary departure from what we normally wear. Fourth, there's a welcome element of escapism and fantasy as we put on a style made famous by a particular star and in so doing we join their fan club and identify with their lifestyle. As Tamara Mellon, owner of celebrity shoe brand Jimmy Choo, said in an interview for *Sunday Times Style Magazine* on 13 July 2003:

> When you buy our shoes, it is like buying a little piece of fantasy, a bit of escapism. It is the fantasy of my lifestyle – the helicopters, the holidays, the marriage, the cars my husband owns, the fantasy fairy-tale elements of my life.

4

Celebrity's impact on property

People have always been drawn to famous buildings, whether on a pilgrimage to a cathedral or a sight-seeing trip to a skyscraper. Whole cities have become closely identified with monuments and it's hard to think of New York without the Statue of Liberty, Paris sans Eiffel Tower and London missing Big Ben. Realizing the power of these 'celebrity properties' to attract visitors and revenue, the politicians and planners have seized the potent cocktail of 'name architect' and 'landmark building' and used it to regenerate whole cities. Since its opening (on 18 October 1997), the Guggenheim Museum in Bilbao, designed by Frank Gehry, has had a major impact not only on the city, and a region previously mainly known for terrorist violence and kidnapping, but also on the Spanish economy. The stunning museum attracts nearly a million visitors each year, almost half of them foreigners and over 80% of them say they came to Bilbao exclusively to see the Gehry building or had extended their stay in the city to visit it. The 'Bilbao effect' continues to contribute over £100 million annually to the Basque economy.

The power of famous buildings to attract people in a leisure or commercial context also extends into the private choice of where to live. Celebrity has an effect on the price of property and is another extraordinary manifestation of the influence of the famous on the public. People have long been fascinated by the places where celebrities have lived and visiting the homes of the rich and famous has become something of a cottage industry in places like Beverly Hills. TV programmes looking into celebrities' homes in the USA and UK are testimony to our interest in famous people's lives.

In the UK glazed Doultonware 'Blue Plaques' are fixed onto a building to commemorate the fact that a famous person once lived there. Nominations for these English Heritage Blue Plaques are suggested by members of the public and, like so many other aspects of celebrity, the process is essentially

Figure 18 *John Lennon's Blue Plaque.*
Source: English Heritage.

democratic and created by popular demand. There are now about 800 in London alone, with about 20 new ones being added each year. The plaques don't just honour the great figures of the past, such as Karl Marx, Vincent Van Gogh and Sylvia Pankhurst, they also recognize more contemporary figures. On 8 December 2000, John Lennon became the first British rock musician to be honoured with a Blue Plaque in recognition of his contribution to popular music and his undisputed status as an icon of the 20th century (Figure 18).

The impact that the arrival of famous people in the locality has on property prices and the premium placed on houses or apartments for sale or rent if they have had a celebrity owner occupier is further evidence of this love affair. It seems that the mere proximity to a celebrity excites in people an enhanced sense of value and leads them to be prepared to pay a significant amount extra for any given home. Notting Hill Gate in London, once a quasi-slum, a prostitutes' dormitory for central London, and scene of the infamous Notting Hill riots of 1958, has become highly desirable over the past ten years. Market factors such as relative affordability compared to neighbouring Holland Park and the perennial appeal of the market in Portobello Road have contributed to the area's gentrification, but it's mainly because celebrities have chosen to make their homes there. This has both been stimulated and capitalized on by the eponymous film *Notting Hill* starring Julia Roberts and Hugh Grant and produced by local residents Tim Bevan and Eric Fellner of Working Title Films. Indeed, the blue front door of the house in the film attracted so many tourists that the owner was forced to sell it and replace it with one of a different colour! Caroline Freud, who bought the house which was once owned by the film's producer and screenwriter Richard Curtis, put the blue door up for auction after she realized she was living in a tourist attraction which drew in crowds of people posing for pictures outside her house. In

1999 it was sold at Christie's in South Kensington for £5750 to a Portobello Road antiques dealer. Not everyone was pleased by this sale and John Scott of the Notting Hill Improvement Group was reported by the *Kensington & Chelsea News* as saying: 'Although we live in a free world, the door will be sorely missed. When the Farmer's Market is on I stand in the street giving out leaflets and for the last few months, I've been inundated with tourists asking where they can find the door. I think the owner of the house should get another door, identical to the original to keep the tourists happy and to retain the character of the area.'

A survey of 1000 estate agents conducted by the internet property company Fish4homes.co.uk revealed that a large majority of those responding believed that a celebrity owner could add as much as 25% to the value of property, all other things being equal. Indeed, an A-list celebrity such as Bill Clinton, Madonna or Mick Jagger moving into the locality could increase the value of the property they purchase by as much as 35%. For example, the house recently bought by Madonna and Guy Ritchie in Marylebone, London W1, for an estimated £5 million has reportedly already increased in value by a cool £1 million, simply because of the megastar rating of its new owners. While the particular property targeted by celebrity will appreciate in value instantaneously by these enormous percentages, it also seems to be the case that the neighbours will also benefit from the pulling power of a star moving into their area. According to the survey, neighbouring houses will also go up by up to 11%, with the rest of the street adding value by up to 8%.

Dan Wakeford, of *Heat* magazine, compiled the following table in 2001 and although, by now, out of date, given the pace at which the barometer of fame rises and falls, it is nevertheless more good evidence that celebrity *does* sell.

'A-list' celebrities who could achieve a 20%+ increase in property price

Sir Paul McCartney – St Johns Wood, London and Brighton
Madonna – Marylebone, London
Noel Gallagher – Marylebone, London
Liam Gallagher and Nicole Appleton – Hampstead, London
Kate Moss – Notting Hill, London
Elton John – London W11, Buckinghamshire
Geri Halliwell – Notting Hill, London
Robbie Williams – Notting Hill, London
Victoria and David Beckham – Hertfordshire
Mick Jagger – Richmond, Surrey

Chris Evans and Billie Piper – Knightsbridge, London
Jude Law and Sadie Frost – Primrose Hill, London
Liz Hurley – Chelsea, London
Hugh Grant – Chelsea, London

This phenomenon of celebrities adding value to property is not limited to the entertainment industry. A-list politicians such as Lady Thatcher and Tony Blair can potentially increase property prices by 25%, although this impact remains to be seen in the case of the notorious purchase of the two flats in the Panoramic in Bristol. However, when Prime Minister Blair did sell his Islington home some years ago, it fetched a premium of almost 10%. Copping Joyce, the Islington estate agent, believes that the former Blair home will still be worth up to 5 to 10% more than similar houses next door, even in 40 years' time.

Hundreds of people travelling to Westbourne Grove to see a blue front door and having their picture taken posing in front of it? People paying 20% over the odds to live in an ordinary house once occupied by a Prime Minister? Neighbourhood property prices up by 35% because a rock star has moved in nearby? Really? But perhaps there is a rational explanation for this apparently irrational behaviour, which turns a two-bedroom flat worth half a million to one worth three-quarters of a million with no other changes to its accommodation apart from a previous resident. It may just be that celebrities, being in the swim of the opinion-forming classes, are aware of the next up-and-coming place and perhaps because they have professional advisers, time and money they can snap up bargains before others. And obviously if they are in a clique of people who move opinions, then their collective decampment to a particular postal code can become a self-filling prophecy and produce the rise in property values which benefits them and their friends and associates. In a sense this is 'insider trading' in reputation (Figure 19).

Figure 19 *Celeb 'Flat for sale'.*
Source: Private Eye/Ligger.
© Pressdram Limited 2002. Reproduced by permission.

Figure 20 *Palm Island.*
Source: Palm Island.
Reproduced by permission of Hill and Knowlton.

Rick Stein, who became a celebrity chef through his BBC TV series and his best-selling cookbook *Taste of the Sea*, has had an enormous impact on property values in Cornwall as a result of his entrepreneurial development and promotional ability. Locals refer jokingly to Padstow, the location of his seafood restaurant, bistro, café, patisserie, delicatessen, hotels, cookery school and gift shop empire, as 'Padstein'! Anyone who bought a cottage there 26 years ago when Stein's restaurant first opened will have done rather well, as indeed has he, and now he's embarking on an ambitious project to regenerate surfer centre Newquay in the same way.

Property developers in Dubai are currently promoting an extraordinary concept called 'The Palm' and rumoured to have sold £900,000 villas there to several celebrities including England football stars, with David Beckham and Michael Owen among their number. We await hard evidence that these sales were made, but it's evident that the futuristic resort has already gained great publicity from these reports (Figure 20).

All this reaffirms that celebrities lead opinion and that people are prepared to follow them in the most fundamental of their purchases, in this case the place that they choose to live and invest most of their money in – their bricks and mortar.

5

Celebrity impact on body shape

From mankind's earliest days there have been attempts by human beings to alter their appearance through the use of adornments such as makeup, jewellery and clothing and the mirror has been underrated as one of the key influences on our social development. Women, in particular, have been in the forefront of the use of cosmetics and toiletries to increase their allure and throughout history, society has thrown up iconic figures such as Queen Nefertiti, Helen of Troy, the Queen of Sheba, Cleopatra and Boudicca. These beauties used a combination of shrewd political intelligence and their sexual attractiveness to men to great effect and thereby wielded great power. While there is no doubt that their physical perfection was largely a gift of birth, they were adept at using early forms of cosmetics to enhance it, as well as using spectacular costumes and accessories.

Their example as beauties and role models was preserved for their own people and posterity by portraits and sculpture and we see the same process continuing on into the modern era.

The advent of photography certainly gave an enormous boost to the influence of celebrities over other people and industries such as cosmetics, hair care and toiletries have from the beginning used Hollywood stars and other famous beauties to promote their brands.

But it's not just female stars who have had an effect on women customers. What is striking is the degree to which men too have got involved in the beauty business especially as it's not long since the image of the ideal man was 'macho', as portrayed and lived by the likes of John Wayne. The feminist movement and its successors have increasingly succeeded in changing the balance of power between the sexes in both boardroom and bedroom.

One of the stars who has had the greatest impact on women and their physical self-image and the transference from the feminine ideal of a soft, essentially unathletic and passive persona to one of a more muscular, toned and empowered physique is Jane Fonda. On the back of a movie career based on hits such as *They Shoot Horses Don't They?*, *Barbarella*, *Klute*, *The China Syndrome* and *On Golden Pond*, many of which played to her feminist beliefs, she launched her original 'Workout' video in 1982. Since then she has sold over 4 million videos and been a major contributor to the global exercise and gym phenomenon, educating and enabling millions of people to achieve a healthier balance between 'calories in' and 'calories out'. Quite recently there has been such an enthusiastic take-up and vocal endorsement by stars such as Ben Affleck, Jennifer Aniston, Geri Halliwell and Catherine Zeta-Jones of the Atkins Diet, that it has now become world famous. This regime increases substantially the proportion of protein in the daily diet and reduces carbohydrate significantly (Figure 21). Despite its controversial nature millions of ordinary people have taken it up. Indeed its adverse effect on proprietary diet brands such as 'Slim-Fast' has led to Unilever blaming it for reduced US revenues and there is even talk of reviving the Potato Marketing Board!

The storylines in movies and TV dramas have reflected the new social reality as it has evolved and perhaps led it too. 'Real men' have become 'new men' and most recently we have discovered the 'metrosexual', a man who displays many character traits and behaviours that would once have been regarded, pejoratively, as effeminate. In line with this, today's male Hollywood stars are quite often physically unimposing with the Schwarzenegger physique somewhat out of fashion and the newer men possessing a sensitivity light years away from the 'Dirty Harry' persona made famous by Clint Eastwood. Today's box-office stars such as Ben Affleck, Tom Hanks, Will Smith, Hugh Grant and Leonardo DiCaprio have all given ordinary men permission to acknowledge their 'feminine side' and this has been reflected in the growth of markets associated with personal grooming.

In the 1950s hardly any men used a deodorant whereas nowadays some 84% do. Many men have always shaved so that in itself is not a development but it's interesting to see that the concern over skincare has resulted in a significant increase in the use of shaving cream, sticks and foams, as opposed to basic soap, with 70% of men using these products. An example is 'King of Shaves' which contains special facial care ingredients (Figure 22).

There has been a dramatic increase in the numbers using whitening toothpastes as measured on TGI over the past five years from 4.3% of adults in 1998 to 19% in 2003 and most growth in this market has come from male users – up from 1.2% in 1998 to 16.4% in 2003. And how many middle-class kids don't go through the braces phase? Although the absolute numbers are still small there are twice as many adults wearing contact lenses instead of

Figure 21 *Atkins Diet.*
Source: David Eldridge.

glasses, up from 3.7% to 6.1% between 1987 and 2003 with the growth being broadly equal between men and women.

But these are relatively minor physical 'adjustments'. Perhaps 20 years ago only the top Hollywood stars and other very wealthy individuals would have resorted to cosmetic surgery such as facelifts or nose jobs in order to prolong and enhance a youthful appearance. Such operations would have been conducted under considerable secrecy with the patients going away on holiday for some time in order to conceal from their friends and associates the

Figure 22 *King of Shaves.*
Source: KMI.
Reproduced by permission of KMI inc. ltd.

telltale bruising and scars until they had fully healed. While preserving some semblance of discretion and hardly ever admitting it in public, nowadays movie stars and other famous people in the public eye do not seem to make very great efforts to deny that they have had surgical procedures of one sort or another. This laissez-faire attitude has permeated down into the mainstream of the population so that breast implants, eyelid tucks, lip plumping and liposuction are topics of daily speculation, discussion and more than occasional implementation.

In this context the figures from the American Society of Plastic Surgeons (ASPS) reporting the large numbers of people resorting to cosmetic surgery or other 'assistance' are perhaps unsurprising. During 2002, 1.6 million people had elective cosmetic surgery as opposed to outpatient treatments. Five million people underwent cosmetic treatments such as Botox injections. Taken together these 6.6 million Americans spent a total of more than $7 billion (£4.4 billion) on having a nip and tuck, an injection or treatment to improve their appearance. An additional 6.2 million patients had reconstructive cosmetic surgical procedures after suffering disfiguring accidents or undergoing serious surgery – one wonders what proportion of these owed at least a little something to vanity?

The increase in the preparedness to go through these painful and potentially dangerous procedures is remarkable. In 1994 only 39,247 women in the USA had breast augmentation surgery, but by 2002 the number had increased sixfold with 236,888 women having it done and this represented an 8% increase over 2001 alone. Interestingly, while the number of American men undergoing cosmetic surgery remained constant year on year, in 2002 40% of them were less concerned about improving a weak chin as opposed to looking less fat, with the number having tummy tucks nearly trebling to 5145. The ASPS is naturally in the business of promoting cosmetic surgery and helpfully provides a menu of procedures and costs. Figure 23 lists the figures for female procedures in 2002.

The United States of America is not alone in this. It's reported that between 25,000 and 27,000 Brazilians have breast surgery each year and indeed a Brazilian company is the world's third largest supplier of breast implants. According to Mintel, the market research company, in a report called 'Health and Beauty Treatments' based on a sample of 2000 adults, consumers in the UK spent £1.3 billion in the year 2002 on health and beauty, with the average customer spending £95 a year. This represents a 44% increase over 2000, when the expenditure was £0.9 million. One of the main reasons for the increase, according to the report, is as follows: 'The influence of celebrities on consumers attitudes towards their own appearances is becoming significant, particularly among those aged under 35.' This trend has been further fuelled by the plethora of celebrity-focused publications and mainstream newspapers and magazines covering the topics of body shape and cosmetic surgery in their editorial. As is so often the case, advertising picks up on and reflects themes and trends from society, and cosmetic surgery and the preoccupation with body shape are no exceptions. Figure 24 shows an amusing topical example from the award-winning Beck's campaign by M&C Saatchi.

Procedure	No. of patients	Average cost
Liposuction	230,079	$2,074
Nose reshaping	209,123	$3,469
Eyelid surgery	186,522	$2,455
Facelift	105,850	$5,352
Botox injection	991,114	$422
Microdermabrasion (skin blasting)	771,314	$171
Sclerotherapy (removal of spider veins)	495,610	$242

Figure 23 *Cosmetic surgery procedures undertaken by females.*
Source: ASPS.

Figure 24 *Beck's 'Cosmetic Surgery'.*
Source: Beck's.
Reproduced by permission of M&C Saatchi.

In an article by Antonella Lazzeri for the *Sun* newspaper on Thursday 6 June 2003, it was reported that actress Demi Moore had invested in the region of £250,000 in order to reinvent herself and relaunch her career. The once A-list star, having had three children with husband Bruce Willis (Rumer 14, Scout 11 and Tallulah Belle 9), seemed to hit premature middle age and was photographed looking significantly overweight. In order to counteract this Moore embarked on a determined regime combining cosmetic surgery, diet and exercise. Lazzeri put together an astonishing but probably plausible menu of items on her shopping list and the costs attached:

- brow lift, mini-facelift, chemical face peel, collagen and Botox injections: £95,000
- reduction of breast implants: £15,000
- personal training sessions at £75 per hour: £14,000
- yoga personal training at £80 per hour: £16,000
- liposuction of hips, thighs and stomach: £90,000
- Pilates sessions at £75 a throw: £75
- delivery of her 'Zone Gourmet' diet meals: £5000

The results of this were pretty impressive in terms of physical appearance, with Moore securing a part in the Charlie's Angel sequel *Full Throttle* and beating both Rachel Hunter and Catherine Zeta-Jones to be voted runner-up to Elle 'The Body' MacPherson in a 'sexiest star mum' poll in *FQ*, a new magazine for dads.

Fashion is at work in cosmetic surgery as well as everywhere else. The latest thing, according to the ASPS, is the buttock implant and there is even a website devoted to promoting its benefits produced by Thomas Harris, a surgeon from South Carolina: www.betterbuttocks.com. So far the number of operations is small, with only a reported 614 buttock implants carried out in 2002 in comparison with the 250,000 breast implants executed in the same year, but it's another good example of where celebrity has led the way. The trend has been triggered by the spectacular success of singer Jennifer Lopez, aided and abetted by Kylie Minogue and tennis star Serena Williams. All three of these global stars have shapely bottoms and rather than trying to minimize or flatten them to conform to the Caucasian ideal of body shape, they have decided to glorify them. In so doing they have crystallized the idea in the Hispanic and African American communities that their own genetic disposition towards a 'big butt' can be something to be proud of. Given that the Hispanic population in the USA has become the single largest ethnic group, this has been a pretty smart move from a commercial point of view.

Consumers are increasingly willing to part with sums of money in order to acquire characteristics reminiscent of their idols. Dr Richard Fleming, a leading Beverly Hills plastic surgeon, spends about 40% of his practice hours working on celebrities and he reports that Nicole Kidman's nose is one of the body parts most requested by his clients. This sort of request has been made to him so many times that Fleming has taken to compiling an annual list of the favourites. In 2003 the year's most asked for eyes belong to Heather Graham. Halle Berry's are the cheekbones most aspired to. Denise Richards possesses the most kissable lips and the most requested jaw line is that of Cate Blanchett, while Britney Spears possesses the top body shape. As in so many other things men are following the female lead and now half of Fleming's clients are male. They usually end up looking for Edward Burns' nose, Johnny Depp's jaw line and Will Smith's physique. The irony of all this is that the star whose body part is the reference point may not herself have acquired it at birth but as the result of a cosmetic procedure of her own, perhaps inspired by a movie star of the previous generation! Thus these idealized body shapes are evolving through a process of celebrity-driven R&D, which is increasingly distant from an individual's genetic inheritance (Figure 25).

Figure 25 *Celeb 'Cosmetic surgery'.*
Source: Private Eye/Ligger.
© Pressdram Limited 2002. Reproduced by permission.

Celebrities are giving us ideas on how to dress, what to say, what to do, what to eat, what to buy, how to have sex and with whom, where to live, what to drive and where to go on holiday. Increasingly, they are telling us how to modify our appearance, not just by means of cosmetics, clothing and other accessories, but by use of medical treatments and cosmetic surgery. The fact that such a significant number of people are actually going through with this, often using celebrity features as a reference point for their surgeon is indicative of the powerful influence that stars can have. If people are prepared to have a scalpel put through their flesh on the inspiration of celebrity, it's hardly surprising that they might buy a soft drink or a packet of crisps that has been endorsed by a star.

PART II

Why Celebrities Work
for Brands

Introduction

In Part I we saw the all-pervasive influence of celebrity and celebrities on our everyday lives. In this context it is right to assume that stars can have a powerful effect on the fortunes of the brands that they endorse. But before getting into the practicalities, it's worth considering, at a more general level, why celebrities work for brands. As we shall see, the use of the famous in advertising and other forms of marketing communications is by no means the only successful creative route open to marketers and their agencies. In fact, only about 16% of the top performing campaigns, according to a number of authoritative sources, utilize celebrities. Other techniques, such as product demonstrations, side-by-side comparisons, slices of life, mnemonic devices, brand characters, humour, analogy and fantasy, among others, can also be very effective and each of these needs to be considered in any given brand situation.

However, there are three macro factors at work that may mean the use of celebrity is a particularly appropriate one nowadays and which could potentially lead to its increased use in future. The first of these factors to be explored is the increasing potential for interactivity between brands and their customers. Indeed, it looks very likely that the traditional separation between brand or 'theme' advertising, which adds value to the image and reputation of corporate, product and service brands and response or 'scheme' advertising, which is often seen as discounting it through price offers and other promotional techniques, is ending. The future is 'brand response', a form of communications that combines both added value and some form of interactive sale-closure process, which in itself adds value.

Analysis of the IPA Effectiveness Databank reveals a slow but sure increase in the number of different means of communication being used by winning campaigns. In 1998 the average was 3.97, in 2000 it was 4.06 and in 2002 it rose to 4.20. We can expect this number to increase in the coming years. Within the mix, TV remains the single most important medium employed according to the analysis and it has a powerful 'leveraging' effect on an

Figure 26 *The relative interest of brands and celebrities to a customer.*

integrated media campaign. This is key to success and given that 'brand response' is the future, it seems likely that TV, already arguably the most powerful medium, will become even more so as increasing numbers of media platforms offer audiovisual capability and, of course, this suits the use of celebrities extremely well (Figure 26).

The second of these factors is the 'era of consent'. It seems plausible that we are moving steadily to a situation in which customers will have much greater control over the commercial communications messages they receive. 'Gatekeeping' through either personal or technological intervention will become commonplace. If brands are increasingly going to have to seek permission from people in order to communicate with them then it is obvious that only the brands that are desirable will qualify for access. In establishing the necessary customer trust and credibility it seems likely that celebrities, who themselves have a high standing in the public eye, could be one of the more powerful tools for brands in gaining the necessary customer permission.

The third macro factor has been widely documented and that is the phenomenon of increasing media fragmentation and commercial communi-cations clutter. This, in combination with consumers' innate ability, honed by much practice to screen out unwanted information, means that it is increasingly difficult for brands to gain a customer's attention. This is a real problem for marketers and their agencies, as attracting attention, and thus achieving a high degree of fame, is key to building their business. Again it would seem that celebrities, who by definition have considerable fame of their own, and who are much more attractive to customers than brands per se, can, if harnessed correctly, create the necessary 'cut through'.

6

Celebrity and interactivity

There is an overall explosion in the availability of commercial communications media. For many years in the UK there were only three or four TV channels whereas nowadays there are over 500 and the radio airwaves are now supplied by almost 300 stations, let alone the plethora of unlicensed ones operating on the web. One clear consequence is that the sheer volume of advertising has increased steadily over the years and will continue to do so. Already in the UK people are watching 3.54 hours of commercial television daily. But those who have computers are spending an average of six hours a month online on top of their TV viewing, according to AC Nielsen. Indeed the Which Internet Survey 2002 revealed that half of all internet users spend more than five hours per week online and 9% of them spend more than 20 hours per week online, which means this small but growing segment is watching as much web as it is TV.

And digital technologies are also enabling unprecedented levels of interactivity, which is going to increase and become much more sophisticated over the next few years. As a result we are witnessing the gradual emergence of a new phase in commercial communications, that is the convergence of so-called 'brand and response' advertising. For people in communications agencies and marketers in client companies, this represents advertising's Holy Grail. No longer will they need to work hard building brands up using added-value advertising imagery and then knock them down by retailer-driven price promotional activity at the point of purchase.

Increasingly there is the potential for building brands up and enhancing them further by giving customers a really rewarding interactive experience through the manner in which they respond to them and purchase.

In this new and far more complex media environment it will be important to produce integrated brand communications that can work across any number of technological platforms. A particular challenge for creativity in this context is the widely varying advertising formats that will need to carry the brand message. From a practical point of view consider the varying specifications for an image which might appear on a website, on the tiny screen of a video phone or as an HTML file attached to an email, to say nothing of the technicalities of producing a 30-second TV or radio commercial, a 96-sheet poster, a colour spread in a magazine, a black-and-white page in a newspaper or a direct mail letter.

While there are many different creative approaches to producing big ideas for brands which can work across all these sorts of platforms and be adapted to the requirements of each particular medium in production terms, it seems obvious that the use of a celebrity can provide one of the most powerful pieces of image 'glue' that can hold an integrated communications campaign together.

We can already see this in work in the context of the traditional mail-order businesses as increasingly they migrate to the internet producing online versions of their hardcopy catalogues. Within this enormous market, worth £8.35 billion in 2002 in the UK alone, there is the beginning of a celebrity segment. For example, Martha Stewart, with her lifestyle catalogues existing both on and offline and complementing her TV show, books and videos, makes a total brand presentation in a multi-channel context. That the use of direct and interactive response media is on the increase is evidenced by the strong growth of direct marketing expenditure over the last six years as reported by the Advertising Association (Figure 27).

The Bellwether Report, produced for the IPA by NTC Research, is published once a quarter and the sample of respondents is a panel of

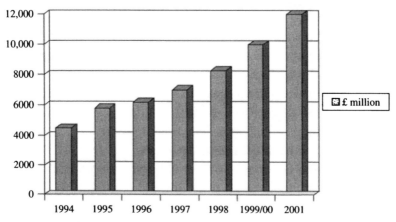

Figure 27 *Direct marketing expenditure.*
Source: Direct Marketing Association/Advertising Association.

about 250 senior clients who are decision makers on their company's marketing communications expenditure. They are asked to report whether their marcoms budget is up, down or the same as the last time they responded and these questions are asked for each segment of their expenditure. Since the Bellwether Report began in 2001, the marcoms sector has been in recession, but in virtually every period the budget allocated to direct marketing has been up compared to all other media. The resilience of the internet sector during the downturn has also been impressive. This implies that DM in its widest sense is gaining market share of all forms of advertising and marketing communications (Figure 28).

Some commentators believe that the swing to more measurable media such as direct marketing is a temporary and cyclical characteristic typical of recessionary times, but given the other change factors at work, and especially the convergence of brand and response advertising, it seems likely the trend to DM will continue in better times too.

Despite the dynamism of the direct mail sector there has so far been relatively little use of celebrities in this medium. One recent exception is for esure featuring Michael Winner. This could be to do with the fact that famous people are generally much more wary of allowing their image to be used in print advertising materials per se and rather more willing to do so on television which they see as a more aspirational medium. And it may also be to do with the relatively poor image of 'junk mail', which celebrities may wish to disassociate themselves from. We can but hope

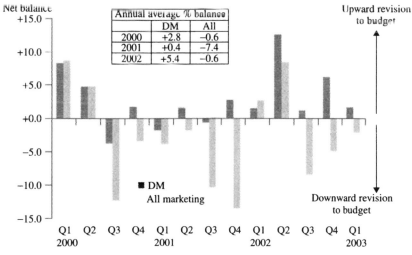

Figure 28 *Bellwether suggests increased direct marketing share.*
Source: NTC research for IPA.
Reproduced by permission of NTC Research Limited.

that, as the users of direct mail take advantage of increasingly sophisticated databases and get their customer relationship management skills much more finely tuned, the scattergun approach to the medium will be replaced by much more tightly targeted and appropriate rifle shots. Experiments in responding to sales leads with individually tailor-made and produced one-off car brochures costing £40 each have proven more cost effective than using the traditional one-size-fits-all catalogue. If the creative quality of the pieces mailed to customers continues to be enhanced by improved production values, affordable because of the improved responsiveness resulting from greater accuracy, then celebrities may be more prepared in future to allow direct mail to be included in their contract for usage.

The increase in the use of interactive media for commercial communications purposes will be facilitated by new technologies. Already 80% of households have a mobile phone. As a result there has been an extraordinary explosion in short message service (SMS) or texting, a medium that some people say was invented almost by accident. Sixteen billion text messages were sent in the UK alone during 2002 and the growth rate looks to be almost exponential (Figure 29).

As the UK mobile phone market approaches 100% initial market penetration, the next generation video phones and personal digital assistants (PDAs) are arriving and are already gaining share. It's likely these will incorporate more sophisticated biometric security features such as fingerprint reading, voice recognition and iris scanning. This will make them highly

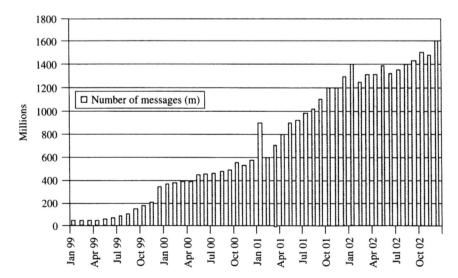

Figure 29 *There's a meteoric growth in text messaging.*
Source: Mobile Data Association.

personalized portable teleshopping devices with credit account facilities and thus there will be the potential for brand advertising with an instant purchasing response channel. We have already seen the use of celebrities such as David Beckham, with his reported £1 million Vodafone deal, in promoting these new generation mobile phones and their instantly recognizable faces are perfectly suited to the screen size constraints of the new medium.

There is a very significant growth in the penetration of personal computers both at the office and at home. TGI data show that the number of households with personal computers has risen from 29% in 1995 to 60% in 2003. As a result, growth in internet usage is also rapid and by about 2006/7 roughly 80% of all UK households will be online (Figure 30).

This has led to a whole new communications channel, that of email. The widespread success of Hotmail is attributed to 'viral marketing', giving it over 40 million users in less than three years, courtesy of the 'Get your free Hotmail' notice and link at the bottom of every Hotmail email sent by users. In January 2002 the number of emails sent between households was 550 million, exceeding the volume of postal items by some 300 million, and as the bandwidth increases people are circulating pictures, music and movie clips. So-called 'viral advertising' has taken off as a result of this and brands such as John West Salmon have benefited enormously from the free circulation of their commercials on the internet (Figure 31).

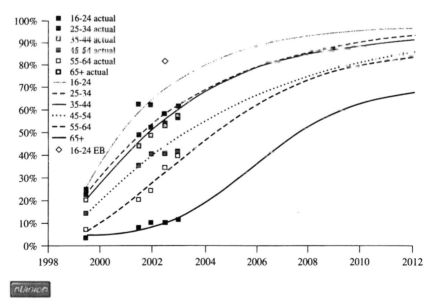

Figure 30 *Massive increase in internet usage in the UK.*
Source: 'Changing Lives'/Eurobarometer/nVision.
Base: 0154 adults 16+, living in the UK.

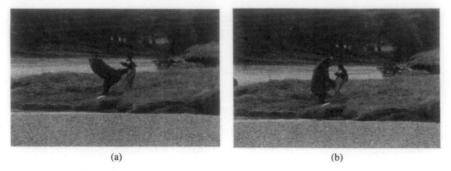

(a)   (b)

Figure 31 *A highly amusing bit of 'interactivity' in Leo Burnett's John West commercial.*
Source: Leo Burnett.

Some estimates suggest that over 100 million people have seen copies of the Budweiser 'Louie Lizard' commercials created by DDB Chicago on the internet and several witty home-made versions of Budweiser's 'Whassup' commercials have been created and circulated adding to the campaign. The case history on this campaign won a Silver Award at the 2002 IPA Effectiveness Awards, confirming the potency of an offline/online media mix.

Given the power of stars it is likely that high-quality, amusing and engaging commercials featuring them will have great potential for viral distribution adding significantly to the value of the brand campaign. BMW, and their USA agency Fallon, have already exploited this opportunity via specially commissioned short films made by famous Hollywood directors such as John Frankenheimer, Ang Lee, Tony Scott and John Woo.

Broadband is not developing as quickly as basic internet, but about 6.5 million households are forecast to have fast connections by the year 2006. There is also a very interesting race going on between platforms (Figure 32). Who's going to win this battle for customers, is it going to be the internet or is it going to be computers? Is it going to be web television or is it going to be interactive TV, terrestrial or satellite or cable that commands the audiences of the future?

Either way the forecast of the number of households with digital television is about 16.5 million by December 2006, but meanwhile traditional TV is already well established as a shopping channel. QVC has developed a very big business in the UK as Figure 33 shows and teletext has an astonishingly high level of usage, especially in the travel sector, despite its low profile as a medium. According to TGI, 19,847,000 UK households had teletext in 2002.

As a result of these new technologies people are shopping on the web in a big way and at Christmas 2002, eight million people in the UK bought something via the internet. Companies such as Amazon, eBay and

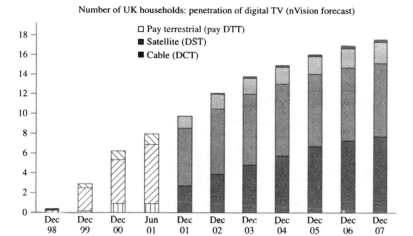

Figure 32 *There's a race on between platforms.*
Source: The Future Foundation/nVision.

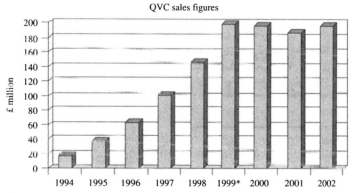

Figure 33 *Teleshopping has arrived.*
Source: QVC

lastminute.com have recently gone into profit and so after a very shaky start and near collapse when the dot.com bubble burst in 1999, it really does look as if online e-commerce is becoming a fact of life and a major route to market for brands (Figure 34).

Some market sectors such as travel are now largely on the web and there is increasing availability of content online, such as games, gambling, music and video (Figure 35). The music market is almost entirely driven by celebrities and nearly all music stars have their own websites. The more sophisticated of them run their fan cubs online and sell music as well tickets to their concerts

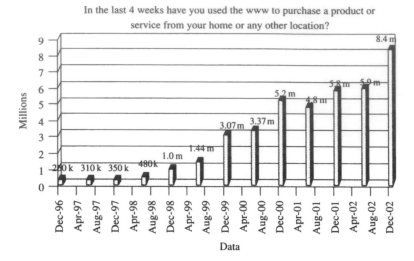

Figure 34 *Web shopping is booming.*
Source: NOP.

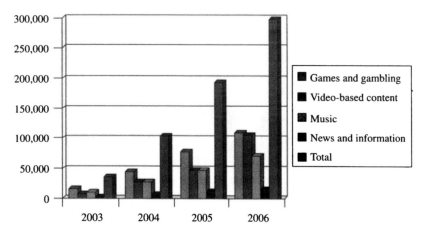

Figure 35 *They're getting lots of content online.*
Source: Datamonitor.

and a whole range of their own brand merchandise. Despite the current limitations of the technology and the lack of availability of bandwidth, there have already been some huge web-based celebrity events. For example, in November 2000, while 3500 Madonna fans at London's Brixton Academy, including music industry figures and celebrities such as Mick Jagger, were able to view her performance in person, it was broadcast over as many as 100,000 simultaneous audio and video streams to an estimated 200 million web users in more than 15 languages.

Interactivity penetration at home via PC, TV and/or other means* – nVision forecast

*Access via mobile phone, PDA, or any other device except television or PC

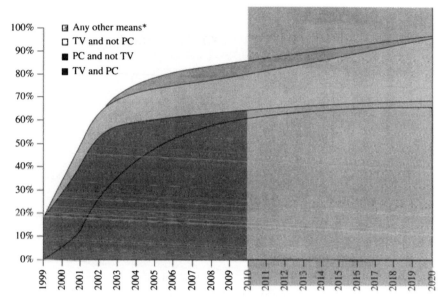

Figure 36 *Eighty per cent interactive access at home by 2006.*
Source: The Future Foundation/nVision.

The overall picture is that by 2006/7 around 80% of all households will have some means of interacting at home with companies and their brands by a computer, TV or mobile device (Figure 36).

All this potential for interactivity is an exciting but challenging prospect for marketers as brand and response communications come together and the balance of power between 'push' from the manufacturer and 'pull' from the customer shifts towards the latter. In this environment it seems very likely that much of the content will be of a televisual nature and that goes for the editorial as well as the advertising. The internet and its major websites will progress from being largely magazine formats to a TV hybrid, with increasing proportions of audiovisual material. Meanwhile, digital interactive television will increasingly offer movie images with the potential for click through to further text and picture content. It's obvious that celebrities will perform extremely well in this context as they have always had the ability to bridge all media and specifically from static media such as print to moving media such as video.

7

Celebrity in the era of consent

We are witnessing the gradual emergence of a new phase in commercial communications, which is the 'era of consent'. As we have seen there is an explosion in the availability of media, a massive increase in the numbers of commercial communications messages being sent to customers by brands and a greatly enhanced ability for people to interact with them. The latest estimate of the commercial portion of our daily media diet, if we wish to consume it, is in the region of a phenomenal 5000 brand communications per person per day. While most people might accept intellectually that this is roughly the right amount, it's doubtful whether anyone believes that they personally are engaged by anything like that number in practice. According to Robert Heath and his theory of 'Low Involvement Processing' (LIP), we may well be absorbing much more information at a subconscious level than we realize and this is a significant contributor to our perceptions in general, and thus of brands too. More work needs to be done in order to take full account of LIP, but at a conscious level we can see the human being is remarkably adept at screening out irrelevant messages. How often have we observed people flicking through pages of advertising in the newspaper or magazine that they are reading in favour of the celebrity editorial they bought it for? How often have we asked ourselves a few minutes after a commercial break what commercials we have just seen and been unable to recall most of them?

Many would argue that this screening or blinkering facility is becoming ever more finely tuned as the explosion in media continues apace around us. We have a picture of the archetypal customer, surrounded by a fortress built of his or her own indifference to brands. The customer lives safe inside this 'castle', protected by a moat and accessible only by a drawbridge that is seldom let down and a portcullis which is rarely raised up. At a conscious level the customer selects which communications to be interested in and, while entertainment is a key factor, usually this interest is purposeful. If they are looking for some product or service, they will selectively perceive relevant brand messages. Statistically, this means that at any one time a relatively tiny proportion of the customers will be 'in the market' for a particular product category or item within it. This is why the big users of direct mail and loose inserts, such as credit cards and banks and insurance companies, usually rely on an essentially commodity approach to their marketing and why they are satisfied with response levels that are perhaps only 1% or 2% from the millions of items distributed. This editing process comes naturally to all of us and very few of the 5000 commercial messages we receive daily are consciously allowed in. But, increasingly, brands are allowed to communicate with us by invitation only and we are rapidly entering the era of permission marketing. In this new environment brands will have to make themselves sufficiently attractive and trustworthy in order to be invited in over the drawbridge. An association with a desirable celebrity is likely to be a powerful way to achieve an 'access all areas' pass to the customer's castle.

One result of increased interactivity in commercial communications is that brands are able to collect very much more detailed information about their customers and to build databases which can be interrogated to produce increasingly sophisticated segmentations. Marketing programmes can then be constructed that are tailored very specifically to particular segments and enable customers to receive appropriate communications, benefits and offers in a highly cost-effective manner. In this context it's hardly surprising that some of the fastest, almost exponential growth in direct marketing is coming from the more 'intrusive' media such as direct mail, tele-marketing, email and SMS. Unfortunately, too many people are bringing the commodity mass mailing mentality from direct mail to these new technologies. But in the digital world there's no excuse for accepting a response rate of 1.5%, because of the potential for genuine one-to-one dialogue. Plus the irritation factor of 98.5% spam in an inbox, let alone intrusions on voice mail or on a landline, is out of all proportion to what it might be on the doormat and thus much more damaging to the brand responsible.

In the most well-established direct marketing medium, direct mail, we are now seeing extraordinary growth with 5000 million items of direct mail sent in the UK in 2002 according to the Royal Mail. Meanwhile, as more operators are being awarded government licences to operate in the deregulated UK market, the likely result is that poorly targeted 'commodity' direct mail will increase. This may well provoke a customer and political backlash,

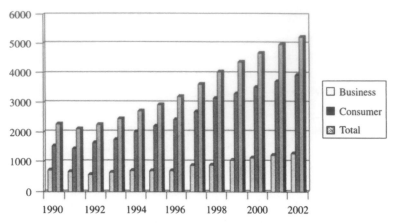

Figure 37 *Over 5000 million items of direct mail sent in 2002.*
Source: Royal Mail.

led by environmentalists among others, who resent the waste involved in the process (Figure 37).

Telephone marketing is another intrusive medium enjoying rapid growth. For many years companies have provided telephone helplines in order to assist their customers and the telephone has also been used as a highly effective mechanism for receiving responses generated by advertising and other marketing communications. There is a highly variable quality of service being offered by companies in this way and many appear to be in the business of creating 'helpline hell' as opposed to providing 'helpline heaven' for their customers. One-to-one communications can enable extremely accurate targeting, genuine personalization and real relationship building, but contrary to common belief, doing it properly doesn't come cheaply. Only too often a massive investment in advertising and marketing communications can be fatally undermined by a poor customer interface with call centres. As with so many new technologies, cost reduction, rather than quality improvement, seems to be the initial driver for their adoption by companies, hence the trend to 'offshoring' contact centres to India. The voice of marketing arguing for using them to increase quality is usually heard too little and too late, and often after much damage has been done to brand reputation.

A clever use of new interactive technology involves sending audio ads direct to mobile phones via voice mail and, given the distinctive voices that many celebrities have, this new medium offers great potential for using them. However, a recent example of creativity involving a celebrity in this way ran into trouble, illustrating how difficult it is to get things right in this newly emerging arena. The voice mail ad was for the hit movie *Minority Report* and the audio message started with a man (the actor Tom Cruise, who starred in the film) drawing breath. He asked slowly 'Where's my minority report?' and then breathed heavily before screaming 'Do I even have one?' He then paused to breathe heavily again before repeating, 'Do I have one?' A girl's voice replied, 'No'. The voiceover then said, 'Don't miss out on your minority report. Buy it now on DVD and video. Click below to hear the message in full.'

Unfortunately, 18 people complained to the Advertising Standards Authority (ASA) about this innovative audio ad. The advertiser, Twentieth-Century Fox Home Entertainment, argued that the audio ad was sent only to those who had registered their contact details on its website, including their mobile phone numbers and who had agreed to receive information on future film, DVD and video releases. In this context Fox contended that those subscribers would be familiar with the film and with Tom Cruise's voice and also felt that it was clear from the end message that the audio was indeed an ad. However, the ASA considered that the message could be seen as menacing, was not revealed to be an ad until too near the end and might have to be paid for. Thus, it upheld all aspects of the complaints.

Marketers are also increasingly taking advantage of the extremely low cost per unit of email and text to send millions of messages. In the first half of 2003 nearly 45% of all UK email was 'spam', i.e. largely unsolicited, unwanted and unwelcome commercial messaging. The electronic version of the fraudulent 'Nigerian deposed dictator's fortune' letter made an early appearance on the net and most of these junk emails are selling dubious financial or medical products, the latter being very often of a pornographic nature. E-junk is seemingly growing at an exponential rate: MessageLabs scanned 134 million emails in May 2003 and found that 55% of those were spam. That's an increase of 40% on the previous month. BT OpenWorld reported that of 11 million emails sent over a six-day period in March 2003, 41% were detected and trapped as spam (Figure 38).

Unless we stop it, it will stop us. In the USA, around 9 billion emails per day, i.e. about 90% of the traffic, are junk. About 180 companies that send 90% of it dominate the spam industry. Experts believe that if the level of junk email is allowed to grow at its present rate, within eight to 12 months it will provoke a meltdown in the global email system because servers cannot cope with that amount of traffic. This is quite apart from the threat posed by pernicious viruses such as Sobig.f, which may be the product of malicious pranksters or, more sinisterly, the creature of commercial spammers experimenting with new ways to proliferate their unwelcome messages. AOL, Microsoft and Yahoo!, among others, have struck back, and in 2003 AOL won a big lawsuit against a 'spammer', so hopefully the tide is turning and will continue to do so with the support of new, tougher legislation.

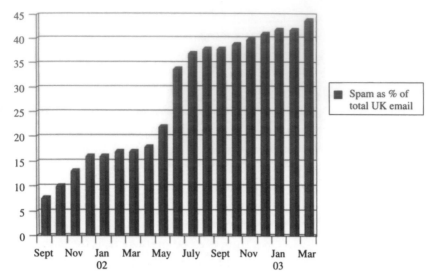

Figure 38 *Now nearly 45% of all UK email is spam.*
Source: Brightmail.

The EU Directive on Privacy and Electronic Communications (2002/58/EC) was published on 31 July 2002 and EU member states had until 31 October 2003 to enact it into national law. In summary, webmasters must provide clear and comprehensive information about cookies somewhere on their site. Unsolicited emails or SMS may not be sent to someone where there has been no prior customer contact at all, unless there has been a specific 'opt-in' by the individual granting permission to the sending company. Existing customers (and the precise definition of what counts as an 'existing customer' is still a grey area) can be emailed or texted with similar product or service offers, but can still opt out of receiving them in future, if they so wish. Subscribers to directories must be informed about the purpose of a directory before their inclusion and given the option as to whether personal data are published. These legislative measures, supported by self-regulatory activity, are both reinforcing and building the trend towards an era of consent and the age of permission marketing wherein customers will become more and more aware of the value of their personal data and wary of trusting other people with it. Only brands that behave with a good set of manners will survive and prosper in this environment.

But, in the meantime, the level of complaints is increasing and this is hard evidence that customers are fighting back against unwanted marketing communications and are sending out a powerful signal to brands that in future they will need to seek permission to communicate with their customers. Year on year 2002 versus 2001, the overall number of complaints to the

Authority	2001	2002	%
ITC	7796	7830	+0.4%
ASA	12,451	13,959	+10.8%
DMA	169	194	+14.7%
Total	20,416	21,983	+7.7%

Figure 39 *Complaints are on the increase.*
Source: ASA, ITC, Direct Marketing Authority.

Independent Television Commission, the Advertising Standards Authority and Direct Marketing Authority in the UK increased by 8%, with the strongest growth recorded by the DMA (Figure 39).

As can be seen from Figure 39 the absolute number of complaints is relatively small when taken in the context of the millions of advertisements and commercial communications that are sent out annually. And it's also true that a tiny proportion of these complaints are upheld by the various authorities and result in the offending material having to be amended or withdrawn. Nevertheless there is an indication that customers are becoming more prepared to complain and that there is a greater awareness of the mechanism to do so. This is a healthy situation for the UK which has a market that is largely self-regulated as far as advertising is concerned and one in which the brand owners are increasingly taking responsibility for all their communications, because they understand the importance of maintaining public confidence in them.

However, as well as complaining after the fact, customers are putting up the barriers to prevent communication and there are very significant increases in people taking advantage of the various 'preference services' on offer in the UK. Research suggests that many of the people who are doing this are relatively upmarket and high net worth individuals, i.e. just the sort of valuable customers that many brands wish to communicate with (Figure 40).

Perhaps the most dramatic example in recent times of customers putting up the barriers and creating the era of consent, or permission marketing, has been the June 2003 launch of the 'Don't Call Me' service in the USA which attracted 23 million people who wanted to stop telesales calls to their numbers in the first two weeks alone. By September the total had reached 50 million. The Federal Trade Commission originally forecast the

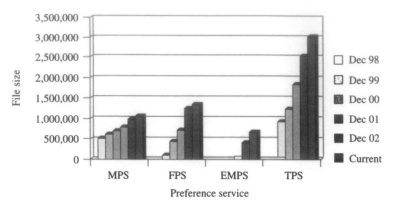

Figure 40 *Increased use of preference services.*
Source: DMA.

registration of up to 60 million phone numbers in the first year out of an approximate total of 166 million residential phone numbers in the United States, i.e. 36% of all numbers, but on the basis of this initial avalanche this may even be a conservative estimate.

It's easy to see that brands which behave badly are going to be very quickly eliminated from customer communications portfolios by the use of services such as 'Don't Call Me' and anti-spam software. It is argued that personal video recorders and electronic program guides operated by devices that can be programmed to eliminate advertising, will undermine the implicit contract between viewers and broadcasters under which they get free programming in exchange for being exposed to commercial communications. However, sensible advertisers have always appreciated that they are intruding on people's leisure time when they appear in the pages of their newspaper or magazine or on their TV screen and thus in principle nothing has really changed. Advertising has always had to add value, whether by imparting news, education, or sheer entertainment, and the era of consent simply puts a greater premium on brands doing this well. Given the power of celebrity and its attractiveness for millions of people, it seems highly likely that the role of famous people in promoting companies, products and services will grow and be one of the best ways of securing permission to communicate with customers.

8

Fame is the key

Nowadays brands have to work very hard on their communications to give customers a 'reward' for letting them into their mental 'castle'. Useful information or 'news value' is a tried and tested route. Many brands, and indeed whole corporate brand philosophies such as that espoused by Procter & Gamble, have been based on the idea that advertising and marketing communications should concentrate primarily on conveying rational and functional benefits, and preferably by imparting 'new news' to current and potential customers. This continues to be a viable option for brands, despite what people say about the inability to maintain product differentials.

Another way over the 'drawbridge' is through added value of an emotional and psychological sort, perhaps in the form of humour, entertainment or romance that rewards the customer and seduces them into giving their time and attention to the brand and its communication, which also contains sales messages. This particular style of 'soft' salesmanship can be very successful too.

More recently, during the 1990s and into the early part of the new century brands have begun to develop other 'moat-crossing' techniques, which make appeals to the emerging consumer interest in higher order values. So now we have brands that are declaring a political, ethical or even spiritual 'credo'. Corporate social responsibility has become a key aspect of brand positioning and a focus of reputation and risk management (Figure 41).

If we accept that we are rapidly entering the era of permission marketing in which customers are going to be increasingly willing and able to put up barriers to entry, then the challenge for brands is to create a sufficiently attractive total persona to which people wish to subscribe as if it were a club they want to belong to. Consumers are increasingly going to be able to 'pull' communication from brands in addition to allowing certain brands to 'push' messages to them.

Figure 41 *The Brand Manners Book of Life.*
Source: *Brand Manners*, Hamish Pringle and William Gordon. 2001.
© John Wiley & Sons Limited. Reproduced with permission.

In his chapter in *Advalue*, 'Advertising and the non-conventional brand', Leslie Butterfield describes his 'subscription' model and the decision process involved (Figure 42). He writes as follows:

> Work that I have done on countries, issues, causes and charities, political parties and people brands confirms the generally accepted view that two of the key drivers of identification – a kind of surrogate for 'subscription' – are 'awareness' (have I heard of them?) and 'familiarity' (do I know anything about them?). But drawing from some of the theory about how interpersonal relationships are formed, I would interpose between these two in a subscription process 'visualisation' (do they conjure up an immediate picture?).

Thus the Butterfield model sets up the context in which celebrities can work so well in the promotion of brands. The crucial thing about the executional technique of using celebrities to convey any or all of these brand values or information is that famous people are very much more likely to be 'invited in' by customers. Stars, by definition, have very high public

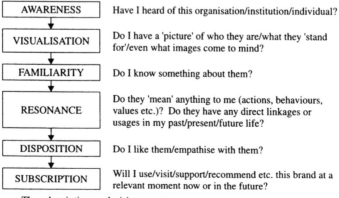

The subscription on decision process

Figure 42 *The subscription decision process.*
Source: *Advalue* by Leslie Butterfield (ed.) (2003).
Reprinted by permission of Elsevier Limited.

"I don't know who you are.

I don't know your company.

I don't know your company's product.

I don't know what your company stands for.

I don't know your company's customers.

I don't know your company's record.

I don't know your company's reputation.

Now—what was it you wanted to sell me?"

MORAL: Sales start **before** your salesman calls—with business publication advertising

McGRAW-HILL MAGAZINES
BUSINESS•PROFESSIONAL•TECHNICAL

Figure 43 McGraw-Hill's 'The Man in the Chair'.
Source: McGraw-Hill.
© The McGraw-Hill Companies, Inc. Reproduced with permission of The McGraw-Hill Companies.

awareness and people are able to visualize them very easily as they are so familiar with them. And if the celebrities are carefully chosen to suit the brand they will provide the meaningful resonance and positive disposition which leads to 'subscription' and the building of a successful relationship. Perhaps this is why the use of celebrities is one of the more powerful techniques in advertising and marketing communications.

There is a clear link between higher awareness, or 'fame', for a brand and more favourability towards it. Sheer 'likeability' in a brand's advertising and marketing communications aids awareness, thus completing a virtuous circle for the brand. The fundamental idea that the first step towards building a customer relationship is simple awareness was brilliantly encapsulated by the famous McGraw-Hill advertisement reproduced in Figure 43.

At its most basic, raising the pure level of awareness and familiarity and putting a smile on the face of this grumpy customer is how advertising and marketing communications can ensure brands are more positively received. Familiarity easily translates into favourability or likeability, the most powerful component in a brand's reputation. Hard evidence that familiarity and favourability have a close and positive correlation is provided by the long-standing MORI tracking research study of corporate reputation. This can be seen clearly demonstrated in Figure 44.

The McGraw-Hill advertising proposition that a higher spontaneous brand awareness translates into a greater propensity to do business in reality is supported by data from the financial services industry provided by Ipsos-UK in Figure 45.

Clearly spontaneous brand awareness reflects the level of 'marketing push' by the company – how effectively they have drawn consumers' attention to the brand. Hence awareness rises and falls in response to marketing activity. Related to this but on a deeper level, a sense of familiarity and understanding of the brand's proposition has been shown to be the more important aspect of awareness, in terms of driving a stable, long-term desire for the brand. Figure 45 illustrates the connection between awareness and brand success, but other brand building blocks such as the relevance of the offer, the differentiation of the brand and the quality of its services need to be included to create a complete picture. Successful brands tend to score highly for all these aspects.

Work carried out by Marilyn Baxter and Leslie Butterfield on the PIMS database and published in *Advalue* demonstrates very clearly that brands which outspend their competitors, and thereby gain relative share of voice,

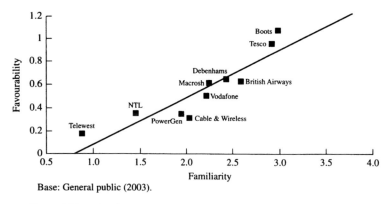

Base: General public (2003).

Figure 44 *The MORI study of corporate reputation.*
Source: MORI.

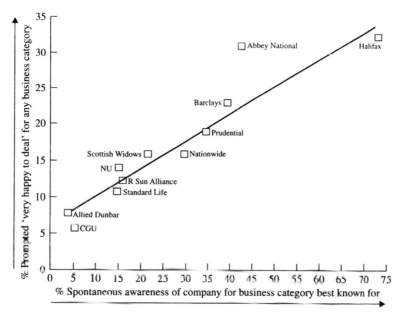

Figure 45 *Brand awareness and propensity to do business.*
Source: IPSOS RSL.

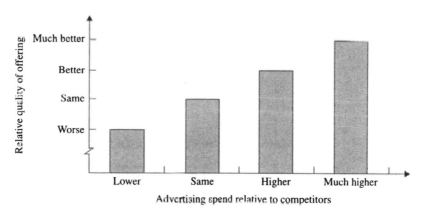

Figure 46 *Impact of advertising spend on product image and reputation.*
Source: PIMS.

also gain improvements in the relative quality of their offering and in the perception of their relative product image and company reputation (Figure 46).

This is why brands that do not cut their advertising communications expenditure during a recession or a downturn generally fare better than those companies that do. This analysis of the large PIMS database of

European consumer goods businesses also suggests that it is not just any old advertising that matters, but rather advertising that succeeds in building quality perceptions of the product, either directly or through the intermediary of product image and company reputation.

At its most basic, the brand must ensure that it achieves high awareness, favourability and likeability. If it does these really well, then the next step for the brand is to create a reputation for living up to its promises. Doing this will establish real customer trust. Advertising and marketing communications are also essential to achieving this too. One way of doing this is to associate the brand with another personality in whom the public have confidence and whose opinion they respect. The right celebrity, who is established with an audience or fan base which is relevant, and who has created an atmosphere of trust around themselves, can give the brand a powerful third-party endorsement and positive halo effect by agreeing to be associated with it.

We know that a consistent and engaging brand 'story' effectively told by the leaders of the corporation, retold by its employees and made public by advertising helps enormously in motivating the whole organization and aligning its efforts behind common goals. Hence the success of entrepreneurial brands such as Purdue Chickens/Frank Purdue, Body Shop/Anita Roddick, Virgin/Richard Branson and easyJet/Stelios Haji-Ioannou. The same dynamic has worked for major corporations such as Microsoft/Bill Gates, Oracle/Larry Ellison, General Electric/Jack Welch and IBM/Lou Gerstner – major corporations led by charismatic celebrity leaders. These individuals are walking talking brand stories that provide their companies with a compelling narrative drive and constantly generate valuable publicity.

However, not all corporations, companies or brands have the benefit of such people. An attractive alternative is to incorporate a celebrity dimension to the company story as this can add enormously to the narrative drive, simply because the chosen star has a life of their own which runs in parallel to that of the brand, but then interlinks with it as each episode of the commercial communications unfolds. The corporate 'story' as communicated through advertising, websites, public relations or events, creates drama, excitement and momentum and even more so when it has the added glamour contributed by a star. These are especially important elements in building and maintaining employee morale and never has it been more important than in these disintermediated times when more and more brands are in direct contact with their end users through websites, email and call centres.

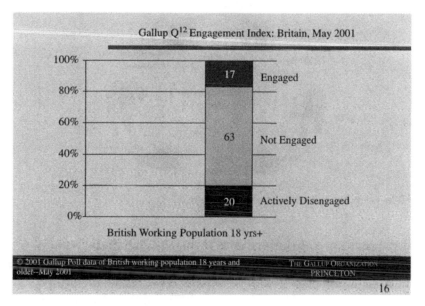

Figure 47 *Gallup chart on employee satisfaction.*
Source: Gallup.

Brands are no longer insulated from their customers by wholesalers, retailers or other intermediaries and their frontline employees, whether on their payroll or contracted out, deliver thousands if not millions of 'moments of truth', which can keep, reinforce, undermine or break the brand promise. In this context, research findings by Gallup in 2001, which indicated that six out of ten employees are 'not engaged' and that 20% are 'actively disengaged' gives considerable cause for concern (Figure 47). How likely is it that employees who fit this profile can be positive ambassadors for the brand? Companies that give their people more than material reasons to 'get out of bed in the morning' reap enormous rewards in terms of increased employee commitment and it seems highly plausible that an association with a famous celebrity can contribute significantly to the job satisfaction and even sheer enjoyment of working for the brand.

For a brand to succeed in the modern social, economic and political environment and the rapidly approaching era of permission marketing it has to concentrate on doing three interrelated things really well: being famous, being likeable and being consistent (Figure 48).

Effective advertising and marketing communications, linked to consistent and transparent brand behaviour, are fundamental to achieving them and the power of celebrities can be harnessed to increase the chances of success significantly.

Figure 48 *Celebrity can help to get three key things right.*

Further evidence of this dynamic is the 'Ads That Make News' survey, produced by Propeller Communications, with data from Durrants Media Monitoring, in association with www.brandrepublic.co.uk (Figure 49). This regular survey measures the volume of coverage national newspapers give to ad campaigns. Nearly all the most written about ads in UK national newspapers between January and November 2002 were those involving celebrities. This additional free exposure makes a significant contribution to offsetting the cost of the campaign and the building of brand fame.

	Advertiser	Campaign
1	Pepsi	David Beckham
2	Sainsbury's	Jamie Oliver
3	Walkers Crisps	Gary Lineker
4	Nike	Thierry Henry et al.
5	Anti-euro	Cinema ad featuring Rick Mayall as Hitler
6=	BT	Chameleon Phone/Bringing people together
6=	M&S	Xmas celebrity campaign
8	Lotto	Billy Connolly
9	ITV Digital	Johnny Vegas/Monkey
10=	Halifax	Howard & Angela
10=	Pot Noodle	Slag of Snacks

Figure 49 *Top ten ads that make news.*
Source: Propeller Communications.

PART III

How to Choose Celebrities for Brands

Introduction

As with any decision which affects the perception of the brand, be it the way it is named, what its predominant colour is, how it's packaged, the look and feel of its logo, its handwriting in terms of typeface, the places in which it is seen and sold, what's said about it by third parties in the press, what promotions it runs in shops and other outlets, what sort of mail shots or door drops it carries out and, of course, what kind of advertising campaign it runs, the choice of a celebrity identified as being best for it is one of the more important decisions that will ever be taken for the brand. In a sense the brand's image and its customers' self-image will be 'refracted' through the 'prism' of a star's persona and produce a new set of perceptions.

These are very serious considerations and taken with the amount of money involved, which is often considerable, makes the choice of celebrity a big decision. Celebrities are brands in themselves and thus in choosing such a partner the brand is in effect getting married to one of its own. And the marriage analogy is not a bad one to use. As in human relations compatibility is crucial. In the many articles that appear in the media advising people on how to increase their chances of finding a suitable partner, a common success factor is the degree to which people are similar to each other and have shared backgrounds, views and aspirations. The theory that 'opposites attract' on a long-term basis does not often seem to be borne out in practice and, as with so many other areas of human activity, people seem to prefer positive and reinforcing reflections of themselves, rather than diametrically opposed challenges. And, of course, this relationship is not just about a couple, it's a ménage a trois because the customer is involved too, making it a triangular one. Three personalities have to gel if the brand campaign is to work (Figure 50).

Figure 50 *A triangular relationship.*

Fortunately, there is a wealth of experience both in market research terms and in life case histories, which can give marketers and advertisers plenty of guidance in this tricky area. And, of course, the reason it is tricky is that celebrities are unusual brands in that they talk back and they may also change their behaviour, their views and their perceived personality quite quickly, literally making them not the person they used to be and certainly not the individual with whom the brand originally partnered.

9

Understanding where the brand is now

The starting point for any brand communications campaign is the client brief* and a vital component of a good brief is a brand audit which establishes a full understanding of the brand 'territory'. The 'territory' is the mental space that the brand occupies in customers' minds and represents the essence of the corporate, product or service promise that constitutes the brand. Before embarking on any kind of marketing or advertising, the brand manager and any agencies involved must be able to answer the key question about the nature of that brand promise and its status in the marketplace, which can be summarized as: 'Where are we now?'

In this respect the use of celebrity in advertising is no different from any other creative or strategic approach. It's absolutely essential for the brand marketer and their agencies to have a deep understanding of what actually constitutes their brand. There are many different models for doing this, but one which may be especially useful in the context of the use of celebrities is that of 'brand anthropomorphy'. This model builds on our tendency to personify inanimate objects in human terms and to ascribe attitudes and values and even behaviours to brands. In focus groups it's quite easy for customers to describe packaged goods or service products as if they were real people and to ascribe emotional, psychological and other attributes to them. The logical conclusion of this process for marketers is to treat the brand as if it were a person and to analyze it in all the human dimensions possible (Figure 51).

In the brand anthropomorphy model there are three main constituent areas that are relevant. The first of these concerns the rational or functional benefits which underpin the performance of the product or service brand. In the 1950s this approach to branding was in its heyday and was typified by Rosser Reeves of agency Ted Bates, with his Unique Selling Proposition, or

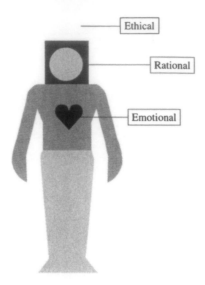

Figure 51 *Brands now have all these dimensions.*

USP. Many brands in the household cleaning markets in particular thrived on a succession of new improved miracle ingredients which advertising focused on single-mindedly. This rational or functional approach still has a place despite the subsequent shift in emphasis towards emotional, psychological and other brand values. It is often said that nowadays product differentiation on the basis of these practical aspects is not possible to sustain in the long term because of the ability of competitors to imitate and copy any innovation remarkably quickly. However, as Niall FitzGerald, Chairman of Unilever, has observed:

> A common reason for a brand's decline is complacency. The story is a familiar one. A company or brand builds a good reputation, sits back and rests on that reputation, only to wake up one day to discover that faster, hungrier, more innovative competitors have passed them by. IBM is a good example, not least because it's a company that, since feeling the pain, has successfully reinvented itself.
>
> The sequence of events goes like this. To begin with, you are, for example, a very technologically advanced company – and deservedly very successful. As the market becomes more and more competitive, you realize that you need both product performance and brand character to stay ahead. Brilliantly, you build a great image for the brand, so that users not only respect the company but feel loyal to it as well. You grow even more successful.
>
> Then comes the critical stage. You become such an enthusiast for the notion of brand personality – and become so fixated with your own – that you come to believe that competitive product performance is no longer your highest priority. So you neglect to innovate, you neglect to invest in R&D,

you stop listening intently for those faint murmurs of discontent – and for a month or two, or even a year or two, your success continues and your profits mount. You may even be tempted to believe that you have discovered the secret of perpetual motion.

Then, with savage suddenness, your once healthy brand becomes an invalid, losing share and reputation with precipitate speed. What has happened? Your market has discovered what you have done, and suddenly realized a once-loved brand has taken its users for granted. The response of its users is brutally unforgiving. What happened to a computer company has happened to car manufacturers, to retailers, to banks, and to fast-moving consumer goods companies. Complacency is one of the easiest ways to bring a brand to its knees.

Indeed, it often seems to be the case that brands with the richest and most vivid imagery and personality are the ones that have their feet on the ground when it comes to practical product performance, which they constantly strive to improve.

Thus the brand can be conceived as an inverted pyramid with a very broad top expressing powerful values supported by a key point, which represents a core nugget of product truth. Robin Wight, eponymous founder of leading UK agency WCRS, has a pithy saying which encapsulates this approach to branding, as exemplified in his agency's outstanding campaign for BMW. Wight exhorts his agency to: 'Interrogate the product until it confesses to its strengths.' And it's certainly true that major advertisers such as Procter & Gamble in particular continue to build enormous businesses with brands that are largely based on outstanding functional performance: soap powders that wash whiter, toothpastes that make teeth brighter and floor cleaners that produce more of a shine.

Thus the key part of understanding where the brand is now is having a full appreciation of its performance on these rational attributes. It's also important that these are benchmarked regularly against the competition, especially if other brands are introducing new formulations, in order to avoid the risk of falling behind. There are many examples where celebrities have been used to reinforce these kinds of brand attribute and it does seem that the authority a famous star brings to the presentation of a product benefit can have a powerful impact on the audience. It also seems that a sprinkling of glamour can increase the appeal of what may seem rather utilitarian aspects of product or service performance.

The second area in which brand anthropomorphy can be used to establish the starting position for a campaign is in assessing the emotional and psychological benefits that surround the brand. These benefits came to the fore in the 1960s and 1970s as a result of the application of psychology to the marketing and advertising business. As the motivational psychologists discovered then, and as we appreciate today, customers can describe products and services in remarkably colourful language. They can ascribe the whole range of human virtues (and vices) to their favourite chocolates and equally to their less than favourite insurance companies. Leading UK agency Bartle Bogle Hegarty has used the term 'Emotional Selling Proposition', or ESP, to describe the kind of brand platforms that are based primarily on personality and image attributes. In understanding the nature of the brand image and the personality it presents to the world in terms of dimensions such as friendly or unfriendly, traditional or modern, dynamic or relaxing, the brand manager and agency team can assess the strengths and weaknesses of the brand character and consider in which direction its persona needs to be moved in order to increase its appeal to the relevant target audience. If, for example, the brand is seen to be somewhat parochial compared to its more cosmopolitan competitors, the use of an appropriate celebrity could be a fast acting way to remedy these negative perceptions.

The third area in which brands can be assessed as if they were people is on the higher order issues of ethics, politics and social responsibility. Mass market concern about these more rarefied matters has emerged over the last ten to 15 years and in turn customers have looked to brands and begun to critique them on the same dimensions. There seems to be strong evidence that customers in Westernized economies are reaching the top of Maslow's pyramid (Figure 52).

Brands ignore this important social trend at their peril and the list of famous companies which have run into trouble due to allegations of unethical, exploitative or socially irresponsible behaviour is already quite a long one and the alarming rapidity with which firms such as Andersen, WorldCom and Enron disappeared has compelled chief executives to look much harder at their own corporate behaviour. Stock exchanges and investment analysts are increasingly scrutinizing the ethical positions of the companies whose performance they follow and they are being assisted in this by new indices such as the FTSE4Good, the KLD-Nasdaq Social Index and the Dow Jones Sustainability Index. Brand owners live in an increasingly litigious environment, particularly in the USA, as evidenced by the massive class actions that have been fought and sometimes won against the tobacco companies. These legal threats are now threatening to engulf food-manufacturing corporations and thus the importance of measuring and performing in terms of the 'triple bottom line' has never been greater.

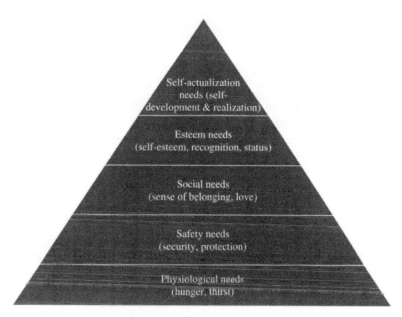

Figure 52 *Maslow's hierarchy of needs.*

In the 21st century companies must continue to deliver their economic bottom line and reward shareholder investors with an adequate return on their capital. However, companies have a second bottom line, which must also be measured, and that is their impact on the environment in which they operate. Then, there is the social bottom line, which is increasingly preoccupying governments, NGOs and citizens. This is concerned with assessing the contribution of corporations to their communities and the degree to which they are putting something back into society. Taking these issues together they can be regarded as a basket of values, which represent the brand's 'credo' and these should be seen as incremental to the rational and emotional values which are more familiar to us.

It's clear that the role of celebrity in addressing the higher order values of brands is in its infancy. So far, most of the activity involving famous people in this domain has been in the context of charities and good causes as opposed to the commercial sector. However, there seems to be no good reason why celebrities should not be deployed to vouch for the credentials of a brand in terms of its ethical, political or even spiritual values. Assessment of the brand's current position must include an appraisal of its merits and demerits at this higher level and consideration needs to be given to ways and means of enhancing its performance in this area as in any other (Figure 53).

Figure 53 *Celeb 'Pope'.*
Source: Private Eye/Ligger.
© Pressdram Limited 2002. Reproduced by permission.

[*For more detailed guidance on how to develop a good brief for a brand communications campaign, please see the joint industry best practice guidelines developed by ISBA and the Communications Agencies Federation, whose members are the IPA, the MCCA and the PRCA. 'The client brief, a best practice guide to briefing communications agencies' can be downloaded free from www.ipa.co.uk.]

10

Seeing how a celebrity could help the brand

Having completed the brand audit and thus being able to give a comprehensive answer to the question 'Where are we now?' on behalf of the brand and to define its composition in terms of these three distinct but related sets of values, the brand manager and the agencies involved need to be clear about where the 'centre of gravity' of the brand's personality and promise to its customers actually lies. There is absolutely nothing wrong with a brand being centred on rational or functional dimensions, with relatively weak attributes in the emotional, psychological, ethical or political ones. By the same token, there may well be brands that are heavily reliant on their emotional and psychological appeals. Increasingly we're seeing the mergence of brands that are centred on corporate social responsibility and thus their ethical, political and even spiritual values are key. Sometimes there might be a situation where there is a happy pairing of polarities – the ethical bank which invests money with an eye to the behaviour of the investee companies, but also manages to serve its customers with high technology in an extremely efficient manner. It is also likely that certain market sectors may favour certain attribute mixes, but even if there appear to be norms shared by a particular set of competing brands it may well be that a contrarian approach using a different mix of values could be highly effective. Once it's clear what the brand's individual position is and its territory is mapped out, the way forward can be planned with confidence, regardless of whether or not a campaign involving celebrity is deemed to be the most fruitful executional approach.

Having defined 'where the brand is now', the next task is to agree on a desired destination by asking the question 'Where do we *want* to be?' and answering it in terms of the objective for the brand. In the context of the dynamics of the particular marketplace, the positionings of other brands and forecasts of likely directions for the market, the brand manager and the agency have to construct the future scenario and the required values for their brand to achieve increased competitive advantage. In this context the role of advertising and marketing communications usually acts for a brand in one of three main ways: launch, reinforcement or repositioning.

The first of these opportunities to consider is in actually launching the brand in the first place. Here the use of a celebrity can be particularly powerful, especially if the brand is establishing a new category where customers need the reassurance and leadership an appropriate star can give them. The early adopters will follow this lead and often create a mutually reinforcing 'virtuous circle' for the new brand (Figure 54).

The second way in which advertising can be very effective is in maintaining and reinforcing a brand's competitive position in the marketplace. Again the use of celebrity can be very effective in this instance, especially if other brands have entered the marketplace and have changed its dynamics. The third way in which advertising can work for a brand is in repositioning it in the context where market development and the maturing in the evolving of customer taste have created greater potential in a different sector of the market than the one in which the brand is currently positioned. An appropriate celebrity can be used as the focus of the brand communications and as a signal to customers that its positioning is changing to suit a new and perhaps emerging target audience.

In each of these scenarios the market analysis can result in a brand-positioning map of which the one in Figure 55 is the first in a series of hypothetical examples. In this instance, the key dimensions in the marketplace are represented by 'traditional' and 'modern' and 'luxury' to 'everyday'. Here we have a situation where a completely new market opportunity has been identified and the marketing company decides to launch Brand A, positioned as a traditional luxury product.

Figure 54 *The celebrity virtuous circle.*

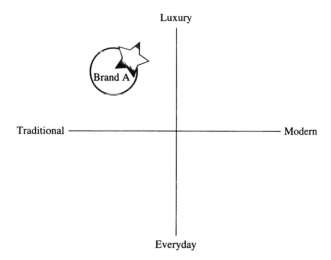

Figure 55 *Brand A: traditional luxury product.*

Having taken account of the nature of the target audience and where the intended 'centre of gravity' of the new Brand A's personality should lie, a famous celebrity might be chosen to complement this positioning and personify all the traditional luxury values to be ascribed to the brand. The star in the brand campaign can be used to play back to the customer their values, aspirations and desires in a heightened and enhanced manner.

Parker Pens used Penelope Keith in this way in a memorable commercial called 'Finishing School' created by seminal agency Collett Dickenson Pearce and directed by Alan Parker (Figure 56). Using her plummy aristocratic voice and trading on all her heritage as the star of long-running TV series 'To the Manor Born', Keith admonishes an upmarket girl pupil in a cheque-signing class who asks how to spell the word 'pence', saying she won't need to worry about that!

Much advertising works in this way, based on one of the world's oldest sales techniques: creating empathy, delivering flattery and satisfying desire. In a sense this sort of advertising holds up a 'pink mirror' to a customer and enables them to see an enhanced version of themselves brought to them by the brand. When their reflection is refracted through a celebrity this can be even more effective.

Let's assume that Brand A is a great idea and does indeed succeed in creating a new market segment focused on 'traditional luxury'. In this case it is highly likely that competitive entrants will quickly follow Brand A's lead and before too long the marketplace is rather more complicated, with two other brands adopting different competitive positions in the traditional

Figure 56 *Penelope Keith.*
Source: CDP.

luxury market segment. As a result of this Brand A finds itself pushed out of its original launch position by Brands B and C, which have outcompeted it on the dimensions of tradition and luxury. Brand A now wishes to reassert its position and move back to where it was before (dotted edge circle) (Figure 57).

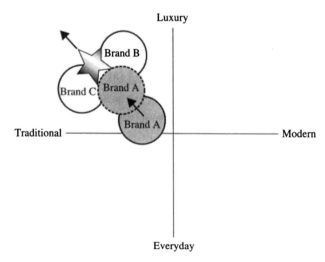

Figure 57 *Brand A needing to reassert itself.*

One way in which the brand can do this is by employing a new celebrity with a personality that has a heightened set of values in terms of luxury and tradition and use this reinjection of star quality to achieve the objective.

After a few more years the market has matured further and now there are three brands occupying the 'luxury traditional' quartile and one in each of 'traditional everyday' and 'modern everyday'. The brands in the 'traditional luxury sector' have been losing share, as has Brand D in 'traditional everyday'. However, the overall market is in growth and this is being driven by Brand E in the 'everyday modern' sector and by Brand A (Figure 58).

Exploratory qualitative research among customers of the competing brands in this maturing market has given greater insights into the market dynamics. The marketing and agency team have come to the conclusion that repositioning their brand away from its prime competitors in the 'traditional luxury' sector into the new market space of 'modern luxury', i.e. the noticeable gap in the top right-hand quartile is likely to be the best option to create future growth in brand share. Thus the objective for Brand A can be defined as 'To increase £ brand share by 5% in a market forecast to grow by 2%', as a result of the repositioning (Figure 59).

The next important question that needs to be answered in developing the brief that could lead to a celebrity solution is: 'What are we doing to get there?' Clearly advertising alone is unlikely to bring about a successful migration from one market quartile to another. Improved formulation can create the core product truth and the foundation for a rejuvenated Brand A. Refreshing the brand identity with associated repackaging may well be

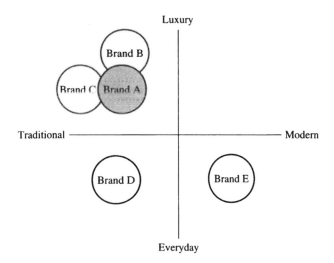

Figure 58 *Brand A mature market.*

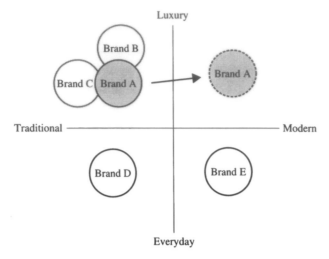

Figure 59 *Brand A repositioning.*

required and pricing could need to be pushed upwards at the same time: luxury goods often need to be seen to be expensive. It may also be important to readdress the distribution channels used by the brand. Personality and image are so often a function of the company that is kept and that includes the retail environment: in fulfilling the new strategy the more traditional outlets stocking the brand will probably need to be replaced with ones of a more contemporary nature (Figure 60).

All these elements of the marketing mix need to be working in harmony with each other in order to generate the desired positioning of 'modern

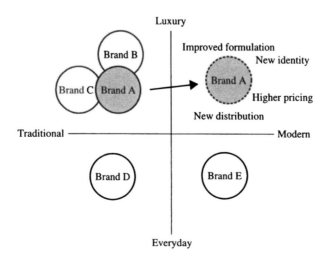

Figure 60 *Brand A: what are we going to do to get there?*

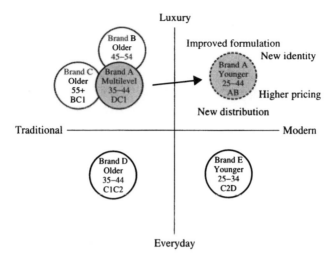

Figure 61 *Brand A: Who do we need to talk to?*

luxury' and very often the glue, which holds them altogether and then delivers the new brand promise to prospective customers, is advertising. This leads on to the next in the series of key questions that need to be answered on the way to an effective creative solution for the brand and this is perhaps the most crucial: 'Who do we need to talk to?' (Figure 61).

In our hypothetical example the analysis of where Brand A is now in the context of its competitors and the proposed repositioning has led to a definition of the desired future customer as being younger and slightly more upmarket than Brand A currently enjoys. Such basic socio-demographics are a pretty blunt instrument to describe the target audience with, and it would be much more helpful to bring the current and future customers to life through the use of qualitative research. From the insights gained through focus groups much more vivid and meaningful pen portraits can be drawn of the people with whom the brand wishes to have a meaningful conversation. The same sort of research can establish the likely reactions of the brand's existing customers to the new direction. Very often older users are flattered when their brand is marketed to a younger audience with more contemporary imagery, but beware changes in formulation that may undermine the rational and functional reasons for loyalty!

Having been briefed clearly in terms of where the brand is now and agreed its future destination as being a positioning of perceived modernity and luxury in the eyes of a defined target audience, having put the other elements of the marketing mix into line and having agreed that an advertising and marketing communications budget is necessary for the task, it's now up to the creative people to come up with a big idea for the brand which will transport it from where it is now to where it wants to be.

Clearly, there are many different ways in which 'luxury' and 'modernity' can be expressed in terms of imagery and brand proposition and the use of a celebrity is but one of the routes that may be considered. In this particular hypothetical example it again might look as if the use of an appropriate star could be a very quick way of signalling the change that the brand is making and therefore finding a famous person with whom the younger more upmarket customers would associate a luxury brand, and whose image is sufficiently current to communicate modernity, could be a very effective solution for Brand A.

De Beers is an excellent example where the use of a celebrity has helped create a new brand identity and positioning in a market with strong tendencies to commodity. In 2001 the diamond giant made a decisive switch from a supply control to a demand-led business model. As a key part of this new approach a joint venture was formed with LVMH, the luxury goods group, called De Beers LV to create upmarket jewellery shops. A new logo and brand identity were created and the retail venture's diamonds are branded with the name 'De Beers' indelibly imprinted in minute characters on each stone larger than 0.25 carat. In order to create greater impact and relevance to a younger contemporary market, supermodel Iman was engaged as the face of the brand in the campaign created by agency J Walter Thompson. Iman brings with her the heritage of Africa and the added cachet of rock star husband David Bowie and for months the Bond Street building site was a mega-poster of her for the brand (Figure 62). The flagship store was unveiled on the corner of Bond Street in London in November 2002 and in September 2003 its first three retail outlets opened in Tokyo department stores.

The demand-led strategy spearheaded by the Iman campaign has generated additional spend on marketing by the diamond jewellery industry of some $180 million, double the previous year, and it looks as though it is starting to pay off. In the ten years prior to the change of direction in 1999, the compound annual rate of decline in diamond jewellery consumption was minus 2.5%. But since 2000 the annual growth rate has been plus 3% and in 2002 retail consumption grew by 4% worldwide. At the end of July 2003, De Beers posted a sparkling set of results showing diamond sales up 2.75% to $2.92 billion against $5.2 billion for the whole of the previous year and profits up by 34% to $414 million for the first half of the year.

In choosing the right celebrity the marketing team can draw on all the background research about Brand A and the insights that have been

Figure 62 *Iman.*
Source: De Beers LV Ltd.

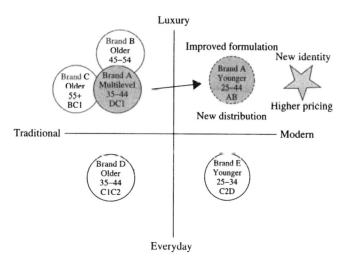

Figure 63 *Brand A: choosing a celebrity.*

gained into the prospective customers for a rejuvenated modern luxury brand (Figure 63). The profile of the celebrity can be matched very precisely to that of the new Brand A, but after that creativity, intuition and sheer good luck will all come into play in matching the right celebrity with the brand and, after all that, there's just the fee to negotiate and the contract to get signed!

11

Researching the effectiveness of celebrities

As with any other type of advertising, market research can be extremely useful in developing a celebrity campaign for a brand. Indeed, it would be a foolhardy marketer or advertising agency which decided to proceed with the kind of major investment that an association with a famous star represents without having taken the precaution of exploring fully the relevance and appropriateness of it. After all, a relatively modest expenditure of under £20,000 on exploratory qualitative research and perhaps double that on a quantitative check could significantly increase the effectiveness of the campaign. These sums pale into insignificance when compared with the hundreds of thousands of pounds that a TV production or major print campaign is likely to cost, let alone the budget to be deployed in the media, which could easily be £1 million or more, to say nothing of the fees due to the celebrity.

One of the joys of using celebrities in advertising in research terms is that by definition they are extremely well known to the public. Therefore when discussing ideas in individual in-depth interviews or in group discussions with people chosen to represent the target market, it's very easy for respondents to talk about the brand in question in relationship to a whole range of stars who might be considered to have a relevant association. Exploratory qualitative research can be used to gauge the best fit between a particular celebrity and the brand and the appropriate degree of intimacy that can work commercially and practically. It's also important to gauge the receptiveness of the customers in a particular market to the use of celebrities per se. It may be that, for whatever reason, people in a certain sector do not see the use of famous people as relevant, or it might be that other brands that compete in the same area are already using stars and thus there isn't really a gap in the market for another brand using that creative vehicle. Some brands may have such strongly established personalities due to their longevity or to previous advertising campaigns of a non-celebrity sort that research indicates it's unlikely that adding a star endorsement will actually work.

Assuming that, in principle, using a celebrity for the brand seems to be a viable route, then qualitative research can also be used to pre-test creative executions of a campaign idea featuring a star. All the evidence suggests that campaigns featuring celebrities are no more likely than those featuring any other sort of creative idea to be successful – simply putting a famous person on the screen or in a magazine juxtaposed with the corporate, product or service brand is simply not enough. Particularly in the more sophisticated economies of the world, customers have got used to a high standard of advertising and know very well how the 'marketing game' is played. They appreciate that celebrities are 'doing it for the money' and if that's all they are seen to be doing in the brand campaign then it's unlikely to be particularly successful and could even be counterproductive. Qualitative research can be used to establish whether there is genuine added value in the creative idea, which is using a celebrity as a key part of it, and to use the diagnostics from the focus groups to develop it further and make the most of the investment in the star. After all, a poor script can cost the same to make as a great one that would increase the impact of the campaign enormously.

While creative people are usually comfortable about the qualitative research process, they are often sceptical about the ability of quantitative market research to assess the true merits of an advertising concept before it becomes a reality in the media. And it's true – sometimes it's very hard for people in a market research situation to grasp a truly innovative creative idea as evidenced by several campaigns which 'failed' in research, but which were produced and run anyway by brave clients and turned out to be great successes. Examples often cited in this context include CDP's Heineken 'Refreshes the parts' campaign launched puzzlingly, but engagingly, with a commercial in which policemen had their feet revitalized. Prior research had recommended that the execution not be made because refreshment was not 'relevant' to the lager market! The British Telecom 'Beattie' ads by AMV BBDO featuring Maureen Lipman had a narrow escape, since research suggested that she was likely to depress calling volumes, particularly among higher calling women, who were likely to distance themselves from her behaviour. In practice 'Beattie' became one of BT's most successful celebrity spokesmen in a long-running and successful campaign. The Audi 'Vorsprung durch Technik' campaign by BBH, which ran the risk of confirming all the worst fears about German characteristics – towels on the sun loungers before dawn etc. – was brought back from the brink by the addition of the ironic and self-deprecating voiceover by Geoffrey Palmer.

However, given the scale of the investment entailed in a celebrity campaign and their intrinsically high-profile nature, with consequent loss of face and damage to mutual reputation in the case of failure, many clients and their agencies use quantitative pre-testing as a key final stage in the developmental process. This process is best carried out using a completed TV commercial as the stimulus material for the research and, of course, producing a film is an expensive process. Film-making nearly always has an element of risk attached and this can often be heightened when a celebrity is involved. Thus there has to be a good level of confidence in the celebrity script idea based on the qualitative research, which gives the client and agency the green light to shoot the commercial, using a director and production company with the necessary experience and expertise. Having got to a provisional edit of the ad, then there are a number of market research agencies that have expertise in carrying out quantitative appraisals of them. Usually they have a substantial history of previous tests and thus are able to compare the results of the proposed commercial against the 'norms' for the market sector and even by the type of creative execution.

Millward Brown is acknowledged to be one of the leading UK research companies in the specialist field of quantitative pre-testing of commercials and they have amassed a substantial database of tests, which is sufficiently large for comparisons to be made between ads that featured celebrities and those which have not. Analysis of the Millward Brown database shows that in the three years 2000–2002 an average of 18% of all the commercials they tested have featured famous stars (Figure 64). This is a little above the incidence of celebrity campaigns in the IPA Effectiveness Awards database of case histories which is about 14%.

Their experience overall is that celebrities can be used successfully to grab attention and generate interest in involvement in the brand. They can also be used to establish a brand 'cue', which can in turn aid recognition and communication and they have also found that the 'right' celebrity can add values by association. Their research suggests that as long as the star doesn't 'upstage' the brand it's often beneficial if the celebrity is used for what they are famous for already and for the brand to borrow and build on their existing persona. Generally speaking, Millward Brown find that humorous ads communicate better than 'straight' ones and that spoofs or parodies can be especially effective. But, like all the best advertisements, those featuring celebrities need to integrate the brand and the message in the execution rather than falling into the trap of a simple 'bolt-on' juxtaposition, where the brand is a passenger in a star vehicle and is easily substitutable for another. It's in the nature of celebrities that they have not only their ardent fans, but

UK finished films

| | With celebrity | Non-celebrity | | |
Year	No. of tests	No. of tests	Total	% with celebrity
1991	12	94	106	11
1992	13	112	125	10
1993	14	92	106	13
1994	18	153	171	11
1995	17	134	151	11
1996	10	136	146	7
1997	17	113	130	13
1998	25	171	196	13
1999	23	145	168	14
2000	34	130	164	21
2001	34	158	192	18
2002	39	187	226	17

Figure 64 *Percentage of advertising campaigns featuring celebrities.*
Source: Millward Brown 2003.

also those that hate them. Thus one of the lessons learned through these tests is that having a star with a generally likeable personality is more likely to make for success.

However, the data also suggest that commercials featuring celebrities are no more likely than any other to perform in the top quartile or indeed the bottom quartile of all commercials, regardless of creative device. Indeed, across a raft of measures Millward Brown can find only one area in which there is a slight difference between celebrity commercials and non-celebrity commercials when it comes to the top performers. This difference is small but nevertheless noteworthy and it consists in the degree of correct attribution of brand to commercial, when no pack shot is shown in the stimulus material (Figure 65).

There is also a minor degree of difference in the overall level of branding for a commercial when a celebrity is employed (Figure 66).

Overall there's no getting away from the need for a really good creative idea and an excellent script if the asset that the celebrity represents is to be truly exploited for the benefit of the brand and ideally in so doing enhance the reputation of the star too.

mruk is a UK research organization with particular strengths in the regions and is the licensee for the Add+Impact system, which employs a

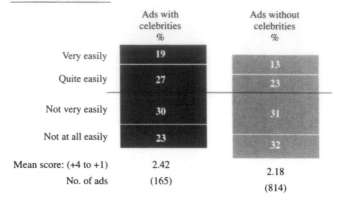

Celebrities can act as a brand cue

If the logo and PACKAGE?PRODUCT were taken out of this advert, how easily could you tell it was for XXXX?

UK finished film norms

	Ads with celebrities %	Ads without celebrities %
Very easily	19	13
Quite easily	27	23
Not very easily	30	31
Not at all easily	23	32
Mean score: (+4 to +1)	2.42	2.18
No. of ads	(165)	(814)

Figure 65 *Celebrities can act as a brand cue.*
Source: Millward Brown 2003.

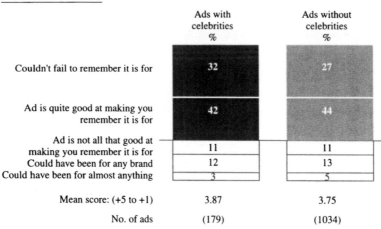

Branding mean scores
You've just watched an advert for XXXX. Which one of the phrases below applies to this advert?

UK finished film norms

	Ads with celebrities %	Ads without celebrities %
Couldn't fail to remember it is for	32	27
Ad is quite good at making you remember it is for	42	44
Ad is not all that good at making you remember it is for	11	11
Could have been for any brand	12	13
Could have been for almost anything	3	5
Mean score: (+5 to +1)	3.87	3.75
No. of ads	(179)	(1034)

Figure 66 *Branding mean scores for celebrity and non-celebrity ads.*
Source: Millward Brown 2003.

combination of both qualitative and quantitative research methodologies to assess advertising executions across all media. They too have a very large database of tests, with over 2322 having been conducted to date worldwide, of which 337 have been categorized as featuring a personality or celebrity, i.e. around 16%. A key part of their system are measures of the proportion of the target audience who indicate first the level of 'attention' given to the advertisement, second, the level of 'commitment' to the product or service having viewed the ad and, third, the level of 'acceptance' of the advertisement being relevant and appropriate to them, i.e. the degree of 'bonding' with it. Analysis of the mruk results confirms the Millward Brown finding that as a genre of advertising, executions that use celebrities are substantively neither more nor less effective than other types (Figure 67).

Comparison of Add+Impact data from three different geographical areas, namely Europe, Asia and Australasia, also indicates that there is little difference in the effectiveness of the use of celebrity ads in different parts of the world. Perhaps this is not surprising given the global nature of the phenomenon of fame and its application to advertising for brands all over the world (Figure 68).

However, when the data on celebrity ad effectiveness are broken down to product category level, some substantial differences are revealed which could have significant implications for marketers and their agencies. On this analysis, it looks as if there is a heightened degree of effectiveness when a celebrity is incorporated into the advertising and marketing communication for brands where there is either personal consumption or personal appearance involved (Figure 69).

Advertising genre	Level of target audience attention	Level of target audience commitment	Level of target audience bonding	Base number of ads
Fantasy	63%	48%	57%	253
Analogy	61%	45%	54%	104
Celebrity	60%	46%	57%	337
On/off camera drama	60%	46%	57%	1051
Product display	56%	45%	60%	313
Demonstration	53%	44%	61%	264
			Total	2322

Figure 67 *Advertising effectiveness by genre of ads.*
Source: mruk Research.

Geography	Level of target audience attention	Base number of ads
Europe	57%	106
Asia	62%	155
Australasia	62%	54

Figure 68 *Effectiveness of celebrity advertising around the world.*
Source: mruk Research.

Product category of advertising content	Change in % attention (compared with average)	Base number of celebrity ads
Food and drink	+7.2%	75
Alcohol	+7.1%	24
Personal appearance	+5.4%	47
Soft drinks/snacks	0	47
FMCG	−0.5%	53
Healthcare	−1.0%	40
Finance and services	−4.5%	85

Figure 69 *Effectiveness of celebrity advertising by product category.*
Source: mruk Research.

The UK supermodel was not well recognized in the
USA, but she was felt to be very appropriate

Q. Do you recognize the model in the ad?

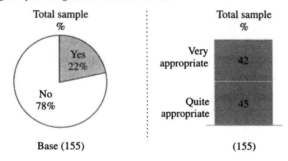

Base (155)   (155)

Figure 70 *Millward Brown supermodel research for cosmetics brand.*
Source: Millward Brown.

In this context, a test that Millward Brown carried out for a major cosmetics firm in the USA gives a very useful insight into how a celebrity can work for a brand. In this particular instance, the advertising execution was intended to launch a lipstick brand in the United States, but the UK supermodel to be used in the commercial was not especially well known on the other side of the Atlantic, with only 22% of the sample recognizing her. Despite this, she was felt to be a good choice with a total of 87% of the respondents feeling she was either very or quite appropriate to the task (Figure 70).

However, at a prompted level, the communication taken out of the commercial was significantly enhanced among those who recognized the supermodel. These included key dimensions such as 'Is in tune with the latest trends' (68% v 49%), 'Gives my lips great colour' (62% v 49%), 'Is moisturizing' (85% v 48%), 'Draws attention to my lips' (68% v 51%) and

Communication take out was better among those who recognised the model

Prompted Communication	Recognised %	Didn't recognise %
Is in tune with the latest trends	68	49
Gives my lips great color	62	49
Is moisturising	85	48
Draws attention to my lips	68	51
Makes my lips look fuller	50	34
Base:	(34) low base	(121)

Figure 71 *Millward Brown supermodel prompted communication.*
Source: Millward Brown.

'Makes my lips look fuller' (50% v 34%). Similarly, all the key measures such as 'enjoyment', 'involvement', 'branding' and 'understanding', plus the overall level of 'likes' was significantly higher among those recognizing her (Figure 71).

At a rational level the UK supermodel also performed well with 'news content' (88% v 63%), 'distinctiveness' (35% v 29%), 'relevance' (84% v 73%) and 'credibility' (55% v 43%) all being communicated much better to those familiar with her. All these data testify to the power that a celebrity can have in advertising communication terms. However, the real clincher was in terms of purchase intention: 74% of those who recognized her saying they would either 'definitely' or 'probably' buy the lipstick at a price of $4.97, compared to 56% among those who did not recognize her. These results show the importance of celebrity, as it is clearly sheer fame that grabs attention, generates increased interest and involvement, aids communication and increases persuasiveness. The use of a beautiful woman in promoting this lipstick did work pretty well, but when she was recognized as a celebrity supermodel the impact was considerably greater.

HPI, another leading UK research company, has developed a model for the various ways in which celebrities work for a brand and is clear from this that establishing a true connection between the famous person and the brand is central to the success of the campaign (Figure 72).

In HPI research terms an example of a 'testimonial' would be the role of Carol Vorderman in the Benecol advertisements where she is essentially acting as a spokesperson or mouthpiece for the brand. Their definition of 'imported' is where the celebrity performs a role that is already well known to the audience through TV or film appearances. Examples here

TESTIMONIAL

HARNESSED   IMPORTED

OBSERVER   INVENTED

Figure 72 *Five ways a celebrity can work for a brand.*
Source: David Iddiols, HPI Research.

would be Neil Morrissey and Leslie Ash reprising their roles from hit TV show 'Men Behaving Badly' in commercials for UK DIY retailer, Homebase. 'Observer' is where the celebrity takes on the role of commenting about the brand in question, for example as a customer, as Alan Davies did for Abbey National. Their definition of 'invented' is where the celebrity plays a part which has been developed exclusively for the brand and which only exists in that context. This was the technique underlying the appearance of Nicholas Lyndhurst in a portfolio of roles in ads for WH Smith. Finally, their interpretation of 'harnessed' is where the celebrity persona is wedded to the storyline of the brand advertising and as such the character of the celebrity him or herself can be evolved through the vehicle. This has been done with comedian Johnny Vaughan for Strongbow cider. Clearly, these five areas can overlap with each other and, indeed, a celebrity campaign may evolve from one to the other over time. Indeed, in an appendix to this volume, you can find details of the winning papers in the IPA Databank of Effectiveness Awards case histories that used celebrities. This suggests that the five HPI categories can be sub-segmented and that there may be at least ten different creative approaches to using celebrities in advertising.

HPI's research suggests that customers perceive the use of celebrities in 'testimonials' or in 'imported' mode as being imposed on the brand and less effective for it. Stars in the 'observer' mode can work well, but when they are 'harnessed' or 'invented' there seems to be a much greater degree of integration between celebrity and brand. As a result of this the correct brand attribution is very significantly higher with characters like Gary Lineker for Walkers and Jamie Oliver for Sainsbury's scoring in the high 80%–90%, whereas testimonials by Anthony Hopkins for Barclays, Denise Van Outen for Nescafé, and even Richard Branson for the Post Office, languish under 15% in terms of attribution. The high standards of British advertising have created high expectations and thus audiences perceive the straightforward brand spokesperson role or testimonial route as rather mundane and probably being done just for mercenary reasons. Contrariwise, there is much more audience reward to be derived from the storylines of commercials which give the opportunity for the celebrity to show some genuine engagement with the brand and therefore be enjoyed to a greater degree. There seems little doubt that admired advertising can lead to admiration for the brand. The sensitive and creative use of both qualitative and quantitative research can be a vital aid in achieving this.

PART IV

How to Use Celebrities for Brands

Introduction

This part is all about how to use celebrities in the service of a brand. Clearly, there are as many ways of doing this as there are ideas in the human imagination, but there are some broad principles that can guide marketers and their agencies in the utilization of stars. At its most basic there is a relatively simple equation between the degree of intimacy between the celebrity and the corporate, product or service brand and the effectiveness of the endorsement. The more closely involved the celebrity is with the brand, the more they commit themselves and the more they are seen to be inextricably associated with it, the higher the cost in financial terms. But beyond the monetary considerations, in the ideal relationship between a brand and the star there needs to be a real sense of commitment and engagement between the two.

The important thing is that the marketer and their agency should go into the partnership with the celebrity with a very clear view of the financial constraints imposed on situation by their budget and therefore a realistic expectation of the degrees of intimacy that are achievable with any given status level of star. For example, it might be better to use the voiceover only of a very famous movie actor in a long-term campaign for the brand rather than to employ a much lesser star as a lead artist in a one-off commercial. There is enormous scope for creativity in this arena and there are many different ways of making the best of famous people in the service of brands, but the guiding principles should be the optimization of 'fit', 'fame', 'facets' and 'finance' (Figure 73).

The marketer and their agency need to ask themselves the following questions before embarking on the use of a celebrity:

'How well does this particular celebrity fit in with the brand?'
'How famous is the star?'

Figure 73 *Four 'Fs' in using a celebrity.*

'Which facets of this high-profile person can best work for the brand profile?'
'How much of this can the brand finance?'

All the research suggests that the more intimate the relationship between the brand and the celebrity chosen to be its partner in commercial communications, the more likely it is to be effective in the marketplace. So, ideally, the marketer and the agency should strive to create as inextricable a bond between their brand and the star as possible.

However, celebrities are brands in their own right and are constantly seeking to maximize their own reputation and perceived value in the eyes of their fan base and the public at large. In trying to develop their own careers they are helped, and sometimes hindered, by an army of interested friends, relatives, advisers, agents and producers. Thus the world in which they live and operate is a complex one where decisions are taken for all sorts of reasons, which may or may not appear rational to a brand owner seeking to establish a commercial relationship with the celebrity. The star may therefore resist well-meaning attempts to create intimacy and fend off a close relationship with the brand on any number of grounds and only settle for a relatively 'cool' association such as a product placement, rather than a 'hotter' one such as direct employment. And, of course, money will be a big factor in all this. Celebrities and their agents understand very well the power that they wield and the increase in their impact on the brand that will result from an increasingly wholehearted involvement with it. Thus, quite naturally, intimacy comes with a high price tag.

For all these reasons the nature and depth of the relationship does need to be explored in some detail. Figure 74 sets up a model of the six main ways in which the celebrity can be involved with a brand. Inevitably, there are overlapping areas between them, but it is helpful to discuss each of these in turn and the subsequent chapters do this.

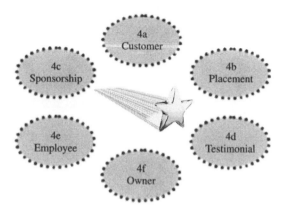

Figure 74 *Degrees of star involvement with a brand.*

For example, it might be that the celebrity has already chosen to be a customer of the brand, but how widely known is this usership? Could it become the basis of a more formal association?

If a brand owner discovers that a famous person is already a customer, then it could be a useful strategy if the celebrity is provided with the favoured product or service for free resulting in more conspicuous consumption of it. This has been done with cars, for example, and is essentially a form of one-to-one product placement, which can, of course, be taken much further in the context of placement in movies, TV shows or even books and songs. Or it might take the form of a sponsorship, that is to say paid for representation by wearing the brand logo as part of the sort of sponsorship agreement commonly found in sports. The relationship could go further into a full-blown testimonial in which the star actually talks about their brand usage and makes favourable comments about it in the script of a commercial or in interviews set up for public relations purposes.

At another, much deeper level of engagement, the celebrity might be hired as an employee of the brand, for example as a sports team member, a name designer for a haute couture house, a star analyst in the financial services sector, a conductor for an orchestra, as temporary guest editor of a magazine or even as the CEO. Finally, it could go all the way to the most intimate of relationships, that of ownership, where the celebrity actually develops and markets their own brand, either on their own using the brand owner as a 'white label' manufacturer or in a co-branded joint venture.

12

Celebrity customers

Even celebrities have to eat and drink, find somewhere to live, go shopping and generally behave like customers, albeit ones with considerably greater spending power than ordinary people and the ability to influence the buying decisions of others simply by what they choose to buy for themselves. The role-modelling effect, whereby people seek to emulate their favoured celebrities, presents an opportunity for the brands, which are either lucky enough or shrewd enough to become patronized by famous people (Figure 75).

The building of a brand by association with customers whom other people respect, aspire to or even simply want to copy in order to be part of their peer group is probably as old as human society itself. In feudal times kings, queens, dukes, duchesses and the other noble folk who comprised the court were the fashion and style leaders of their day. At the beginning of the last century their majesties George and Mary were sufficiently enamoured

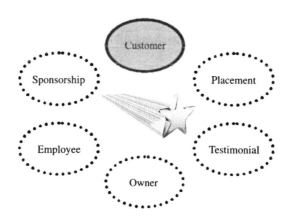

Figure 75 *Star involvement with a brand – customer.*

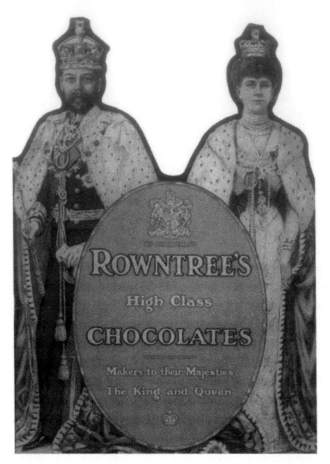

Figure 76 *Rowntree's Chocolates display card image of 1911.*
Source: HAT/Nestlé.
Image of an advertisement for Rowntree's Chocolates from 1911 is reproduced with the kind
permission of Société des Produits Nestlé S.A.

of Rowntree's 'high-class' chocolates to allow their likenesses to be used in
Rowntree's publicity (Figure 76).

In more recent times the honour of being a supplier to royalty has
been formalized in the UK by the creation of the Royal Warrant Holders'
Association. There are roughly 800 warranted companies, all but 40 of
whom are association members, and they qualify to display the royal crest
of the royal patron to whom they supply their goods and services. It is hard
to quantify the value of this royal association but there's no doubt that
it has some power. One of the side-effects of the spectacular falling out
between Mohammed Al Fayed, owner of Harrods, and the royal family was
the removal of both Queen Elizabeth's and the Duke of Edinburgh's Royal

Warrants from the façade of the Knightsbridge department store. This once pre-eminent retailer has recently been eclipsed by a resurgent Selfridges in Oxford Street and is now reputedly up for sale – was the loss of the warrants mere coincidence or a portent?

With or without a warrant, the evidence suggests that royal patronage in the UK is a valuable thing for a brand. The shares in Scottish & Newcastle, owner of HP Bulmer, were a direct beneficiary of Prince William's comment in his interview marking the end of his second year at St Andrews University when he said: 'Everybody thinks I drink beer, but actually I like cider. I do think I'm a country boy at heart.' Bulmer's spokesman George Thomas said at the time: 'Cider is popular with the 18-to-24 age group so, at 21, Prince William is the perfect target market. It is terrific news for the cider industry.' When photographs of Zara Phillips, daughter of Anne, the Princess Royal, were widely publicized, showing her horsing around at the 2003 Badminton horse trials wearing a distinctive pink and white sweatshirt, it must have done wonders for the profile of Hackett, its maker.

Exploiting a celebrity customer for the benefit of the brand is obviously a delicate matter. In encouraging further purchase by the provision of advantageous terms or even free products and services is one way of doing so, but even a celebrity and their entourage can only consume so much of any particular brand. There's also a risk that the brand may be taken advantage of by the many 'wannabe' stars who attempt to exploit what minor fame they may have, and the promise of more to come, by soliciting freebies. Thus the brand manager and any agencies involved have to approach this area with great caution and perhaps it's better simply to rely on the basics of outstanding product delivery and great customer service rather than a surfeit of gifts.

Old-style Italian restaurants often used to cover their walls with autographed photos of famous customers glad-handing the owner and would provide free meals to ensure they visited again. But this seems decidedly uncool nowadays and was never likely to be a feature of the marketing of a restaurant such as the Ivy in West Street, near Leicester Square in Central London. Jeremy King and Christopher Corbin acquired the Ivy in 1989 when it was long past its best, but by the time they sold it to the Belgo Group, along with sister restaurants Le Caprice and J. Sheekey's, in 1998 for £13.4 million, this duo had turned it into one of the world's most famous restaurants, with food that was excellent without aspiring to Michelin stars, but a following among celebrity guests to die for.

What they did so skilfully is an object lesson for any luxury brand, which aspires to develop its celebrity customers and indeed probably provides good guidance for the mass brands that will almost certainly find famous customers hidden away in their database, if only they took the trouble to identify them. Corbin and King made it their business to know their customer base extremely well and not just the celebrity lunch or dinner guests themselves, but their secretaries, personal assistants and agents who very often make the bookings on their behalf.

They were also assiduous in understanding the industries from which a majority of their customers come which, given the location of the restaurant, and its history, tend to be concentrated in the movie, TV, show business, media and literary worlds. The restaurant produces their own weekly in-house news bulletin with items summarized from the newspapers and key publications such as *The Stage, Screen International, Broadcast* and *Campaign.* As a result of reading the relevant trade press and being genuinely interested in these creative industries, they are able to recognize famous people or celebrities in the making and converse with them in a well-informed manner. Indeed, there is now an expectation among customers that the Ivy team will be au fait with the latest news in their sector and this adds value to the dining experience. Combined with a shrewd allocation of tables and careful placement in the restaurant, the Ivy has managed to create an ambience that works as well for the stars as it does for the business clientele, which likes to rub shoulders with them. Current manager Mitchell Everard has continued this deep customer understanding and commitment to outstanding service, which should be the stock in trade of any professional brand owner.

The Ivy has never used a public relations agency, but instead has kept a very tight control on its own profile and relied purely on positive word of mouth from customers to spread the reputation, first through the key London market, then internationally to New York, Los Angeles and now worldwide. If a restaurant enjoys a celebrity clientele, the temptation for staff to tip off the paparazzi when a star guest is in the house is high, but this is a dismissible offence at the Ivy and their celebrity customers gain comfort from this policy. Despite this strictly enforced house rule, some of the people emerging after a meal do occasionally oblige door-stepping photographers with inside information. As a result many free column inches have appeared as the likes of Tom Cruise or Nicole Kidman are captured on camera emerging from the restaurant into a waiting limousine, with the way cleared for them by the Ivy's distinctive top-hatted doorman.

With this outstanding attention to detail the Ivy has little need of giving away free meals to celebrities in order to ensure they return again and again. But King and Corbin did set up a symbolic little club for those customers who have eaten there on every single day of a week. Those who have joined this select group only know they have done so when a dessert that they haven't ordered arrives at their table. This is a large dish with dark chocolate decoration around its edge and a blue glass bowl at its centre containing some delicious chocolate truffle sticks. Even the most blasé of customers cannot fail to be touched by this stylish acknowledgement of their loyalty to the restaurant!

As an extension of treating celebrity customers extremely well and building word-of-mouth reputation among their peer group, there is the tacit agreement whereby a product is named for a famous customer in the hope that there will be an increased halo effect on the brand. There is a long history of this practice and it does seem acceptable when there actually is an existing buyer–seller relationship. This was the case when Dame Nellie Melba, the famous singer and toast of the Covent Garden Opera House from the 1890s to the 1920s, was a favoured customer of the Savoy Hotel in London. The chef there, Auguste Escoffier, created the 'Peach Melba' pudding in her honour. More recently, but in the same vein, the ex-Mrs Noel Gallagher, Meg Matthews, a prolific Bond Street shopper, bought so many shoes that she has had a £565 pair of scarlet sequined open-toed Gina ankle boots named after her. It also seems legitimate where the celebrity has been a genuine inspiration or muse to the creator of the product. The German nail varnish company Tennails, owned by SB Beauty Marketing Limited, launched a new range of nail polishes. In their Star Collection, all the colours are named after famous celebrities including Catherine Zeta-Jones, Angelina Jolie and Minnie Driver. They have also launched three other labels in the same mode. Items in the first range, called 'Some like it Hot!', are named after classic screen icons such as Marilyn Monroe and Katherine Hepburn. The second is 'The Name's Bond' with such labels as Pussy Galore and Miss Moneypenny, and finally 'Catwalk Stunners', which covers the big names in the fashion world: Elle MacPherson, Naomi Campbell and Christy Turlington. The key with this strategy is to ensure that the celebrities involved *are* involved – if such a naming exercise turns out to be a superficial PR stunt then it may damage the brand severely.

If a celebrity chooses to buy a particular product or service of their own volition and as a result of a preference derived from their own experience, then this constitutes the most intimate of relationships that the brand can achieve and is extremely valuable as a result. But because it is, at least to start with, a relatively private and personal buying decision, it is hard to turn this to commercial advantage without damaging the very relationship that the brand is seeking to develop. The best advice for the marketer and agencies is to do unto celebrities as they would wish to be done to themselves. That is to say to treat them in an adult-to-adult manner with real consideration and sensitivity. The first step in doing this successfully is, of course, to identify whether the brand has any famous customers already – it's surprising how few have taken the trouble to find this out, given the potential benefits that they could bring to the business.

13

Celebrity product placement

Judging the dividing line between a celebrity customer and the initial stages of celebrity product placement is extremely difficult. Perhaps one way of looking at it is that when the celebrity is deliberately using the brand as part of a piece of conspicuous consumption which in some way is going to benefit them, then it moves beyond the straightforward private purchase and becomes a commercial act. In a sense the celebrity is using the iconography of the brand to build his or her own distinctive identity. At the other end of the scale, of course, the lead is taken by a brand, which seeks to enhance its own positioning by a close commercial association with a celebrity, thus acquiring some of their iconic status for itself (Figure 77).

At the beginning of the last century artists Georges Braque and Pablo Picasso, the founders of the Cubist movement, innovated by incorporating elements of everyday objects in their paintings and collages: Braque's 'Still Life on a Table' features an advertisement for Gillette razors cut from a newspaper. But the incorporation of iconic brands into modern art really

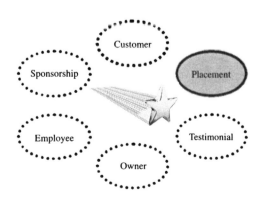

Figure 77 *Star involvement with a brand – placement.*

began in earnest with the irreverent work of Andy Warhol in the early 1960s. His silkscreen series of Campbell's soup tins and three-dimensional sculptures of Brillo boxes turned these ordinary consumer goods into works of art, which became famous worldwide. Not only did these artworks give enormous free exposure to the brands involved, but also reinforced their own status as iconic representatives of American consumer culture.

However, it's not always the icon brands that benefit by being adopted by creative people in the worlds of the arts and music. Many fashions over the years have been spawned by famous people who have expressed their individuality by choosing to associate themselves with obscure brands rather than with the more mainstream ones that ordinary people use. Sometimes it just turns out that a rock star such as Janis Joplin really likes to drink Southern Comfort while performing on stage. Then along comes Keith Richards of the Rolling Stones and pulls the same stunt, but this time with a bottle of Jack Daniels. Lesser known and more contemporary band, Alabama 3, with its own cult following, have a particular thing for Tenants Super Strength lager and have written a song about it eulogizing the 'Ole Purple Tin'.

There are very strict rules surrounding product placement in UK TV shows so what good fortune it was that the men in 'Men Behaving Badly' just happened to imbibe cans of Stella Artois on a pretty regular basis, if not every episode of the 'non-commercial' BBC series. In an episode of 'Sex and the City', Jessica used a baby 'rock-a-tot' product and sales rocketed. Liam Gallagher, bad boy frontman for UK rock band Oasis, adopted the then unfashionable Kangol brand and appeared wearing it at concerts and on shows such as 'Top of the Pops', turning it into must have clothing for a whole generation of fans. In many of these cases the brand owner stumbles on the association by chance or has it drawn to their attention by a fan or a mention in a press article. Once this has happened, the marketer has to approach the situation with great caution in case he or she accidentally compromises the star making them feel exploited and causing them to drop their usage, thus killing the goose that lays such valuable eggs for their brand.

Adidas executives got it right in 1986 when they spotted major hip-hop stars Run DMC performing their song 'My Adidas' in front of fans who immediately reacted by holding up their own Adidas shoes. The company acted immediately and signed the three artists to a $1.5 million sponsorship contract. In the year 2002 artists Busta Rhymes and Puff Daddy collaborated on a song called 'Pass the Courvoisier Part II'. Despite rumours to the contrary, Courvoisier claimed that there was no prior involvement between the company and the duo, but in any event the association reportedly led to a sales increase of 20% as the fans of these celebrated hip-hop stars flocked to emulate their heroes' drinking habits. This vogue for cognac has turned around the fortunes of a key French industry, which had been in long-term decline. Bemused French producers have now been on familiarization trips to the United States in order to try and understand this extraordinary phenomenon whereby hip-hop culture has adopted one of the icons of French culture for its own. The most expensive French champagnes, Cristal and Krug, which are celebrity brands in themselves, have also been major beneficiaries of the new money generated by rap music.

These rising stars rely on celebrity brands to ensure maximum credibility in their conspicuous displays of wealth. Lucian James, a brand and marketing strategist working out of San Francisco, monitors the Billboard top 20 to identify songs that carry brand names and then ranks them on his website 'American Brandstand'. On any given week there are between 20 and 50 brand references in the top 20 songs! Given that these are the most listened to tracks in the USA, and this popularity often leads to international chart success and worldwide exposure, this is a very valuable form of product placement for brands. The beneficiaries of this tend to be luxury goods such as Mercedes-Benz, Lexus, Burberry and Gucci, but the list of brands also extends to the likes of mid-market Abercrombie and Fitch and then as far down the market as Burger King and Payless Shoes. This form of 'accidental' product placement, which as John McKnight, drinks guru of agency BMP.DDB, would say is 'apparently untouched by the hand of marketing', can be very powerful influence on young adults, who themselves are seeking their own identities.

Those brands, which are really serious about making celebrity product placement work, have to take a strategic approach and leave as little as possible to chance. They also have to commit significantly greater financial resources to the process. The same rigour must be applied to this technique of applying celebrity to a brand as any other, with the same detailed analysis of the appropriateness and relevance of the fit between the brand and the star, plus the context in which this product placement will occur.

Ford have recently signed up soccer prodigy Wayne Rooney to drive their 'Sportska' and thereby help position it away from their 'Ka' model, which is widely perceived to be a vehicle for women. At 17 years of age the Everton star was the youngest England player ever to score a goal for his country when he did so in the match against Liechtenstein in September 2003. In this context Ford's reported payment to him of £1.5 million to secure a promotional deal and get him to drive the 'Sportska' looks as if it could pay off.

Nearly all the most successful executions of the product placement strategy occur in movies, especially those made in Hollywood, and there is no guarantee of box-office success at the time the placement is being negotiated. Long experience, close personal connections, good judgement, creativity and a healthy dose of luck are all required to produce the kind of returns that RayBan got from its reported $60 million investment and its sunglasses' iconic role in the *Men in Black* movie starring Will Smith and Tommy Lee Jones. *MIB* became a global blockbuster generating audiences in excess of 300 million and ticket sales revenues of $577 million. Reportedly, RayBan's sales increased by 20% on a worldwide basis and revived the fortunes and fashionability of a brand that had been suffering at the hands of newer arrivals on the eyewear scene such as Oakley, Chanel, Dolce & Gabbana, Gucci, Porsche and Prada. The brand has continued this successful strategy with Keanu Reeves in the *Matrix* movies.

Because of the risks involved in making movies, where the statistics show that the tiny proportion of the feature films made which are successes subsidise the vast majority that are not, it's not surprising that marketers and the agencies involved tend to gravitate to the key protagonists who have the best track records. Directors, producers, scriptwriters and stars who have delivered hits in the past probably stand a greater chance of doing so in the future and nowhere has this been better demonstrated than in the extraordinary sequence of Bond movies.

As a result of their success and perceived bankability, these Broccoli Saltzman productions have become a magnet for product placement. Perhaps the epitome of such deals was the decision by BMW to use the film *Golden Eye* to launch its new Z3 Roadster car in the year 1995. This might have been seen as foolhardy were it not for the track record in box-office terms of the Bond movies and the extraordinary PR spin-off that accompanies each new release. BMW's confidence was rewarded and *Golden Eye* achieved a worldwide audience of 200 million and a box office of over $351 million. The car went on to be a great success and its first-year sales totalled over 10,000, making it one of the most successful new car launches the company has ever seen. Indeed, the car sold out completely in its first year of production! Several other brands have hitched themselves to the Bond bandwagon and these include Rolex, Omega, Visa, Avis, Smirnoff, Heineken, Ericsson, and L'Oréal. Maybe this is just a virtuous circle in which the strong get stronger, but these brands do seem to be some of the most successful ones and several are among those most committed to celebrity.

Negotiating product placement deals in movies is extremely difficult and there are a number of specialist companies, mainly based in Los Angeles, which operate in this area on behalf of both producers and brand owners. For this process is a two-way street as the income from product placement has grown over the years to the point where it has become a significant element in the financing of a film production. The product placement industry in the USA has its own trade body, the Entertainment Resources and Marketing Association, where the names of some of the leading companies who operate in the sphere can be found.

The proliferation of TV channels and the voracious demand for content that this has created means that broadcasters' production budgets are stretched ever thinner and the independent production houses are under relentless pressure to reduce the cost per programme hour. This in turn has created many more opportunities for product placement in TV shows. However, in the UK, the rules are strict. Under the ITC Code of Programme Sponsorship, product placement is defined as: 'the inclusion of, or a reference to, a product or service within a programme in return for payment or other valuable consideration to the programme-maker or ITC licensee (or any representative or associate of either)'. In essence, this is not allowed. Meanwhile the BBC's Producer's Guidelines on Programme Funding and External Relationships state that: 'A product or service must never be included in sound or vision in return for cash, services or any consideration in kind. This is product placement and it is expressly forbidden in BBC programmes. It is illegal to make any such arrangements in the UK or anywhere else within the European Union.' It goes on to say that:

> BBC programmes need to reflect the real world and from time to time reference will be made to commercial products and commercial concerns. However, programmes must never give the impression that they are endorsing or promoting any product, service or company. References in programmes to all products and services must be editorially justifiable and not promotional.

Nevertheless, within this highly constrained environment the major UK car brands such as Ford and Vauxhall vie with each other to provide the vehicles for police dramas and there is a useful quid pro quo for the production companies given the wear and tear involved in dramatic car chases which often end up in accidents and even total write-offs! Its reported that Ford may have provided as many as 500 cars in any one year for filming purposes. Perhaps it's a function of the complexities surrounding the negotiation of these product placement deals and the participants' mutual desire to maintain confidentiality, but one of the results of the somewhat shadowy nature of this activity is that there is a paucity of facts and figures on what it costs and on the results that are generated. However, one guiding principle can be relied on, which is that as in the direct marketing field, if a brand continues to use a particular media channel, in this case prior placement in close juxtaposition to stars, then that's a pretty good sign that it is working profitably.

14

Celebrity sponsorship

As with product placement, there is a wide spectrum of associations between celebrities and brands, which could be defined as sponsorship. However, the definition of the word sponsorship itself is helpful in clarifying the role of the brand in relationship to the celebrity. In its original sense there is a meaning of the word sponsorship, which implies 'helping, supporting, and acting as patron' (Figure 78).

From the earliest times, wealthy people with a love of the arts, music, architecture, or fascinated by outstanding prowess in the fields of sporting endeavour, have been attracted towards those with outstanding talents in these areas. While the wealthy patron may have had some personal interest derived from a modicum of ability of their own they recognized that their talent was but a pale reflection of the expert's. Very often these talents, although outstanding, need nurturing and training, and herein lies

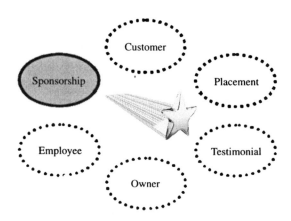

Figure 78 *Star involvement with a brand – sponsorship.*

the opportunity for a reciprocal relationship. The talented protagonist very often lacks the financial resources to develop their talents to the full whereas the gifted amateur patron has the wealth to provide equipment, coaches and other support to enable the professional to achieve their full potential. Thus the patron can bask in the reflected glory of the artist or athlete, knowing that their support has made a real contribution, giving them a vicarious sense of achievement too.

Over the centuries the talents of great artists such as Mozart and Michelangelo have been supported by patrons, such as Archbishop Hieronymus Von Colloredo, Emperor Joseph II and the Medici family, all of whom have had the vision to recognize great talent and the sensitivity to manage what was very often a turbulent relationship. The same process is at work in the modern era and there are lessons in the history of sponsorship for the marketer, brand manager and their agencies. Customers nowadays are very sophisticated and they see with great clarity how the worlds of marketing, advertising and branding operate. In this context, sponsorships of celebrities by brands where the brand is bringing little more than hard cash to the table are much less likely to be successful beyond a low-level association and an increased potential for brand name recognition (Figure 79).

There's no doubt that sports celebrities are a powerful motivator, especially for men, and this has been confirmed (as if it needed to be!) by research

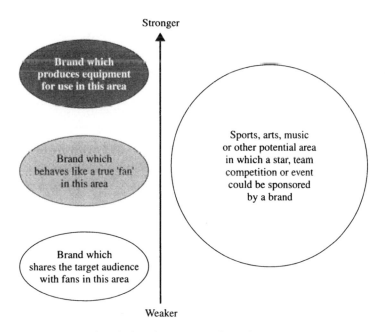

Figure 79 *Relative strength of the brand-sponsoring relationship.*

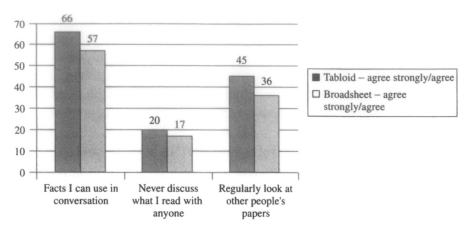

Figure 80 *Sports news as social currency.*
Source: NMA/BMRB/Davey Bioletti Planning and Research.

from the newly formed Newspaper Marketing Agency (NMA). This shows the vital role that sports news plays as a social currency among men and therefore why linkage with stars, especially football ones, can be so effective for brands in the UK (Figure 80).

What is more newsworthy is the priority that readers put on the sports pages in their papers. Some 54% of tabloid readers claim to treat back page as their first port of call and while the average broadsheet reader is less likely to claim back page first readership, over one-third still opt for back page as their first access to paper. This rises to 69% including those who scan front-page headlines and then turn to the sport section. Reebok's involvement with footballer Ryan Giggs is a good example of a sports brand working successfully with a soccer star and the IPA Effectiveness Awards case history from the early 1990s showed a dramatic increase in sales (Figure 81).

A sponsorship is much more effective if customers perceive the brand to be adding value to the relationship because of its own skills and provenance. This is why some of the most obvious sponsorships are also the best. Many of these do occur in the world of sports and can emerge from very small beginnings and grow to be mutual associations of enormous benefit to both parties. For example, the parents of young kids embarking on a career in tennis are not always from the well-off middle classes and they face years of significant expenses in terms of tennis shoes, clothing and rackets, to say nothing of the travel and accommodation costs involved in going to the many tournaments in which their children must participate in order to improve their ranking. This is a happy hunting ground for brands, which want to sponsor the up-and-coming talent and which, if they get lucky and

Figure 81 *Ryan Giggs.*
Source: Reebok UK.

pick a winner early in a young career, can negotiate a very attractive deal. Many of the leading sporting brands have close contacts with the coaching staff of the sports in which their brand specializes and are either in receipt of requests for sponsorship or in the market actually offering it proactively to those kids and parents who seem to have the greatest potential.

Even at this very young level there's another lesson to be learned by brands operating in this core area of true sponsorship. This is the basic reality that outstanding people, whether in sports, music or the arts, wish to maximize their performance and any equipment that is involved in the process has to be of the very highest quality in order to make the most of their ability. Happily, this relationship is a reciprocal one because the use of the equipment under the most demanding competitive conditions is a very effective form of research and development for the brand (Figure 82).

Thus apart from sponsoring a young performer by providing them with equipment and a financial contribution towards their living, travelling and training expenses, for which of course the brand gets the usual recognition in terms of logos and photo opportunities, the company is also receiving regular feedback on how the latest version of their racket, instrument or computer is performing. When an average club tennis player sees Tim Henman at Wimbledon playing with a Slazenger racket, he or she is right to assume that Henman is not just using this racket because he's been paid to do so – his career is too important for that – but that he really believes Slazenger rackets are the best he can get to suit his particular game.

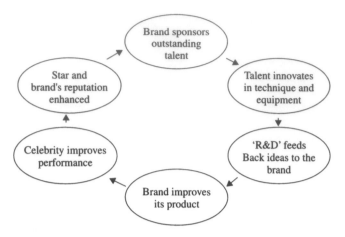

Figure 82 *The mutual benefit of celebrity sponsorship.*

This kind of sponsorship, between a sporting equipment brand and a sports celebrity, is one of the most direct ways in which famous people can sell. Quite rightly, customers perceive outstanding performance to be inextricably connected with a piece of sporting equipment and can assume with a high level of confidence that if they too were to play using that particular piano, guitar, racket, bat, club or pair of boots, then their own personal performance would certainly be no worse than it would be anyway and quite likely to be much improved.

The obvious downside of sponsoring an individual performer in the area of sport, the arts or music is that they may not do as well as hoped and their star may wane instead of wax with possible negative associations for the brand. Many of the investments made at the junior levels of sports by brands wishing to sponsor a future winner have turned out to be unlucky gambles. This is why many brands choose instead to sponsor teams, events or competitions which are populated with large numbers of celebrities so that it doesn't matter which individual wins or loses, because the brand is associated with the general aura of star activity. Clearly, the association with a group of people is intrinsically weaker than with an individual, but if the sponsorship is well managed, the presence of the brand is shrewdly negotiated and organization immerses itself as if it were a true fan, then it can work very well. As with any sponsorship, the brand must negotiate as many access rights to spectators and viewers as possible and use all the available opportunities for database building by involving people in competitions, prize draws and websites (Figure 83).

There's hardly a football team playing in any level of the multi-layered English Football Association that does not have a sponsor of one sort or

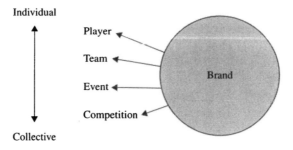

Individual

Player

Team

Event   Brand

Competition

Collective

Figure 83 *Potential points of sponsorship.*

	Premiership Team	Sponsor
1	Manchester United	Vodafone
2	Arsenal	02
3	Newcastle United	NTL
4	Chelsea	Emirate Airlines
5	Liverpool	Carlsberg
6	Blackburn Rovers	AMD Processors
7	Everton	Kejian
8	Southampton	Friends Provident
9	Manchester City	Eidos
10	Tottenham Hotspur	Thomson Holidays
11	Middlesbrough	Dial a phone
12	Charlton Athletic	All:Sports
13	Birmingham City	Phones4U
14	Fulham	Betfair.com
15	Leeds United	Strongbow
16	Aston Villa	Rover
17	Bolton Wanderers	Reebok
18	West Ham United	Dr Martens
19	West Bromwich Albion	West Bromwich Building Society
20	Sunderland	Reg Vardy

Figure 84 *Premiership shirt sponsors.*
Source: IPA.

another. The list of the shirt sponsors for the UK's Premier League is a rollcall of leading brands (Figure 84).

The individual Grand Prix within the Formula One circuit represent good opportunities for an event sponsorship and the R&D process in action, as many of its supporters are providers of components to the motor industry. The British F1 Grand Prix is sponsored overall by Fosters, however the *full list* of sponsors for F1 includes:

Altea (Marlboro)	Imperial Tobacco (Gold Leaf)
Benetton Group	Imperial Tobacco (JPS)
Beta Tools	Japan Tobacco (Mild Seven)
Brembo	Martini & Rossi
British American Tobacco (Lucky Strike)	Orange
Brooke Bond Oxo	Parmalat
Champion	PlayStation (Sony)
Compaq	Politoys
Computer Associates	Red Bull
Copersucar	Reemtsma (West)
Crédit Suisse	Saudia Airlines
DHL	SEITA (Gitanes & Gauloises)
Eifelland	Sonax
Federal Express	STP Corporation
First National Bank	TAG-Heuer
Fondmetal SpA	UOP
Gallagher (Benson & Hedges)	Valvoline
History of sponsorship in Formula 1	Villiger (Tabatip)
Hong Kong & Shanghai Bank	Vodafone
Hugo Boss	Warsteiner Brauerei
Imperial Tobacco (Embassy)	Yardley

Compelling though this sport is for millions, perhaps even this list could be a little overlong?

The world of the arts and music also provides many opportunities for one-off event sponsorship. For example, recent exhibitions at Tate Modern include 'Cruel and Tender', sponsored by UBS and the Unilever Series of commissions in Tate Modern's Turbine Hall. And the Royal Opera House in Covent Garden recently had an evening sponsored by Audi. Each of these events offers the brand the opportunity to match its target audience with the paying visitors and to use corporate hospitality to good advantage with trade customers and other intermediaries. These set-piece occasions are often quite well publicized and the brand will get exposure in that context. Crucially, and very much depending on the negotiation, the brand name may be included in the title of the event and assuming this is picked up by journalists and broadcasters can add a very important additional dimension in terms of media exposure and resultant recognition.

There is hardly an area of human leisure activity that does not exhibit this potential synergy between its great exponents and the brands which provide their equipment. What to the mass market may seem a minority pursuit is to the aficionados an all-consuming passion. Although much smaller in number, the fans of inline skating or early English chamber music are as committed to their activity as the followers of baseball or pop. By definition the brands which operate in these markets and thousands of others like them have to be deeply imbued in the culture and to be continuously involved in spotting new talent, discerning any innovations that they're making, often through their own inventiveness and experimentation, and then adopting and adapting these ideas into their manufactured branded product.

Of course, it's not essential for the sponsoring brand to be directly involved in the activity which it is paying to support and put its brand name to. But in these cases it is very important to exhibit at least some of the characteristics of the true fan of the sport or activity, i.e. loyalty and commitment, if the association is not to be seen by customers, participants and fans alike as merely an exploitative one. Indeed, the power of the celebrity sponsorship dynamic is such that a brand with the right level of resources and credibility in one market sector can use a famous celebrity to establish its position in a completely new sports arena where it had no previous reputation. Nike's incursion into the highly contested and long-established world of golf equipment using Tiger Woods as a spearhead is an example of this strategy. It hasn't been all plain sailing for Nike, given Tiger's form in 2003, but overall the brand has made a major incursion into a completely new sporting category populated by some very powerful and deeply entrenched competitors. It's hard to believe the brand could have done this without celebrity support.

15

Celebrity testimonial

Introduction

The celebrity testimonial is the most widely used technique by which a brand can enhance its reputation. It means literally a 'formal statement testifying to someone's character and qualifications or a public tribute to someone and to their achievements'. There are a very wide range of ways in which a testimonial can be provided with implied degrees of intimacy between brand and star. There is overlap between these, but for ease of use this chapter is itself divided up into sub-sections dealing with the main ways in which a celebrity can provide a 'testimonial' including voiceovers, music, faces and photography, TV and live appearances (Figure 85).

There is ample evidence that the public responds almost immediately to a recommendation made by a famous person whom they respect, especially when an endorsement is given as a part of a TV programme. Celebrity chef

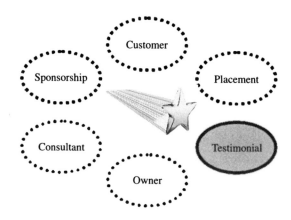

Figure 85 *Star Involvement with a brand – testimonial.*

Delia Smith created some extraordinary sales effects as a result of what she said about ingredients and equipment during her 'How to Cook' BBC TV series. Sales of eggs increased by 54 million during her first six-week BBC2 series in 1998. Delia also had an extraordinary impact on a small frying pan manufacturer by recommending their £10.95 omelette pan as a 'little gem' on another of her programmes. The maker, Lune Metal Products based in Morecambe, Lancashire, saw sales of that particular pan increase from 200 a year to 90,000 in four months! Jeremy Clarkson, the UK journalist and broadcaster is well known for his passion for sports cars and famous for his often acerbic appearances in BBC's 'Top Gear'. In the programme aired on 20 October 2002 Clarkson raved about the quirky Citroën Berlingo Multispace, referring to it as 'astonishing value for money'. In the previous month Citroën had sold just 200 of these vehicles, but 600 were sold in the 11 days after the 'Top Gear' plug. These examples of celebrity testimonials are editorial in nature, but the same effects can be achieved in a commercial, paid-for context, if well managed.

Voiceovers

The price attached to a celebrity testimonial will not only be a function of the status of the star and the extent of the usage over time and in terms of geographies, but will also be directly related to the degree of intimacy and sense of commitment conveyed. At one end of the spectrum, it is quite possible to use a celebrity voiceover without the personality appearing at all. This has been done very effectively in a series of highly successful animated films. Although Disney retains its popularity and money-making ability – it holds the top three positions for gross profit from an animated film – DreamWorks has become an impressive rival, with films such as *Shrek* holding fourth place in the rankings with $455,100,000 according to imdb.com. One important competitive difference that exists between these two animation giants is the relative use of celebrity voices. Traditionally, Disney chose unknowns to talk and sing for its cartoon characters and it is only in the last eight years that it has turned to using celebrities. Their much younger challenger has been much more committed to the use of star voices, which have brought an added dimension to the characterizations in their animated films and celebrities such as Michelle Pfeiffer, Joseph and Ralph Fiennes, Brad Pitt and Eddie Murphy have been used to great effect.

Some advertising campaigns have also used celebrity voiceovers very successfully. For decades, Orson Welles was the sonorous voice which intoned 'Probably the best lager in the world' for Carlsberg. While not strictly a celebrity testimonial in the context of this book, it's worth noting the example of Mr Kipling cakes, a brand invented in its totality by J Walter Thomson in London. The eponymous Mr Kipling never appears in the TV commercials but his persona as a traditional purveyor of cakes of high quality is almost entirely conveyed by the voiceover, which is that of actor James Hayter. Humorist and broadcaster Paul Merton has succeeded Richard Briers as the voice of the bowler-hatted cartoon character Fred the Homepride flour grader and in a good piece of casting, Paul Vaughan, who had become the face of science on BBC TV, was the voice used consistently for all the commercials in the first Orange campaign through WCRS, which established the brand so effectively. In 1997 well-known actor Richard Wilson, who had become famous for his part as Victor Meldrew, the grumpy old man in the BBC TV series 'One Foot in the Grave', became the voice for Flora Margarine. This brand was positioned on a health platform: 'As part of a healthy diet can help to lower cholesterol and to maintain a healthy heart'. So the juxtaposition with the choleric Meldrew, who seemed to run the risk of cardiac arrest in every episode, was an apposite choice. While there are other instances where famous voices have been used as a key part of an advertising campaign, such as Geoffrey Palmer for Audi, it is surprising that it is not a more widely used technique. A famous star such as Anthony Hopkins might charge $750,000 to appear personally in a commercial, but considerably less for a voiceover that will carry a good deal of his imagery, given the distinctiveness of his speech. In the USA, Patrick Stewart of *Star Trek* fame has become the exclusive voice of Citicorp in a deal rumoured to be worth $200,000 a year, perhaps less than one-third of the fee he would command for a TV campaign.

In an ideal world the character of the actor should be relevant to the values the brand is trying to convey through its advertising, and the style and tone of their voice should be sufficiently distinctive to be recognized at some level by the audience. But what is interesting about voiceovers is that even if people cannot name the actor involved it's pretty clear that at a subconscious level there is a familiarity, which adds values to the communication. Perhaps this is why voiceover specialist Enn Reitel, who can produce dozens of different accents and styles of voice, is so popular among advertising agencies. It is also interesting to note that the radio commercial that is consistently voted the best ad of all time in the UK was that for Philips. The famous 'Phirrips' commercial, in which the brand name was jokingly mispronounced to make it sound like one of the Japanese brands which were then dominating the marketplace, was brilliantly delivered in a dialogue between Mel Smith and Griff Rhys Jones. Around the same time they starred in a successful TV series produced by TalkBack called 'Smith & Jones'. Within each episode of the long-running series was a sketch called 'head to head' with the two comedians talking to each other against a black background. Thus the pair's distinctive voices heard on radio had instant resonance with a very amusing TV series. With radio, pictures are being painted with sound and the audience is visualizing the personas based on audio clue. This interaction makes for greater engagement with the brand.

Music

Using the voiceover of a famous star is, of course, only one aspect of the total soundtrack for the brand. The mix can also include powerful mnemonic devices such as that created so memorably for Intel and, of course, celebrity music. Earlier the impact that the mention of a brand name by a famous music artists in a hit song was touched upon. This might have been as a result of serendipity, the star's personal preference or as a subtly negotiated piece of product placement. But although this seems to be a growing area of activity, it's nothing like as widespread as the more conventional use of celebrity music in advertising. The music soundtrack in TV, radio, cinema and increasingly on the internet is one of the most important components of a commercial. Even though it is an indirect way for brands to enlist celebrities to their cause, it is of such a significance that it is treated within this overall chapter on the celebrity testimonial. After all, the music is paid for and the artist has to agree to its usage, thus it fits within the definition of 'speaking for the brand'. Such agreement is often very hard to obtain usually because the musicians do not feel that there is an appropriate fit with the brand making the request or because, on principle, they will not countenance what they see as unacceptable commercialization of their art. Audiences are aware of this discernment being exercised by leading music artists and so when they hear a track being used in the commercial they perceive a tacit endorsement by the artist of that brand.

Celebrity music is a powerful testimonial for a brand because of the rich associations that it has for its fans, which are often tied up with romances, friendships and key milestones in their lives. Coca-Cola's 'It's the Real Thing' commercial of 30 years ago featuring 'I'd Like to Teach the World to Sing' sung by the New Seekers is still more memorable for many millions of people who were young at the time (Figure 86).

Because of the highly segmented nature of the music market, the soundtrack chosen for a commercial can be a very useful tool in positioning or repositioning the brand against a particular target audience. For example,

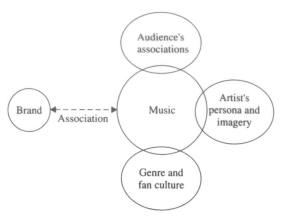

Figure 86 *Brands and music.*

a brand that is targeting people over the age of 50 in a campaign which is running in the year 2004 might choose a 1970s' music track that was a hit 30 years previously when a large proportion of the desired audience were in their teens. Alternatively, a brand that feels that its profile is ageing and wishes to rejuvenate its image, can assist the process by the judicious choice of a more contemporary song. A good example of this, and one that actually involves the music star in the core creative idea behind the brand campaign, is that of Jools Holland and Bell's Whisky. In the commercial produced by agency Miles Calcraft Briginshaw Duffy we see and hear Holland introducing musicians individually in time-honoured fashion to integrate and create the rich and full sound of 'Tuxedo Junction'. He concludes the ad with the phrase 'It's all in the blend', thus encapsulating the brand proposition (Figure 87).

Some brands are prepared to pay very significant sums of money in order to secure what they believed to be an appropriate piece of music for their brand. For example, Microsoft's Bill Gates and guitar nut co-founder Paul Allen were very keen on the idea of using the Rolling Stones track 'Start Me Up' as the soundtrack for their new Windows 95 launch campaign. The perceived link was with the 'Start' button used to open up the software and no doubt the world's leading software company wanted to be associated with arguably the world's leading rock band and harness the energy of one of its great hits (Figure 88).

However, Mick Jagger and Keith Richards, owners of the rights to the songs produced by the Rolling Stones since 1972, had never previously agreed to one of their tracks being used for advertising purposes (although their previous manager Allen Klein, who owns the rights to the songs they wrote before 1972, has been much less squeamish and gave permission to Mars to

Figure 87 *Jools Holland.*
Source: Miles Calcraft Briginshaw Duffy.

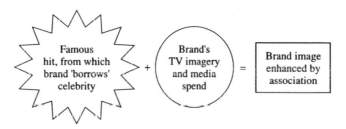

Figure 88 *Brands associating with celebrity music.*

use 'Satisfaction' with their Snickers chocolate bar and 'Gimme Shelter' to motoring organization the RAC). It was only as a result of a long courtship and 'a financial offer that they couldn't refuse' (a sum never disclosed but reputed to be several million dollars) that in the end secured their agreement. Perhaps the Stones were also persuaded by the fact that Microsoft was one of the fastest growing and most powerful brands in the world, that the launch campaign of the latest version of its market leading software, produced by celebrated Portland Oregon advertising agency Wieden & Kennedy, would be global and that the media spend would be $200 million worldwide in the first year alone. Ancillary support deals with clients and suppliers swelled that number to something more like $1 billion, thus giving enormous exposure to the campaign and of course to 'Start Me Up' and the Stones.

Increasingly, music artists are seeing the benefits of this kind of media exposure to an association with the brand. There are many examples where hits have been re-released and become chart successes for the second time on the basis of advertising campaigns and, indeed, where the careers of artist or a band have been resurrected as a result of being reintroduced to a whole, new generation of fans. For example, the Mamas and Papas' 'California Dreamin', was re-released 31 years after its original success in 1966 following agency WCRS's selection of the track for client Carling Premier, and there are many other instances of this mutual benefit as shown in Figure 89.

It's not only popular music that can benefit in this way: some pieces of classical music have also become closely associated with brands. The use of Bach's 'Air on a G String' for Hamlet cigars, and Carl Orff's 'Carmina Burana' for Old Spice are two of the best known examples. They also exemplify the benefits of longevity and continuity in building a brand, as well as taking advantage of music, which is out of copyright. After a composer has been dead for 70 years, the written piece of music is out of copyright, but if the agency wanted to use that same piece of music already recorded by an orchestra for a record company, then that company will have rights and be due fees. The alternative is for the agency to get musicians to record it anew

Artist	Track	Advertiser	Agency	Chart	Year
The Bluebells	'Young at Heart'	Volkswagen	BMP.DDB	1	1993
Stiltskin	'Inside'	Levi's	BBH	1	1994
Louis Armstrong	'All the Time in the World'	Guinness	Ogilvy	2	1994
Babylon Zoo	'Spaceman'	Levi's	BBH	1	1996
Etta James	'I Just Wanna Make Love To You'	Diet Coke	Lowe (US)	5	1997
The Hollies	'He Ain't Heavy'	Miller Lite	BMP.DDB	1	1998
Bran Van 3000	'Drinking in LA'	Rolling Rock	BBH	2	1999
The Wiseguys	'Ooh La La'	Budweiser	BMP.DDB	2	1990
Moby	'Porcelain'	Volkswagen	BMP.DDB	5	2000
Dandy Warhols	'Bohemian Like You'	Vodafone	WCRS	5	2001
Stereophonics	'Have a Nice Day'	The Times	Rainey Kelly Campbell Roalfe Y&R	5	2001
Elvis Presley	'A Little Less Conversation'	Nike	Wieden & Kennedy	1	2002
Room 5 Featuring Oliver Cheatham	'Make Luv'	Lynx Pulse	BBH	1	2003

Figure 89 *Hit music from ads.*
Source: IPA *Campaign/Marketing/Market Week.*

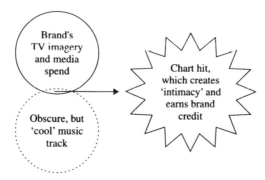

Figure 90 *Brand and music creating intimacy.*

in order to own the rights to it and this may be a cost-effective solution in the long run.

In line with the core principles of the use of celebrity by brands and the desirability of creating intimacy, it's appropriate that many of these chart successes are for relatively obscure songs. Bringing good music of which it was previously unaware to the attention of the audience is a service rendered by the brand, and the public also recognizes that the brand has benefited the artist (Figure 90).

Some agencies and their clients are taking this strategy to increasing levels of sophistication and entering into close partnerships with emerging music stars and using their music for brands in a way which maximizes this reciprocal and symbiotic relationship. Lever Fabergé Chairman Keith Weed and his company take their relationship with the youth market extremely seriously and they have a youth board within their marketing department whose sole purpose is to get close to the target audience by total immersion. Recently, the youth board not only went to Blackpool to go clubbing with students but also got to go to Ibiza on a similar mission! In 2003 Lynx' deodorant body spray brand Pulse used a track called 'Make Luv' by Room 5 featuring Oliver Cheatham, produced by Junior Jack and made by Positiva records, a division of EMI, which worked closely with agency BBH on the project. 'Make Luv' went to number one and was a major club hit. The brand's market share went up by 10% on 2002 and Lynx is now used by 60% of all boys in the UK aged 16 or under and it has 25% of the sales of all male toiletries. Buoyed up by yet another music in advertising success to add to its astonishing track record with Levi's, agency BBH has now set up a joint venture called Leap Music. The company's objective is to acquire the publishing rights in specially commissioned scores and unpublished songs that are exploited through TV advertising campaigns. The massive exposure that a brand campaign generates for the band/composer increases their chances of success and ultimately an opportunity to break through into the charts.

INTERVIEW WITH FRANCES ROYLE, HEAD OF TV AT BBH, AGENCY FOR LEVI'S AND LYNX

Wendy: How do you go about choosing music for your ads?

Frances: Music is very much the responsibility of the producer and the creatives who write the scripts. Traditionally, music is decided on once the commercial has been shot as it has always been felt that you can't decide on the track until you see the first edit. Also on occasions, the music can come from the editor or the director.

As there is little time in the last stage of production (2–4 weeks) we now start briefing music and sourcing music at the first stage of production, i.e. during the first couple of weeks into a production. We write a music brief which is given to our in-house music coordinator whose role is to source music for our commercials via her contacts at record companies, music publishers, band/acts and composers.

Finding the right music is a very important part of producing a commercial as it can add another level of creativity and extend communication to a wider audience. A good commercial can become a great commercial with the right music track. If the music and the idea marry together well they really extend the communication and heighten the emotion, e.g. Levi's 'Odyssey', and ultimately create fame for the client/product and music track.

When the music brief is sent to record companies, and publishers, a proposal is produced which includes the budget we have. As we have a great track record in creating hits off the back of our commercials it means we are in a good position when negotiating with record labels/publishers, as they are much more likely to sell records if their track is used on one of our ads.

No record company can exploit a track the way a commercial does, because they can't afford to put the kind of media spend behind the music that our clients can. Record labels see a commercial as a mini pop-promo for that track. It's a fantastic vehicle to launch a band and a piece of music.

So back to how we choose the music. Ultimately we put the brief out to record companies, publishers and all the music will come back to our in-house coordinator, the producer and the creatives. We go through the tracks and once you've shot the commercial, we try these tracks against the commercial to see which works most effectively.

It's really tough to find the piece of music that (a) works well and (b) is going to be a success. A good example of this is the Lynx Pulse commercial. That was quite an unusual process because we thought up the idea last spring and it wasn't on air until February of this year. The product was called 'Pulse' and we came up with an idea about dance, so our brief was a dance track with a great hook. We had six months to find the piece of music, so we briefed all the dance music companies and they sent in loads of tracks. Then we'd have listening sessions every week to go through all the material and eventually we came up with 'Room 5'.

As music is so subjective it is often hard for everyone to agree on the same track. I may like it, somebody else may hate it. On Pulse the client was unsure about the track but knew it was right for the brand and target audience. To convince our clients further that Room 5 was the right choice, we researched it by consulting DJs and people in the music biz to see if it was going to be a hit. Obviously it had to work brilliantly for the commercial and choreographed dance within it, but also promote the new product. Fortunately, our client really wanted it to be a hit as well as they could see the success could help create further brand fame.

We surpassed everything we wanted to achieve with the commercial and track. Our objective was to create a number one hit and it was number one for four weeks, which is the longest a dance track had been at number one for six years. The choreographed dance featured in the commercial did brilliantly too and was copied by TV programmes and featured numerous times in the press. In addition, radio stations were plugging it, which helped to sell the product/track. The track also exceeded the record label's expectations.

So the whole process and collaboration with the record label was a great example of creating success for the agency, track and client. Also, we synchronised the release of the single with the commercial airdate in the UK and throughout Europe.

Wendy: Is the Lynx ad your most successful example of a song used in a commercial?

Frances: It's the most recent success, but I'd say the big ones were Marvin Gaye, from the first Levi's commercial with Nick Kamen, and then a whole series of tracks from Levi's ads got to number one such as: 'Stand By Me', 'The Joker', 'Should I Stay or Should I Go', 'Spaceman' and 'Inside' by Stiltskin. That one was unusual as the track was specially commissioned for the commercial and then they created a band to front the track because it was such a big hit!

One of my favourites, which also got to number one, was 'Mr Bombastic' by Shaggy. He has said on a various TV programmes that it was totally down to the commercial and Levi's that his track got to number one and ultimately launched his career. Rolling Rock also went to number one with 'Bran Van 2000', which was a track that was about to be deleted by the record label.

Apart from the incorporation of music tracks into commercials, there are other ways of using celebrity music to promote a brand. At one end of the spectrum companies like Pepsi Cola have taken a long-term strategic decision to involve themselves with popular music and over the years have signed deals with a succession of artists representing many different musical genres and thus appealing to youth audiences from all sorts of cultures. In the heyday of 'Girl Power' and the Spice Girls, Pepsi Cola also came to a very important realization in their use of celebrities to promote their brand. Previously, many brands in the soft drinks industry had used the promotional mechanic of customers collecting bottle caps or ring pulls to redeem against celebrity merchandise, tickets or other rewards.

The weakness of the conventional ring pull mechanic is that brand and celebrity can be interchangeable with another brand or celebrity, i.e. the promotion is generic. In many cases the reward was more often than not generic too: a T-shirt a CD or a poster, which might be gained at an advantageous price but which was nevertheless an item available in the shops. Pepsi realized this and in so doing took an important step in getting their brand and the celebrity in perspective. They appreciated that for customers certain celebrities have the magnetic appeal of a planet the size of Jupiter compared to the tiny asteroid that even a brand of Pepsi's stature might represent in their mental universe. If 'celebrity' is what the customers really want to get close to then the role of the brand is not trying to position itself on an equal footing to the celebrity but to offer itself as an intermediary or a conduit through whom customers may pass in order to get to their desired goal. Thus Pepsi, through agency 19 Management, negotiated the contract with the then red-hot Spice Girls by which Pepsi became the gateway to exclusive music and live performances available only to customers who collected the requisite number of ring pulls. This generated massive response because it gave Pepsi customers access to stars they loved and it protected the reputation of the Spice Girls' brand through the promotion's exclusivity.

At the other end of the spectrum the power of music and celebrity media can be linked to great effect in a promotional campaign. Many brands have put together compilations of tracks that have either featured in the brand's advertising or have a related theme, that are appropriate for their customers and can be used as competition prizes and rewards for brand loyalty. These interlinked worlds also offer the opportunity for strategic alliances such as that created for major UK music retailer, Woolworth and celebrity magazine, Heat by agency ZenithOptimedia. A 12-month partnership, starting August 2002, was created that comprised a number of elements each week including key advertising, advertorial and sponsorship positions in the charts, music and review sections (Figure 91).

This continuous stream of Woolworth/Heat items created a strong link that reinforced the retailer's music credentials and produced strong sales results for key releases. The promotional impact can be seen each Tuesday, the on-sale date for Heat, when 80% of copies are sold according to Emap, as each featured product witnesses an uplift of between 39% and 224% on the previous day (Figure 92).

Faces and photography

If celebrity voiceovers and music are literally 'speaking for the brand', the next stage on the spectrum of increasing intimacy and identification is the

Figure 91 *Woolworths and Heat 1.*
Woolworths and Heat 2.
Source: ZenithOptimedia.

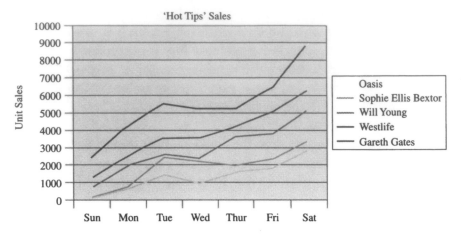

Figure 92 *Hot tips sales.*
Source: Zenithoptimedia.

appearance of the celebrity as the 'face' of a brand. This use of famous people is very well established in the cosmetics and fashion industries where the success of brands can be highly dependent on the model, actress or celebrity with which they are associated and who models their products in advertising and point-of-sale material. Traditionally, the 'faces' of the leading cosmetics brands emerge from the ranks of models who have achieved superstar status or from among successive generations of Hollywood actresses who can capitalize on their fame on screen by judicious appearances on behalf of brands. However, these faces can come from other sources too – for example, former glamour model Heather Mills secured 'A-list' status by marrying the ex-Beatle Sir Paul McCartney and in 2003 she became the face of upmarket US clothing range INC International Concepts.

As with many other areas in the use of a celebrity for a brand, it does seem that continuity is an important ingredient in success. Typically, the celebrity will be contracted for two or three years to a particular brand and the customers will become aware through advertising, PR and references in the media that, for example, Andie MacDowell represents L'Oréal. Brands can also use the careful choice of celebrity 'face' to appeal to very specific target audiences – MacDowell is a good example of an appeal to a slightly older woman who has to acknowledge her age and stage in life, but who can still aspire to look as beautiful as any star who is her contemporary.

Visual association with the brand can be very powerful and seems to work well in the worlds of cosmetics, fragrance and clothing where pictures literally do mean more than a 1000 words and where nearly all the time the celebrity is not required to say anything in print or on camera – unless of course it's the 'Because you're worth it' line in a L'Oréal commercial! One of the more stunningly effective visual associations between a celebrity brand was when Puma created some contact lenses with their distinctive puma logo on them and got Linford Christie, the UK Olympic-medal winning sprinter, to wear them in 1996. The resulting photographs were seen worldwide and spoke volumes for the brand.

A disciplined process needs to be applied to photography or other forms of illustration that might be used to present the celebrity in brand advertising or marketing communications materials. Famous people are quite rightly very particular about their image because they know that, as brands themselves, it is crucial to maintain a combination of consistency and contemporaneity in the presentation of their persona. They are especially aware that the amount of money a brand can put behind the campaign, to say nothing of the free publicity that might result as a result of editorial comment, will result in very significant exposure which will often outweigh the coverage that their latest film, TV series, book or theatrical appearance will generate. The agency, and specifically the art director, and their support in creative services must take the responsibility for obtaining cleared photographs very seriously. Detailed research needs to be done in order to establish whether or not there is an existing image which the celebrity prefers to use and whether they have a favourite photographer that they would like to work with (and this might also mean a particular stylist, hairdresser and makeup artist) or whether they are open to a creative suggestion of using a newly fashionable and up-and-coming one or even an illustrator or painter who might add a new dimension to their celebrity image.

The goal is to get at least one and ideally several cleared images for use in advertising and other applications to promote the brand. An added complexity in this context is that photographers, artists and illustrators retain the copyright in their own work: the agency, acting on behalf of the client, has to negotiate licences and usage fees for their images. So the agency art buyer and art director must go into the negotiation with the artist or photographer in the full knowledge of the goals of the brand campaign, the budget parameters, the geographies and the timescales that are envisaged.

Nowadays it is extremely rare for a photograph of the celebrity to appear un-retouched. Therefore the process of gaining approval for an image is not simply a question of producing a contact sheet, a selection of prints and then obtaining agreement to a few of those. All this needs to be done of course, but then the retouching brief has to be agreed and a range of altered images have to be presented and approved by the celebrity/agent with the client/agency striving to preserve a balance between a glamorized version of the star, which is acceptable to their target audience, and one which becomes too idealized to be credible. As the technology has moved on so has the scope for altering every aspect of a star's appearance. The extent to which this is now possible was brought home to a wider audience with the publication of GQ magazine's front cover featuring Kate Winslet. Many people, including Winslet, believed that her image had been stretched and slimmed to produce an overidealized version of her (Figure 93).

Figure 93 *GQ cover featuring Kate Winslett.*
Source: GQ/Conde Nast.
Reproduced by permission of Conde Nast.

Statements

However, although a picture may well be worth 1000 words, for many other sorts of brands, the addition of a written endorsement makes the communication much more effective than a purely visual one. Well-known people can give quotations which can be used, often alongside their signature, in press advertisements. It's often said that one of the earliest known advertisements was that for prostitutes in the city of Ephesus. It is also said that the first-ever logos, which gave their name to the concept of branding, were the marks made by ranchers with red-hot branding irons on the hides of their cattle to identify them as their own. But in fact it seems more likely that the first-ever advertisements and logos in one were the signatures or autographs of famous people (Figure 94).

Figure 94 *First-ever autograph.*
Source: Schoyen Collection.

The earliest known human mark, which scholars describe as a signature or autograph, dates back to the Sumerian civilization, 31st century BC, thus predating Ephesus and cowboy branding by many centuries. Throughout history the recognizable signature on a treaty, contract, document, painting or other work of art has often been essential in conferring authenticity and can transform a mundane piece of paper, canvas or stone into something of considerable value.

Human society has a great desire for relics of the famous and these artefacts, for example the Turin Shroud, can acquire enormous religious and mystical power. The signature or autograph, which is by definition the most highly personal and unique relic of a person, is also highly collectible and further evidence of the extraordinary appeal of celebrities. Fraser, a subsidiary of the world-famous Stanley Gibbons company, specializes in rare autographs and in May 2003 announced the creation of a top 100 list of the most valuable signatures and signed photographs. The top 20 celebrity signatures and the top 20 celebrity signed photos are listed in Figure 95.

According to Fraser's analysis, the rise in value of the S G 100 index over a five-year period from 1997 to 2002 was some 139% or an average of 19% per annum. Over the same time the *Financial Times* FTSE 100 share price index of Britain's 100 top firms, or 'Footsie', fell by 4%!

Given the attraction of celebrity signatures or autographs it's not surprising that many manufacturers use facsimiles of them on merchandise which is endorsed or designed by a star. However, it is less common to see celebrity signatures used in advertising or other collateral material. Clearly, a printed signature does not have the value of the original but nevertheless as the 'logo' of a famous person it does carry symbolic value with it and therefore brands that have celebrities involved with them should consider the merits of incorporating a signature into their marketing communications materials.

Brands that have used celebrity signatures include Pepsi Cola in Japan (David Beckham's autograph on cans during the World Cup 2002) and Nike, which reproduced Michael Jordan's signature on certain trainers in the Air Jordan range. In the first year alone Nike's Air Jordan line grossed an astronomical $130 million. More recently, Apple has begun selling several limited edition iPods featuring celebrity signatures, including those of Madonna and Beck on the back of the MP3 player.

Press ads often use written testimonials and signatures and can be very effective in direct marketing where customers are buying at a distance and need the reassurance as to product quality and reliable delivery. This is also why the signed 'letter from the owner' is so often seen on the opening page of mail-order catalogues. Whereas with a voiceover it's not strictly necessary

	Undedicated album page signature		Undedicated signed photo	
1	The Beatles	£7500	The Beatles	£12,500
2	Marilyn Monroe	£4950	Apollo 11	£7500
3	Albert Einstein	£3950	Adolf Hitler	£5950
4	Bruce Lee	£3950	Winston Churchill	£4950
5	Lord Nelson	£3950	Harry Houdini	£3950
6	Sex Pistols (inc Sid)	£3950	Princess Diana	£3500
7	John F Kennedy	£3500	Dr W G Grace	£2950
8	Oscar Wilde	£3000	Alfred Hitchcock	£2950
9	Napoleon Bonaparte	£2950	Pablo Picasso	£2950
10	Casablanca stars	£2950	The Who	£2500
11	Charles Dickens	£2500	Neil Armstrong	£1950
12	John Lennon	£2500	Charlie Chaplin	£1950
13	Jimi Hendrix	£2000	England 1966 team	£1950
14	Jim Morrison	£1950	Queen Elizabeth II	£1950
15	Ian Fleming	£1750	Judy Garland	£1950
16	Jim Clarke	£1500	Cary Grant	£1950
17	Buddy Holly	£1500	Bob Marley	£1950
18	Jacqueline Kennedy	£1500	Elvis Presley	£1950
19	Dad's Army	£1250	Rolling Stones	£1950
20	Janis Joplin	£1250	John Wayne	£1950

Figure 95 *Stanley Gibbons 100 Index Top 20.*
Source: Frasers Autographs.

that the celebrity should be contracted actually to use the product that they are endorsing, in the case of written testimonials that will appear in press advertising it is a requirement that they should be customers of the brand. The CAP Code states that:

> Testimonials alone do not constitute substantiation and the opinions expressed in them must be supported, where necessary, with independent evidence of their accuracy. Any claims based on a testimonial must conform with the Code. Fictitious testimonials should not be presented as though they are genuine.

One of the skills in drafting testimonials from celebrities is to capture two things in their statement: first, their endorsement should crystallize the key selling proposition that works most effectively for the brand. Second, the testimonial should be written in words the celebrity is likely to have used. The language of marketing should be avoided at all costs: the goal is to produce a statement which reads as if it is a direct, spontaneous and genuine compliment to the brand from someone who uses it, knows it well and is a genuine enthusiast for it. The problem in practice is that the celebrity, or their agent, is very unlikely to have the time or the inclination to sit down and actually produce such a testimonial. Thus it falls to the agency to tackle the problem.

The best way to go about it is for the copywriter to immerse him or herself in the character of the celebrity and to read or to listen to as many as possible of the public statements they have made and thereby to 'get' their tone of voice and style of speaking or writing. Although it's very difficult to negotiate, given the busy schedule of most desirable celebrities, a personal interview between the copywriter and the star should be arranged. A free-flowing conversation about their latest foray in show business can be used to bring them to a discussion of the brand they are to be promoting and to capture the language and sentiments they have towards the corporation, product or service in question. Some celebrities and their agents may find this process potentially threatening and, as with media interviews, the pill can be sugared by offering them complete editorial control over the published outcome. Given that the brand would not want to be saying anything in its advertising which the celebrity would not fully support, this should not concern the marketer or their agency.

Having done this, and with the full knowledge of the brief for the brand, the copywriter should then draft a series of plausible testimonial options for consideration by the star and their advisers. These statements can be positioned along a spectrum of favourability and emphasis on the agreed selling point of the brand that the celebrity is being hired to articulate. All of them should be couched in language that is sympathetic to the celebrity and, of course, the target audience they will be addressing. The enthusiasm with which they are endorsing the brand should, on the one hand, not be so understated that it doesn't do a convincing job but, on the other, it should not be so full blooded that it doesn't ring true. These statements should be submitted to the celebrity and their agent for consideration, feedback and hopefully agreement. In an ideal world the celebrity will be sufficiently engaged with the project to be prepared to offer constructive criticism and even to volunteer their own version of the statements which, if born out of a genuine experience, will have a ring of truth that can be so powerful for a brand. As with the alternative photography options, the opportunity should be taken at this key moment in the relationship to agree several statements if at all possible, each of which casts a slightly different light on the brand and its benefits for customers. If these can all be signed off formally then the brand has a range of options in the locker that can enable the campaign to have greater flexibility and longevity. There's also the benefit to the celebrity of not having to return to the topic while still getting paid for continued usage.

Television

Putting the testimonial and the visual image together in print advertising to produce a celebrity endorsement can be relatively straightforward compared to the potential twists and turns of agreeing the script for a TV commercial. As is always the case in advertising, but is particularly true when stars are involved, there is a hierarchy of talent, money and availability for any given project. The more successful the production company and the chosen director, the higher the fees that will be charged and the less available they will be to take on the making of a commercial. But, by the same token, TV commercials directors, many of whom are celebrities in their own world, and who have built their reputations by delivering outstanding TV advertising, are always alert for a really good new idea. There is a natural tendency as a director becomes more established and more expensive for the more risk-averse brands with money to gravitate towards them. They do this in the hope that a quality result for their brand can be as near as possible as guaranteed as any creative endeavour can be. The danger in this is that those same risk-averse brands and their agencies often tend to come forward with less adventurous commercials which, while they may pay the rent, are unlikely to add any gloss to the directorial reputation.

Because, as we have seen earlier, celebrity per se is no guarantee of an outstanding commercial communication, it means that a significant proportion of the scripts – perhaps 80% – presented to a director featuring a star will be average or worse. Thus, not only for all the previously described research-based reasons and all the evidence to do with effectiveness, there is another compelling reason for marketers to insist there is a great idea as well as a celebrity in their campaign. This is because in order to get the very best people to work on the brand's behalf, it is essential that there is an idea in the script that moves the commercial up into the top 20% in terms of creativity. If an agency lacks the creativity and innovation to devise a big advertising idea for a brand and just includes a famous person for lack of anything better, then they should not be surprised if the top-flight production companies and directors turn out to be unaffordable and/or unavailable to shoot. If, however, there is a great idea that has wit and charm as well as salesmanship and which reveals a side of the celebrity the public has not seen before, then it's a very different matter. Such an idea could include a star being cast against type, being partnered with another celebrity with whom they are not usually connected or simply playing an exaggerated version of the persona they are already known for. If the idea seems credible in the context of what the audience knows about a favourite star and engages them as a result, it is also likely that the top director will see the opportunity to produce a great commercial and perhaps even a series of them if the idea is campaignable and then, suddenly, everything gets much easier.

However, so far, there has been no mention of the potential role of the, their agent, their advisers, their family and their friends and their star possible input into the script. Within the world of celebrity there is every conceivable type of personality and therefore attitude towards the making of a TV commercial. There will be some who will be sufficiently professional to take the advice of experts and, within reason, go along with what is proposed as long as they have a basic level of confidence in the project. At the other extreme there will be prima donnas of the worst possible sort who will feel the need to take issue over every word or phrase and then still not be happy three weeks later in the post-production studio 15 minutes before the final deadline. The irony is that there is no guarantee, given the nature of the creative business, as to which of these two polarities has the better chance of producing the more effective work. The bottom line is that the agency, and specifically the TV producer working with the creative team, the creative director and the account director, have somehow or other to manage these complex relationships and to navigate the script idea, itself a survivor of a rigorous client approval and market research process, through the shoals, sandbanks, reefs and hidden rocks that are put in its way by all kinds of amateur experts in filmmaking and bring it home to safe harbour more or less intact.

One of the rules in advertising is that there are no rules or, alternatively, that the golden rule is that he who has the gold, has the rule! So a topical and rather successful exception to what's been said so far in this chapter is the current campaign for esure, the insurance company owned by HBOS and founded by Peter Wood, the sector innovator who first made his name and fortune with Direct Line. *Death Wish* film director Michael Winner and 'Winner's Dinner's' restaurant critic is the creator of the campaign, which he has produced direct for HBOS. He pitched his idea to Wood over lunch and he stars in the campaign, which he wrote and directed as well. So far the

Figure 96 *Michael Winner.*
Source: esure.

results are pretty encouraging: in the London and Central TV regions, where the campaign was first launched, the number of insurance quotes requested as a direct result of the advertising has increased by 15%. Research indicates that brand awareness increased by an average of 26% between August 2002 and April 2003 in the regions where the ad has appeared. According to Head of Marketing, Mary Davidson, by September 2003 this had reached a prompted awareness level of 78% and the fast growing company had recruited over 600,000 customers in under two years (Figure 96).

INTERVIEW WITH MICHAEL WINNER

Wendy: Why do you think the esure campaign has been so successful?

Michael: I think it was successful because it was different from the ads they're used to seeing and it was very clear. The message was very clear indeed. You know, I look at a lot of advertisements and I think 'a lot of effort's gone into this but I don't know, I've no idea what this advertisement's selling'.

Wendy: What sells in your ad then?

Michael: I think that it was funny so people wanted to watch it, they didn't want to go to have a piss or a cup of tea you see.

We had a memorable phrase, also I think it was unique. I don't think there has ever been as far as I know in the history of television commercials a commercial where the spokesman for the company suddenly says: 'Calm down, this is a commercial!' You know? It was different, it was also shot in a very simple and direct way, without trying to show how clever we all were which we could certainly do in shooting strangely.

It was a simple direct message and it was funny and it had the most astounding effect there's no question – they took on 600 extra people to deal with the calls.

I think if anything you do is successful it's a great pleasure. I'm delighted that it's a success because I wrote it, from the ground up. I conceived the idea. I was really the advertising agency, the director, the producer, the writer, the actor, the floorsweeper, the postboy, I was everything.

Wendy: The phrase 'Calm down dear' has entered the language now, do people say it to you all the time in the street?

Michael: Oh yes, you walk along the street and people say it. I was walking in Biarritz last weekend on the front and there was a group of four or six English people and it took them a second to realize who I was, then I heard somebody say 'yeah that is Michael Winner that is' and then they all said together, 'Calm down dear!'

The esure situation is a relatively unusual one, but at its heart is the nature of the creative idea and people's perceptions of its merits and potential. Like the commercials director, the celebrity and their agent will look at the script on offer (and if the celebrity has even a modicum of status and topicality there will be many offers from many brands) and they will assess it in much the same way as if they were being offered a part in a movie, a play or a transfer to a new club. That is they will look at it in terms of whether they believe it is likely to enhance their career and their future prospects. If the brand and the script that is proposed plays to strengths in their own persona that they are keen to develop and amplify, then it may well appeal to them. Contrariwise, it could be that they feel that they are becoming typecast in one way or another and that they wish to break out of their existing persona in the soap opera or the basketball team. The young aggressive male lead may wish to show a more sympathetic side of his character; the glamorous actress used to playing romantic parts may wish to demonstrate her ability to express more character in a role; the aggressive defender with an unfortunate reputation for yellow cards may wish to turn over an new leaf and sees a transfer to another club as an opportunity to do so. Celebrities are nothing if not egocentric and a shrewd creative team, which has settled on a range of possible stars for their brand campaign, will be seeking to understand the nuances of their candidate celebrities' careers and juxtaposing the needs of the brand with the needs of their star. If the script for the TV commercial can achieve a win–win for both parties then it's likely that the public will perceive that too and tacitly acknowledge the role of the brand in hosting a new phase in a career or in bolstering the continuing rise of one already established in a particular direction.

Being fully aware of the career ambitions of the celebrity puts the scriptwriter in a much stronger position but there is also a need to understand the technical capabilities of the star. There is absolutely no reason to suppose that a football player who exhibits remarkable fluency on the field of play is going to be able to deliver a script in the studio with anything like the same degree of articulation. The watchword here is to play to their strengths and allow for their weaknesses. A commercial which simply features a famous star visually in an appropriate setting and carrying out some interesting bit of theatrical 'business' with the product or service being promoted can be just as effective and probably more so than asking the star to speak to camera, or engage in dialogue with another actor and be as animated as a piece of wood!

Getting all this right is at the heart of agency creativity and ingenuity and where real value is added to brands. Using celebrities can be an exciting, inspirational, risky and rewarding experience and this quote from George Lois, celebrated US adman and author of *Sellebrity*, sums it up pretty well:

It's a star struck world. We're all suckers for a famous face. A celebrity can add almost instant style, atmosphere, feeling, and/or meaning to any place, product or situation, unlike any other advertising symbol.

You can be victorious playing the Fame Game only if your choice of celebrity is inspired. I use celebrities for the pleasant shock of their seeming irrelevance to the product, for unexpected juxtapositions, for certain connotations and implications, for a marriage between myth and market place, for a subtle but deep credibility.

Using celebrities can be a daunting experience because everything is magnified, money problems, image concerns, schedules, shoots, credits, legalities, directing them, egos, ambitions, fears. It's worth all these magnified problems if the results are fresh, exciting, memorable and truly effective, on the tube, in the streets, in the marketplace. When a Big Idea celeb campaign has the power to become new language and startling imagery that enters the popular culture, advertising communication takes on a dimension that leaves competitive products in the dust.

Earlier the usefulness of test commercials or animatics in research was discussed and there is a further role for them in the context of the use of celebrities in commercials. Whereas with a working actor or actress it is not that difficult to call them in for casting sessions and to require them to rehearse their lines as part of the process, it can be very difficult for logistical or ego reasons to get a famous star to do the same. In this context, having an animatic or test video which is a pretty good representation of what the commercial is to be, can help not only to get a celebrity and their agent to agree to the idea of participating in the first place, it can also be used for them to rehearse their lines. This reduces the chances of a very expensive celebrity turning up on the day of a costly shoot and spending a couple of hours getting the hang of a few simple words and phrases and pushing the whole production into even more pricey overtime.

Live appearances

Finally, in thinking about celebrity testimonial, brands should not forget the impact that a personal appearance by a star can make. The presence of a celebrity at a launch event of a new product or a new store opening can guarantee the presence of the media in a way that a speech by the marketing director never can! Getting the star of a new commercial to appear at the company sales conference can dramatically increase the impact of the campaign by simply motivating the people who have to go out and sell the brand on the back of it. Trade customers can be inordinately influenced by the presence of a celebrity at a company golf day or similar corporate hospitality event.

The presence of a celebrity at a charity lunch or dinner can have a very significant impact on ticket sales and the amount of money raised during the auction, as many a hard-pressed fundraiser will attest. And of course the significant celebrity component of the whole media output, ranging from the TV talk show to the editorial feature, is fuelled by star appearances, which are contractually linked to a new movie, theatrical production or book. If a brand can get its timing right and use a topical celebrity creatively it may well be a beneficiary by piggy-backing on the PR machine.

A rather charming story from UK agency BMP DDB illustrates how celebrity can even be used to reward key employees. In the early 1980s, John Webster's agency wished to acknowledge his extraordinary contribution to its success through the campaigns he had created over the years. Webster produced many excellent live action ads including the great 'Points of View' commercial for the *Guardian*. Awards for this included a Gold Lion at Cannes, an Epica d'Or award, Silver at the Campaign Press Awards and one ad, featuring actor Geoffrey Palmer and a white salad-loving rabbit in an echo of the movie *Harvey*, won that year's Grand Prix at Cannes for Hellmann's Mayonnaise. But he's best known for the many he created featuring invented characters who became brand celebrities, including invisible milk-loving Humphries for Unigate, the Honey Monster for Quaker's Sugar Puffs, the Cresta Bear (inspired by Jack Nicholson) for Schweppes, the Kia-ora crows, George the Hoffmeister Bear, a Dick Tracy-like detective for Tic Tac mints, a hen-pecked flat-capped northern John Smith's tap-room aficionado called Arkwright (loosely based on the Andy Capp cartoon character) and, perhaps most famously, the Smash Martians for Cadbury. Knowing that his true love was cricket, and unbeknownst to Webster, agency director and captain of cricket, Tom Rodwell, arranged for Geoffrey Boycott to open the batting with John at a match against a team of clients at Turville Heath, in Buckinghamshire. The match also made it on to the 'Six O' Clock News' as Geoff Boycott, at that time the country's top batsman, had been banned from playing by Yorkshire, his county club, but was here turning out for a club team! Even though John was out for a duck, he will forever have the score sheet showing Webster 0, Boycott 99. The following year, Geoff was the surprise guest at John Webster's 50th birthday party where he presented John with a painting of the two of them going out to bat.

Summary

As the length of this chapter confirms, there are many detailed considerations to be taken into account surrounding celebrity 'testimonials'. This is one of the most successful ways of involving stars for the brand, but because the stars are brands themselves and the marketer's agency is effectively setting up a dialogue between the two of them in public, it can be fraught with difficulty. Happily, there are many well-documented case histories that demonstrate the enormous contribution to profitability that a celebrity campaign can make. As long as clients, and their agencies, have the necessary expertise and do not attempt to cut corners, especially in cost terms, virtually any sort of brand can benefit from this approach to its marketing communications.

16

Celebrity employees

A brand can benefit enormously from having famous employees. People seem to like working for, dealing with and buying from well-known companies and individuals. Assuming a successful product or service delivery, then a personal association between an individual representative of the company and the customer can create a strong bond. If the company brand ambassador happens to be famous in their own right, then this adds another dimension altogether to the buyer's brand experience. In later conversation the purchaser can not only refer to the various benefits of the brand they have bought, they can also allude to the wider reputation of the associated celebrity (Figure 97).

This phenomenon is most obvious in the case of companies named after the entrepreneurs who founded them, which become very successful and whose reputations create a virtuous circle for their brand. Ferdinand Porsche, Henri Nestlé, John Cadbury, Max Factor and Henry John Heinz are just a few examples where this has happened. Of course there are downsides in

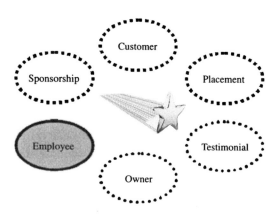

Figure 97 *Star involvement with a brand – employee.*

having a celebrity owner and the question is what would happen to a star-led company if the famous founder were to fall under the metaphorical bus (Figures 98 and 99).

Perhaps with this in mind some of the more notable business empires that have been created over the last decade have avoided using the names of their founders. With the exception of Dell the world of IT is dominated by made-up names such as Apple, Cisco, Intel, Microsoft, Oracle and Sun. However, these brands are still benefiting from celebrity employees at the very highest level and the power of famous CEOs such as Bill Gates, Larry Ellison and Steve Jobs in articulating their individual brand stories, and creating a culture in which so many talented people wish to work, has been a major contributor to these business successes.

The lesson for any company in these media-literate days is that it is very helpful to have a CEO who either already is, or has the potential and the inclination to become, a celebrity on behalf of their company. For those organizations that are doing very well without a charismatic leader it is still worth their while considering the additional benefits that might accrue if they were to have one, and the potential competitive threat from other brands in their sector if they were to take the celebrity CEO approach.

A highly successful way of bringing celebrity into the upper echelons of the company and having a very significant impact on the brand is simply to hire a famous person. The top fashion houses have pursued this strategy successfully for many years. Several of these were classic examples of the eponymous founder becoming a celebrity and creating the virtuous circle around their brand until they lost touch with the newly emerging generations of customers. Yves St Laurent is a very good example of this. As Yves himself has receded the YSL brand has been refreshed by successive injections of talented designers. This strategy has almost become institutionalized in the top couture houses in Paris, Milan and New York: look at the great fashion brands and the new young designers they are employing, who, in a reciprocal and mutually beneficial process, inject new ideas while building their own reputations potentially to the point where they can launch their own house. Stella McCartney secured her first key position with Gucci, then went to Chloe and has now launched her own label and 'Stella', a fragrance to match.

This technique for reviving the fortunes of fashion brands also works well a little further down the market and the case history of Burberry provides an object lesson in this. Not so long ago, Burberry was just another reasonably well-known but slightly faded name in British fashion, perhaps ranking along-side the likes of Aquascutum, Austin Reed, Pringle and Jaeger. In 1997, in a

Figure 98 *Richard Branson.*
Source: Virgin.

Figure 99 *Stelios Inannou.*
Source: easyJet.

move which turned out to be inspired, the board of Burberry decided to make a major investment in a celebrity chief executive/head of design and hired Rose Marie Bravo, who had built a reputation in the USA for running Macy's and Saks Fifth Avenue. Bravo very quickly made her presence felt and with a sure eye and adroit PR sense exploited the well-known Burberry check in an excellent example of 'brand archaeology'. In fact, it was originally by being worn by celebrities Humphrey Bogart and Audrey Hepburn in *Casablanca* and *Breakfast at Tiffany's* respectively that gave the Burberry gaberdine trenchcoat, with its trademark check fabric lining, such huge appeal.

By the clever juxtaposition of what had become a rather dated and slightly trad fabric with trendy items like bikinis and doggie jackets, she turned the check into a surprise fashion hit. She also reintroduced celebrity to the brand via supermodels and shrewd product placement. Burberry advertising through Baron & Baron, the New York-based agency behind a very stylish series of double-page spreads, used stunning black-and-white shots by the star photographer Mario Testino, featuring the likes of Kate Moss and Stella Tennant, that did wonders for the brand in glossy magazines. This newfound fashionability created real excitement and buzz around Burberry and set up a virtuous circle in which all the right people were seen in all the right places, and pages, wearing the check.

The results have been phenomenal. From being a brand close to bottom in both product and retailing terms, Burberry has been floated on the London Stock Exchange at a valuation of £1.2 billion and Bravo has been rewarded with a salary package of £6.15 million making her Britain's highest paid female chief executive. In fact, in 2002, Bravo's total package amounted to £19 million. This included £12.6 million in shares awarded when Burberry floated, £4.1 million as part of a long-term incentive plan and £2.1 million in pay and bonuses. Given her achievement in reviving Burberry through consummate brand management, it's bizarre that some of the investors in the business carped at her salary and bonus award. Clearly, they did not fully understand the underlying value of the brand in the first place and how celebrity could turn it around, otherwise, presumably, they would have taken this action themselves a decade ago.

Markets such as clothing, footwear and accessories seem to be particularly amenable to celebrity input and many brands in the mass market have used famous people across the spectrum of employment from full-time payroll through to ad hoc consultant (where there is clearly overlap into sponsorship) to add value. An important contribution to the resurrection of UK retailer ASDA, now owned by the mighty Wal-Mart, was its 'George' range of children's clothing created by George Davies. He is now part of the

Figure 100 *George Davies.*
Source: Publicis/George Davies.

team working similar magic with Marks & Spencer, which has helped that fallen retail star back to profitability (Figure 100).

George Davies originally made his name when he was hired by floundering UK high street retail group Hepworth to revive their Kendall women's wear brand. This was in the mid-1970s, about the same time as Burton Menswear, then another stumbling giant, took the name designer approach. Burton hired American designer John Weitz to produce a collection under his name, which would be modelled on the styling of the successful European Boss suit range, to be manufactured at the Leeds factory and retailed exclusively at Burton. In short, it was an expensive disaster. John Weitz was not a known name in the UK, Burton's production quality was inadequate and the years of under-investment in their retail outlets, plus the surrounding plethora of sale offers rendered them an inappropriate setting for Weitz's more upmarket range. Meanwhile, the little-known Davies, and to the credit of the board who supported his ideas, took an altogether more radical approach. Kendall successfully evolved into Next and then the Hepworth menswear chain did too. At a stroke the business was completely transformed into a retail and catalogue hybrid, with all the negative baggage associated with the Hepworth brand name being consigned to history. His 'intrapreneurial' task completed, and his fame established, Davies departed from Next and left it in the hands of managers more talented at maintaining and developing a going concern.

The lesson for marketers in these widely differing outcomes from two companies, which started in remarkably similar positions, is that a celebrity designer is certainly not a panacea for all a brand's ills. Hepworth perceived what Burton could not come to terms with, which was that their brand was so deeply tarnished that it would be more cost effective to scrap it and start all over again rather than to continue to pour money into tactical attempts to resurrect it. The Burton Group was subsequently reconstructed and reconfigured, mainly through the development of new brands such as Top Man and Top Shop and later through the acquisition of Dorothy Perkins, Wallis, Burton, Miss Selfridges, Outfit and Evans and is now part of the Arcadia Group which was worth £229 million in 2002. Next was valued at £547 million.

It's not always employees at the top of a company who can be celebrities and do well for the brand. Not all sportspeople make their fortunes out of doing what they love and perhaps only get to the lower representative levels of their chosen game before retiring and taking a more conventional job. However, salespeople who have a reputation for having been pretty outstanding in some sporting activity, as well as having good product knowledge and interpersonal skills, can be incredibly successful. Markets where men are key decision makers are particularly susceptible to this technique and companies operating as manufacturers of sporting equipment are natural homes for ex-players. But many are the companies outside the world of sport which have done rather well by taking on a professional footballer, cricketer or rugby player. Employment legislation in the UK and EU is making it increasingly difficult for any company to discriminate positively in favour of one person over another in seeking particular attributes that are appropriate to their brand. However, without breaking the law, it may well still be possible to recruit one or two celebrities who can act as great ambassadors for the brand both internally and externally.

17

Celebrity brand ownership

The logical conclusion of celebrity involvement with the brand is that the star could end up owning it. Another way of looking at it is that if a celebrity is in effect a brand in his or her own right, then it's quite reasonable for the brand to have its own line extensions. Most naturally these can be developments of the star's core skill and reputation into closely related areas and there are many good examples of this in the worlds of music and sport (Figure 101).

Throughout the history of rock and pop music there have been examples of successful artistes who have developed their own lines of merchandise – tour T-shirts, sweatshirts and other items which are sold at the venues at which they perform and which typically produce revenues which are at least as significant as those generated by ticket sales. The Rolling Stones 'Voodoo Lounge' tour in 1994–95 brought in close to $370 million worldwide while their 1997–99 'Bridges to Babylon'/'No Security' tour did over $390 million and merchandising played a large role in delivering these takings. As the current 'Licks' tour is playing smaller venues the revenue is expected to

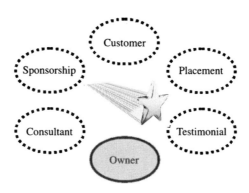

Figure 101 *Star involvement with a brand – owner.*

be lower, but to maximize profitability the merchandising will be more sophisticated than ever with some 50 products on sale including underwear by 'Agent Provocateur'.

One of the most innovative celebrity brand ownership deals yet seen came out of the rock industry. This happened in 1997 when David Bowie wished to take ownership of his complete brand image and its earnings power. He announced that he would issue shares in the Bowie brand to financial institutions and float a personal bond issue. Ownership of the bonds would entitle investors to a portion of his future earnings from royalties on previously recorded material and receipts from future live concert tours. Within an hour Prudential of North America had invested more than $50 million (Figure 102).

There are many famous media brand owners who are celebrities in the sense that they front enormously successful TV programmes, such as that of Oprah Winfrey in the United States, which after 17 years has built up an estimated audience of 21 million viewers across the United States and is broadcast in 109 countries worldwide. (Who says there's no such thing as global culture?) Unlike Jerry Springer, who has also achieved extraordinary levels of viewership with 30 million people tuning in to his show every Friday night, but who is still contracted to the network that hired him as an employed presenter, Oprah Winfrey has achieved such a position of power as a result of her success that she owns the rights to her own show which is a co-production between her company Harpo Films and broadcaster ABC TV. The benefits of a joint venture between a celebrity who owns their own rights to their programme format and the broadcaster who will carry it on air for them are essentially those of greater certainty. In the case of a contracted celebrity there are the well-publicized negotiations every time a contract is due to run out and if the show's successful there is relentless upward pressure on the fees due to the star. By the same token, in a joint venture relationship,

Figure 102 Celeb 'Celebrity as brand'.
Source: Private Eye/Ligger.
© Pressdram Limited 2002. Reproduced by permission.

a longer-term contract can be negotiated to the benefit of both parties: the broadcaster has greater certainty over the future costs of production and the celebrity has the security of a longer run on air even if their star might begin to fade a little during that time period.

The 'celebrity as brand owner' activity long ago spread into a wide range of product areas. Hollywood director Francis Ford Coppola was one of the original celebrity viticulturalists 30 years ago and still produces Rubicon wines from his estate in California. The Seresin wine label in New Zealand is owned by Michael Seresin, one of the world's top cameramen with films such as *Midnight Express*, *Angela's Ashes*, *The Life of David Gale*, *Mercury Rising*, *Angel Heart* and *Fame* on his list of credits. Olivia Newton-John has wines that come in bright blue bottles with red Koalas on the labels and this is produced in South Eastern Australia. Famous French actor Gerard Depardieu has become a successful grower of wine, owning estates in Bordeaux, Languedoc, Algeria and Morocco. Another actor, Sam Neill, has done well with his 'Two Paddocks' vineyard in New Zealand and pop star Mick Hucknall has his one in Sicily, which produces his 'Etna Red' brand, no doubt named with a reference to both his hair colour and his band. Perennial pop star Cliff Richard has also got involved in the area, employing winemaker David Baverstock to produce his Vida Nova, Quinta do Moinho in Portugal, which has been well received by critics.

Celebrities clearly seem to have a bit of a thing for wine and given their predilection for it perhaps it is surprising that the major established companies have not been quicker to sign up famous stars and produce wines for them under their name. Wine consumption in the UK has risen from 18.7 litres per person in 1997 to 21.8 litres per person in 2001 and Britain is now the biggest importer of wine in the world. This increase in market size makes it ripe for further segmentation and there is already evidence that the British are buying more expensive wines: the average price per bottle is now £4.65. Perhaps the fact that many of the great wines are celebrity brands in themselves makes it difficult for them to encompass another famous name within their portfolio, but this should not stop the major chains of off-licences or supermarket retailers that have become so dominant in wine sales.

Celebrity fondness for things culinary also extends into the kitchen where several famous people have got involved with their own brands. Paul Newman has become almost as celebrated for his range of dressings and sauces as he was for his blue-eyed good looks in movies such as *Cool Hand Luke*, *Cat on a Hot Tin Roof*, *The Hustler* and *Butch Cassidy and the Sundance Kid*. The 'Newman's Own' range was launched in 1982 with the now famous Oil & Vinegar Salad Dressing and has become a big business. However, in an early example of cause-related or social marketing, Newman donates all profits, after taxes, from the sale of Newman's Own products to educational and charitable purposes and by 2003 he had given away more than $125 million to thousands of good causes. In a recent development in which a celebrity brand comes full circle to do a deal with a mainstream one, Newman has formed an alliance with McDonald's. This agreement was made in March 2003 as part of the fast food retailer's crucial strategy to reposition itself as a purveyor of more healthy foods. A new advertising campaign created by DDB Chicago supported the launch of McDonald's new Premium Salads with Newman's Own salad dressings and thus gave McDonald's two 'halos', one celebrity and the other corporate social responsibility, in one.

Sauces do seem to be good business for famous people and UK TV personality Loyd Grossman, who achieved his celebrity through programmes such as 'Through the Keyhole' and 'Masterchef', now presides over the most successful single celebrity brand in the UK, worth some £25 million a year. Even royalty gets in on the act, with the Prince of Wales having developed his 'Duchy Originals' organic biscuits brand, which was launched in 1990. The brand was created due to the Prince's firm belief in the advantages of organic farming: the biscuits are made with ingredients certified by the Soil Association and use organic oats and wheat harvested on the Home Farm at Highgrove, HRH The Prince of Wales's estate. No doubt buyers like the biscuits for their taste and these altruistic values, but don't mind the royal connection either!

Another example of a celebrity brand owner with a success in the kitchen is that of George Foreman the ex-heavyweight boxer and this story has an interesting twist. Back in 1994 Foreman was signed up to front Salton's 'Lean Mean Fat Reducing Grilling Machine' in 30-minute long late-night infomercials. The sales took off and Salton launched a series of Foreman-endorsed line extensions such as the 'George Foreman Champ Grill and Bun Warmer'. By 1999 the ex-boxer was so integral to the success of the company that CEO Leonard Dreimann took the decision to sign a five-year deal worth $137.5 million to secure the worldwide rights to Foreman's name and likeness. Not bad for the 54 year-old whose endorsement income at the 1970s' peak of his boxing career amounted to just $20,000! The deal has paid off handsomely for both parties. More than 30 million 'Lean Mean Fat Reducing Grilling Machine' units have been sold worldwide since 1996, with grill sales of $375 million in 2002 alone.

Meanwhile the star has launched his own company, George Foreman Foods, with a portion of all sales going to the eponymous Youth and

Figure 103 *George Foreman.*
Source: Cheetham Bell JT.

Community Centre. So what started as a straightforward celebrity endorsement has evolved into a joint venture licensing agreement and spawned
a star's own brand, thus putting George Foreman among the world's most
successful salesmen (Figure 103).

However, it's not always plain sailing and Naomi Campbell's 'Naomagic'
fragrance, designed in close association with Dorothee Piot of Dragoco
Fine Fragrances, doesn't seem to have made much of an impact on the
marketplace. It's always hard to pin down the precise reasons for failure
but perhaps in the case of Campbell her reputation for being somewhat
temperamental has put off more potential buyers than her undoubted beauty
might have attracted.

In nearly all these cases the celebrity is relying on manufacturers or other
specialists with true expertise in the marketplaces in which they wish to
operate. And herein lies the opportunity for brand owners. Most customers
are not particularly loyal to any one brand in any particular market sector.
Most of the time they make their purchase from a portfolio of brands that are
acceptable to them. Thus the name of the game for any individual brand is
to maintain its place and hopefully improve it in the hierarchy of preference
within that customer portfolio. Sophisticated marketers accept that it is
simply not possible for one brand to have 100% of the available business
from all its customers and this is why many of the bigger manufacturers
operate a multi-brand strategy and attempt to manage a whole category

by clever segmentation and targeting to the various customer subsets that they have identified through research. If a manufacturer has a successful brand operating profitably in a marketplace in which there is not a celebrity brand on offer it may well be worth considering entering into a joint venture with an appropriate famous personality in order to develop a second string to their bow. To this partnership the manufacturer and brand owner brings invaluable market knowledge, production expertise and distribution strength, while the celebrity delivers instant fame and credibility, assuming a good 'fit' with the product category.

Take the example of English actress Jane Birkin, who memorably duetted with Serge Gainsbourg on 'Je t'aime moi non plus'. While her fame peaked in 1969, she is still a celebrity in France. Following a meeting between Hermes' President Jean-Louis Dumas the outcome was 'The Birkin' bag. Top TV series 'Sex and the City' devoted an entire episode to a storyline surrounding the bag and at the time customers were facing a two-year waiting list in order to buy one! Thus Hermes, a classic fashion brand, acquired a celebrity sub-brand, widened its portfolio and created welcome fashion news in the process.

As with any joint venture, the relationship between a celebrity and the manufacturer needs to be carefully constructed and safeguarded from a legal and financial point of view. But over and above this, it does seem that the key success factor is the genuine interest of the celebrity in the product category and the brand to which they put their name. There also needs to be a good level of involvement and engagement between the star and the company so that there is a real sense of commitment and achievement.

The cases that fail are often typified by a somewhat dilettante attitude on the part of the celebrity where the joint venture is seen as either an investment or a plaything, neither of which requires them to have any 'skin in the game'. The dot.com bubble was blown even bigger by ill thought out investments by a whole range of celebrities in new technologies of which they had little understanding and into which they embarked with the goldrush mentality rather than any real commitment to the product or service brand that was being developed.

PART V

How to Manage
the Relationship with
Celebrities

Introduction

It is axiomatic that managing the relationship with stars is not easy at the best of times. People who have become famous celebrities have emerged through the most competitive human gauntlet that exists in the world today. In a relentless and remorseless process of social Darwinism, driven by billions of personal decisions, a tiny number of people emerge on the stage of life as its stars. In order to have got there they have to be very special people and usually they are driven by a powerful cocktail of ego, insecurity, genius, selfishness and desire. Having arrived at their particular pinnacle of achievement, these stars know that just as they have ascended so they will in due course descend, but, of course, none of them wishes to acknowledge this relentless turning of the wheel of fortune. Therefore nearly all of them suffer inner doubts and these insecurities can surface at any time resulting in behaviour which can range from the difficult to the downright outrageous.

And of course brands have egos too! Many of the companies that employ celebrities to promote their brands are very large, have long histories and are proud of their achievements in commercial terms. Very often they are rational organizations that see relationships more in functional than emotional terms. They may well believe that contracting a celebrity is, in principle, no different from contracting a supplier of mechanical parts or product ingredients. Given the different poles from which these two entities approach each other, it's obvious that there is very significant potential for a clash of their egos unless the situation is very carefully managed.

And of course dealing with celebrities and companies is rarely a straight-forward process. On the celebrity's side there will no doubt be an agent, but hidden behind the scenes there may well be a highly influential girlfriend, boyfriend or childhood associate. This person can be a powerful opinion former for the star, who may well not agree to anything until this close adviser is also in accord with the proposal. Marketers are also constrained by other people within their organization: colleagues in purchasing or procurement, the legal department or finance may all wish to get involved in the process and because they are as susceptible as anyone else to the allure of celebrity they may wish to get more deeply into this kind of negotiation than the more prosaic ones which normally fill their day. Very often the marketer will be using an agency or agencies to manage their brand communications and it is likely that the core idea for using a famous person in the service of the brand will have come from one or other of these professional service providers. Within agencies the creative people may have come up with the idea, but it could turn out that an individual in TV production actually provides the key link to the artist's agent. The agency may decide to bring in the outside expertise of a specialist in negotiating with artists' representatives. Then there are the client relationship managers who will be involved in delivering the campaign, to say nothing of the agency's own finance and legal people.

The words 'too many' and 'cooks' rapidly spring to mind! While it is normal for the production of brand communications to involve a team effort involving large numbers of people and it is the special skill of agencies to coordinate these efforts, the case of celebrity adds a further level of complexity and therefore risk just because people are fans as well as professionals. This part of the book is therefore a very important one even though it's dealing with issues of contract and negotiation that may make many people's eyes glaze over with boredom. Nearly all the problems with celebrities can be traced back to a mismatch between the expectations of the contracting parties and it's absolutely crucial to be assiduous in scoping out in great detail the nature of the relationship and the obligations on both sides. On top of that it is essential that the marketer and the agency are hypersensitive to the personality of the celebrity, and their surrounding advisers, and take the managing of that relationship or that set of relationships very seriously indeed.

18

Negotiating and contracting with celebrities

Before embarking on any negotiation with a celebrity or their agent, it's essential to know how much money you're prepared to spend. However, it is beyond the scope of this book to examine the budgeting process for marketing communications campaigns in any detail. There are a number of publications that cover the subject well, including Dr Simon Broadbent's *Spending Advertising Money* and *The Advertising Budget*. There is also a useful summary in the joint industry guidelines entitled 'Finding an Agency', which is available as a free download from the IPA website.

However, without reading any of the literature on the subject of setting budgets for brands, it's obvious that if the celebrity route is one being seriously considered as the creative approach, then sufficient funds must be allowed for. This is in addition to the normal percentage included for production, which is commonly assumed to be between 10% and 15% of the total media expenditure planned. It is very hard to be prescriptive about the precise amount of money that should be set aside for paying the celebrity as so much depends on the particular circumstances surrounding the brand, the campaign and the star. However, it is clear from the case histories published in full in the *Advertising Works* series and available online through www.warc.com, some of which are summarized later in this book, that campaigns featuring celebrities can be extremely profitable. Thus the best advice to marketers and their agencies is to examine these cases in detail, especially those ones for brands in their market sectors, in order to establish relevant benchmarks for their own campaigns.

Another very useful source of information in establishing the likely cost of the celebrity is through the TV production departments of most leading IPA agencies. Many of them will have been involved in producing campaigns featuring major stars in different ways and to varying degrees of engagement. They will, in turn, be aware of the leading agents in the marketplace who act for actors, actresses, musicians and other stars who might be candidates to be featured in an advertising campaign and will be able to give expert guidance on likely costs. However, in order to give an indication of the monies involved and always depending on what was required of them, a mainstream UK presenter would start at around £50,000 to £75,000. A well-known and liked TV personality, Carole Vorderman for instance, would be looking for nearer £200,000 to £250,000 for a year's involvement. Contrariwise, a big US star would be $500,000 to $1.5 million dollars, depending on the package and beware, because in the US pension and tax can bump this fee up another 30%. Hollywood megastars can begin negotiations at $2 million. In a landmark deal announced in September 2003, Elton John signed up to perform 300 concerts in Las Vegas over a two-year period for a fee of £36 million, or £120,000 per show, making him the world's highest paid concert performer.

These artists' agents are by definition acting for their clients and will quite rightly be seeking the highest possible remuneration for them. Depending on the strength of the position of their client, they are likely to quote figures at the very top end of expectations as an opening position in a negotiation. Agency TV production departments have significant levels of expertise in this arena and are familiar with the current prices that are being demanded and the agreements that are being negotiated. However, in some circumstances it may be helpful to outsource the negotiation. There are one or two agents who act on behalf of agencies and clients and in the UK perhaps the best known of these within the industry is Alan Cluer, who has been involved in securing the talent for several of the celebrity campaigns that are familiar to us on our screens. The benefit of using specialist expertise, especially in the more complex and tricky negotiations, is that he or she is in the market all the time and has an intimate knowledge of the career positions of many artists. It may be, for example, that the perception from the outside is that a certain celebrity will be virtually unobtainable either on principle or on price grounds. However, behind the scenes the circumstances maybe rather different, perhaps due to a very expensive divorce, a run of unsuccessful movies or simply a change of heart resulting from a change of agent. These crucial snippets of knowledge can make all the difference in negotiating a celebrity contract and could be well worth paying the fees of an intermediary for.

Having established the budget parameters the next step is to decide in whose hands the actual negotiation should lie. From all we've examined so far, it can be seen that there are three main options, each of which has its pros and cons:

1 agency
2 client
3 agent.

In most cases it makes sense for the agency that has originated the creative idea featuring a star to continue with the process and negotiate the contract with the celebrity on behalf of their client and brand. The agency will have the best possible understanding of the nature of the creative idea and thus is in a position to be flexible (or not) in the process of the discussions with the star and their advisers as to what variations may be made to the core idea in order to accommodate the celebrity's wishes.

Some client companies, such as those in sports or music, whose business is inextricably involved with the negotiating of celebrity contracts, will have an enormous amount of expertise in the area and it would be foolish for them not to use this when it comes to negotiating with the star of a proposed commercial. There may also be circumstances in which it could be advantageous for the negotiation to be led by someone from the client company simply because this could appeal to the artist and his or her advisers. Clearly, if this is the route to be taken, then the client negotiator certainly needs to have the requisite skills.

Finally, there may well be benefits in the agency retaining the services of a specialist agent to act on their behalf in negotiating with the celebrity's representative. This approach may be considered if there's a particular complication involved or where it's perceived that the specialist may have a better connection with the other side.

Whoever is given the responsibility for negotiating the deal must be given very clear guidelines and the authority to reach agreements without constant referral back to other parties. So often a negotiation can come unstuck simply because it loses momentum due to the delays incurred while consultations take place. It is also commonly the case that a given celebrity may be under offer by more than one brand at any given time because they have suddenly become visible as a result of a successful movie, TV, sports, musical or other newsworthy appearance, which has triggered the idea of using them in a number of creative minds around about the same time. Buying a celebrity is a bit like buying a house – you have to know what you want, have the money ready and be prepared to act quickly. You also need to be prepared to walk away!

Another useful approach to negotiating with a celebrity is to maintain parallel discussions with the least a couple of other star options. This can be very difficult to do, especially in the minds of the creative people responsible for the idea, because the concept for the commercial or the campaign may seem to be inextricably bound up with the particular characteristics of an individual star, who thus becomes irreplaceable and a 'must have' for the brand. If the agency finds itself in this position then it is clearly a weak one from a negotiating point of view.

Hopefully, if market research has been used in developing the idea, the agency team will have an appreciation of the underlying mechanics of the idea in relationship to the brand and its objective in the marketplace. They may also be aware of other famous personalities whose names have come up in consumer group discussions or simply as options in conversation with the agency and client teams. Armed with this information, and acknowledging the psychological difficulties of riding more than one creative horse at any given time, it is advisable for the agency to develop alternative versions of the campaign idea featuring different celebrity options. These other stars may be perceived to be less than ideal when compared to the chosen front runner, but assuming they are acceptable per se then these alternatives give the negotiator a much stronger position from which to bargain, especially if it can be made known to the target celebrity and their agent that there are viable alternatives which, in extremis, will be taken.

For the UK launch of the revolutionary GM Card from Vauxhall in the early 1990s, the original first choice for the celebrity presenter was Robbie Coltrane, fresh from his series in which he travelled across America in a pink Cadillac (nice link with the USA where the card originated) and his success as criminal psychologist in 'Cracker' (good serious role in contrast to his usual comic persona and perfect persona for a serious low-interest rate, no-fee, loyalty points credit card). However, Coltrane was contracted to Persil and was in the process of renegotiating that deal. Alan Cluer was the adviser to the agency KHBB and suggested Martin Shaw, star of 1970s' hit series 'The Professionals' (good link with cars; serious police persona) whose career was back on the up with his new role in 'The Chief', as an entirely credible alternative.

Coltrane's agent used the GM Card approach to up the ante with Persil and, in the end, recontracted with them, but meanwhile, Shaw's agent, realizing the impact a £15 million campaign for the first non-'plain vanilla' credit card could have on his client's profile, closed the deal. As it turned out the GM Card from Vauxhall was a huge success, becoming as well known as market leader Barclaycard within six months and recruiting over 300,000 high net worth customers in the first year alone. Martin Shaw's career has since gone from strength to strength with 'Judge John Deed', 'A&E' and 'I Love 1974' TV and movie appearances to his credit.

In making their approach to the desired celebrity, it is crucial that the negotiator should have done their due diligence beforehand as in the GM case just outlined, where Coltrane's position vis-à-vis Persil was key. They need to have an extremely well-informed view on the nature and state of the celebrity's current career and future prospects. They need to know what previous involvement with brands, if any, the star has had and whether or not they have any particular views, for or against, the idea of exploiting their personality in this way. For example, some major Hollywood stars will not agree to appear in commercials for brands that might appear in the USA or Europe, but will be quite happy to do so in the case of advertising which only appears in Japan or elsewhere in the Far East. There is an irreverent website devoted to these celebrities, www.japander.com, and stars who take the Yen include George Clooney, Nicolas Cage, Sean Connery, Cameron Diaz, Harrison Ford, Jodie Foster, Mel Gibson, Brad Pitt and Bruce Willis.

The negotiator has to have very clear guidelines on the parameters of the negotiation they are charged with carrying out. Specifically, they need to know some basic but very important facts about the campaign. The following list is not exhaustive, but covers many of the issues that the celebrity's agent will inquire about and for which the negotiator needs to have 'right first time' answers:

- What is the company and the brand?
- Which agency is responsible?
- Which director and production company are shooting the commercial?
- Which photographer is taking the photos?
- Is the brand seeking exclusivity for the star across all markets, across a smaller group of related markets or just for a particular product category?
- Which media are to be used?
- How many different executions in each media?
- Which markets will which executions appear in?
- How much money will be spent in each medium and in each geography?
- How long will the campaign run for?
- How much of the celebrity's time will be required for the preparation of the creative materials for the campaign?
- What number and type of personal appearances will be required of the celebrity?

It can be seen straightaway that the nature of the answers to these questions will have a material effect on the decision in principle to take part and then very quickly on the price to be demanded. The brand naturally wishes to secure the maximum possible involvement by the celebrity, but is unlikely to be able to afford all the degrees of geographical coverage, duration, exclusivity etc. that it would ideally like. The celebrity, by way of contrast, would like to have the minimum possible involvement with the brand, in order to leave themselves open for other assignments so as to maximize their income, while negotiating very large financial demands for what little they do.

Somewhere between these two polarized going-in positions there has to be a point at which both parties can agree: getting there is very much the skill of the negotiator in understanding the psychology of the celebrity and their agent. Although there are exceptions, it is a rare star who wishes to concern him or herself with the nitty-gritty minutiae of every single deal in which they're involved – that's what they pay their agent to take care of. So what the celebrity wants to hear is a very big 'telephone number' sum of money in exchange for apparently doing rather little. The agent, however, knows full well that they have to operate in the real world and that their skill is in piecing together a deal that delivers that telephone number, but in a way that is acceptable to the party negotiating on the other side's behalf and is affordable for the brand.

The vast majority of celebrity deals are made up of a series of options, with discrete amounts of money attached. The brand, and its negotiator, therefore needs to be crystal clear as to what comprises the core, 'must have', component of the campaign and what it's prepared to pay for it. For example, it might be that the nub of the campaign is a launch 40-second TV commercial, plus two follow-up spots each of 20 seconds in length, which are to be aired in the UK for an initial period of six weeks in total. The agreed fee to the celebrity for this participation might amount to £250,000. However, once additional options have been set out and agreed, covering extensions of the campaign in terms of additional media, geographies and durations plus personal appearances etc., the total sum of money due to the star if all these options were taken up might be £2 million. In justifying this expenditure, the brand marketer and agency will have worked out the potential payback from the campaign as a result of using a multimedia schedule and exposure in additional markets. The brand can also hedge its bets in this way: if the campaign is unsuccessful in its first phase, then the downside in terms of the celebrity fee is just £250,000. Meanwhile, the celebrity and their agent will be looking optimistically at a successful rollout and potential earnings of up to £2 million.

So far there has been a tacit assumption that the celebrity will be paid in cash and while that is commonly the case, it doesn't have to be in every instance. There are more creative ways of paying the star, which can limit the risk to the brand in the short term, but generate much greater rewards for the celebrity and their agent in the longer term. With straightforward cash payments the most common method used is the straight 'buyout' whereby the celebrity receives the agreed sum of money for the agreed participation. A variation on this, which is very widely used for non-celebrity artists who appear in commercials as actors, extras, voiceovers and musicians, is for there to be an initial consideration or 'studio fee' which is then followed by repeat fees payable according to a set formula. In a sense, this latter approach is a form of payment by results and the hope is, from the celebrity's point of the view, that the commercial in which they have appeared will run for some time because it is a success and as a result of that longevity their earnings will be greater. The negotiator for the brand will be able to demonstrate the average number of TV ratings, and therefore repeat fees, which would be paid by the brand on historical precedent and thus the sum that could be due under normal circumstances. On this basis the artist's agent can take a view as to whether it might be advantageous to take a lower studio fee in the hope of recouping greater income overall as a result of subsequent repeat fees.

A variation on the payment by results approach is one where the celebrity might be remunerated by a commission on sales of the brand. Recently there was a well-publicized example of such an arrangement between Manchester United and England footballer Rio Ferdinand and Ben Sherman shirts. This deal was widely reported because of its innovative nature and the belief on the part of the brand and the celebrity that he would be primarily responsible for any significant improvement in sales. Rio Ferdinand signed for three years and is still the face of Ben Sherman, despite the fact that the marketing company, WSS, who brokered the deal, went into liquidation. Herein lies a clear demonstration of the risks to the celebrity in not taking all the money upfront – they and their advisers need to take a view on the likely survival and prosperity of the brand that they're dealing with in exactly the same way as the marketer must take a view on the likely prospects of the star they are using to endorse their product or service.

Finally, the star could be paid by being given a profit share or stake in the business and this represents the most intimate type of involvement between a celebrity and the brand. Depending, of course, on the nature of the contract and a success of the partnership, very significant rewards could accrue to the star if he or she is prepared to take the risk of foregoing fee income in the short term. Keanu Reeves reportedly organized a deal in which he received a low initial fee in exchange for a 15% share of the profits of *The Matrix Reloaded* and *The Matrix Revolutions*, which are now forecasted to earn him between $90 and $200 million. This will enable him to continue his generous habit of giving away personal gifts of several million to many of the members of the crew!

Before closing this chapter on payment of artists it's worth noting that money doesn't always have to change hands. Sometimes a celebrity will do something for a benefit in kind – high ticket items like cars, boats and planes can come in very handy as a part of the jet-set lifestyle and it may be that the marketer sees a placement of their luxury vehicle with a star as being a cost-effective barter.

And, of course, on some occasions, stars will do things for free, especially if it's for a charity or good cause that they believe in. For example, the Lord's Taverners, the cricket-based club and sports charity working for disadvantaged children, fund raises largely through its celebrity members and the events they support pro bono. It's unusual to find a star who does not give their services for free to charity on occasion.

It should be clear by now that negotiating a contract with a celebrity through their agent or representative is a complex matter. It should also be apparent that the sums of money involved are likely to be considerable, especially when taking into account the media expenditure behind the campaign. And there are many pitfalls that can arise in using celebrities. For all these reasons it is absolutely essential that there should be a proper written and signed contract governing the relationship between the star and the brand.

Despite the best intentions of brand managers and their agencies, the tendency to run up to the very limits of deadlines in producing campaigns seems to be endemic in the communications industry. If this is the case with conventional campaigns featuring ideas that are largely under the control of the agency (while acknowledging that many of them are technically very difficult to realize) then when the variable of a celebrity is introduced into the mix it can create very extreme time pressures. Under these circumstances there can be a great temptation to take shortcuts. And one of the shortcuts people may be tempted to take is in the area of the contract. Especially if the negotiations are tortuous or if the celebrity and their representative are in a different time zone making communication difficult, then there is a temptation to go soft and concede issues which, in more normal circumstances and with more time available, would be sticking points. Worst of all, a contract may be negotiated, but not actually signed by the time the shoot takes place. Bitter experience shows that it is far better to lose a celebrity and delay a campaign start date rather than accept a disadvantageous agreement negotiated in a hurry and from a weak position.

The IPA, through its legal team, has produced a template for a 'Celebrity Artist Contract' as the basis for a tailor-made agreement between the brand and a celebrity. Each individual case will have its particular issues, but it is believed that the draft contract covers all the major factors that will need to be addressed in finalizing an agreement, which will be satisfactory to both parties and in their mutual benefit. For example, as well as clearly setting out agreements on such key issues as term, territory, exclusivity and remuneration, the 'death and disgrace' clauses in Section 9, 'Conduct', cover the agency in the event of the celebrity dying before or during the campaign or bringing their brand into disrepute. These insure the agency if the celebrity has done anything that will damage the reputation of their product and gets the celebrity to agree that they will not do anything to damage their reputation in the future. Such clauses would safeguard a brand in a situation such as the one involving Roy Keane walking out on the Irish team during the World Cup. As another protection, the 'Insurance' section (Section 10) allows the agency to take out life/health insurance on the celebrity.

It is in the nature of these things that they get out of date quite quickly, most often as a result of new judgements in legal actions but occasionally because of new primary legislation. Accordingly, the draft Celebrity Artist Contract is available in its current version on the IPA website where it is regularly updated. The draft is free to agencies that are members of the IPA, but is not available to non-members.

It is recommended that marketers, through their IPA agencies, should familiarize themselves with this document, despite the fact that it is nearly 5000 words long and technical in nature, because it does cover all the key considerations surrounding the contractual relationship between the brand and a celebrity. It is therefore very useful not only as a legal document but also as a synthesis of the issues that need to be taken into account when negotiating with representatives or agents of stars.

19

Pitfalls in using celebrities

There are many pitfalls surrounding the use of celebrities by brands and these seem to fall into four main categories:

1 poor celebrity choice
2 video vampires
3 unlawful use of the celebrity
4 scandal involving the celebrity.

First, there are pitfalls to do with the inappropriateness of the chosen celebrity and the lack of proper 'fit' between the star and the brand. When the audience sees that there isn't any real connection between the two they naturally, and probably correctly, infer that the celebrity is 'only doing it for the money' and that the brand is involved in a naive attempt to gain publicity and cachet. Was Joan Collins really a saver with the Bristol & West? There is also a danger in using a star who has been used by too many other brands. There have been periods in the UK when it seemed that Joanna Lumley, wonderful though she was as Patsy in 'Absolutely Fabulous', was plugging one brand after another (Figure 104).

Billy Connolly has also tended to work for quite a few different companies, thus perhaps undermining what is no doubt a valuable talent and one which perhaps would be better off focused on a longer-term relationship with a single brand partner.

Celebrity events can also suffer from the same overexposure and sometimes the 'logo logjam' at major sporting occasions does raise the question of the effectiveness of the activity. For example, during the televised test series between England and South Africa in the summer of 2003 the following corporate sponsors were jostling for position: first, the series sponsor N Power

Figure 104 *Joanna Lumley.*
Source: Publicis.

had a strong presence with a giant logo painted on the grass behind each wicket, a dominant position in terms of perimeter boards and large sight screen posters, and their brand identity was even on the stumps. Vodafone with its £4 million a year deal with the England and Wales Cricket Board (ECB) was also very much in evidence, with its distinctive logo appearing on the right breast and sleeve of each of the England player's shirt, plus perimeter boards. Castle Lager occupied an analogous position on the shirts of the South African team. Meanwhile, the two umpires carried the Emirates airline logo on the breast of their jackets and the slogan 'Fly Emirates' could be seen writ large across their shoulders. Other brands such as Bluesquare, LG, Investec and Friends Provident had perimeter boards and, of course, a number of manufacturers' logos were in evidence on players' bats, including Gunn & Moore and Slazenger. But perhaps one of the most visible brands was the broadcaster, Channel 4, who in a simple but creative coup, had provided spectators with cards bearing their logo '4', which could be seen by millions on TV being waved all around the ground whenever a batsman scored a boundary. Presumably the marketers and agencies involved will all have done their own evaluation of their exposure during the series and hopefully they will have proven to their own satisfaction that it was cost effective, especially taking into account all the other support activities, including corporate hospitality, that will have gone on in the background. Concern about 'communications clutter' will be behind Vodafone's attempt to persuade the ECB to change the England team strip from predominantly blue to red in order to reinforce the mobile phone giant's corporate colours and improve branding.

The second pitfall in using a celebrity to promote a brand is that they can swamp the communication and become a 'video vampire'. The sheer enjoyability of celebrities, either of a genuine variety, or of the more ersatz kind created by brands, is also their weakness. There is a good deal of evidence that the sheer impact of celebrities as brands in their own right is such that while it brings almost instant fame to the brand to which they lend their personality, it does not necessarily impart information of a particularly detailed nature. This has happened often in the financial services sector, and telecommunications and retail are other arenas in which the same syndrome has been observed. Paradoxically, the risks seem to be greater in the low-interest categories. Here celebrities are often used just because the facts and figures, let alone any special contractual or other product details, seem to be so hard to get across interestingly and engagingly by other creative techniques. So often an advertisement or other communication featuring a celebrity 'wins' in research for brands in these more mundane market sectors. Thus one can discern a cycle, which seems to repeat itself in a number of market sectors.

The cycle seems to go a bit like this. The exploratory research on the market and the brand reveals that it has low awareness in a low-interest category. The client and the agency agree that something outstanding has to be done in creative terms in order to break through this apparent customer apathy. The range of options created is tested and an approach using a celebrity emerges as the winner. The celebrity is engaged for the project and the launch commercial sets out the concept, usually with a high degree of initial success. Further commercials follow on from the launch commercial but whereas the initial foray into the market created the exciting 'world' in which the celebrity and the brand can exist together and engaged the public's imagination, the subsequent executions tend to feature particular products and services, the 'meat in the sandwich'. These harder selling 'scheme' commercials are often of a shorter time length and yet are allocated a greater share of the budget than the 'thematic' ones which reward the audience and build brand values. Research on the subsequent commercials often reveals that customers are not 'hearing' or 'taking on board' this vital (as far as the client is concerned) information. The agency or client commissions further qualitative research to examine this problem and discovers that the celebrity is 'vampiring' the communication. This means that that the audience is engaging with the brand at the superficial level of celebrity association, but not at the deeper level of factual communication that is desired.

The agency finds itself in an intractable situation. Faced with having to continue to justify high fees for the celebrity in the face of equivocal results in quantitative communications terms, it often abandons the celebrity route and produces something different in its place. Unfortunately the 'something different' rarely performs as well as the preceding celebrity route and after a couple of years, perhaps coinciding with new management of the brand at the client end, the previous success of the celebrity campaign is rediscovered, the agency is rebriefed, a new celebrity is found and the cycle begins again. Barclaycard and BT would both be examples of brands that have been through this cycle. Perhaps the way to avoid the 'video vampire' effect is to maintain the right balance of 'theme' and 'scheme' communication and to continue to integrate the celebrity with the brand story in a way which creates something genuinely new and rewarding for the customer.

The third major pitfall for brands is the unlawful usage of a celebrity. While dead celebrities are usually fair game in the UK, even here there is a danger if the campaign is pan-global, given the different legal situation in other markets. But with live stars it's tricky and hardly anyone involved professionally in advertising and marketing communications can be unaware that celebrities have rights and are increasingly inclined to assert them. This has been the case for decades in the USA and the litigious tendency crossed the Atlantic years ago. Although it is possible to use celebrities without consent in the UK, it has to be done very carefully: reference to celebrities may be acceptable providing there is no actual or perceived endorsement of the product. Yet despite this, there still seems to be a steady trickle of incidents where these rights are infringed to the detriment of the star and with potentially very expensive consequences for the brand.

Under English law there is no such concept as 'personality rights' as there is in many other European countries and in the United States. In these other countries some celebrities and sports stars including Muhammad Ali and Tiger Woods in the USA, Franz Beckenbauer in Germany, Linda Evangelista in France and Walter Zenga in Spain have all successfully sued for unauthorized commercial uses of their names and images. Indeed, André Agassi is currently suing Rolex in the Nevada court for misusing his image in an advertisement and the industry is currently awaiting the final resolution of a Belgian action being brought by a group of Romanian football stars, who claim that the use of their names and images in computer games infringes their legal rights. However, there have also been some famous judgements in the other direction, as the trustees of the Diana, Princess of Wales Memorial Fund found to their cost when they took on the Franklin Mint which was producing replicas of the Princess's likeness without permission. Even the estate of Elvis Presley found itself in a weaker position than it had hoped when it lost its action against Sid Shaw of 'Elvisly Yours' a small London-based company producing memorabilia without their authorization, but with the protection of a number of UK trade marks registered for 'Elvisly Yours' from 1979 onwards (Figure 105).

Brand owners can learn a lesson from these rulings, which is to ensure that their own trademark protection is adequate. Registering marks in the relevant categories affords significant defence of brand properties and advertising slogans, which have cost millions to establish. In this context the legal fees involved become relatively insignificant, but it's never plain sailing: 'Have a break, have a Kitkat' has been registered successfully, but 'Have a break' was rejected and Kitkat has lost its appeal against the ruling.

However, there are signs that the UK may be falling more into line with the rest of the world. There has been an extension of the law of privacy resulting from the introduction of the Human Rights Act and the Data Protection Act. There have also been some high-profile high court decisions

Figure 105 *Sid Shaw of elvisly-yours.com.*
Source: IPA and Sid Shaw.
Sid Shaw wears the 'I AM NOT LICENSED BY GRACELAND' t-shirt at his 233 Baker Street shop in London holding the Bank of Scotland 'Elvisly Yours MasterCard' and the 'DON'T BLAME ME – I VOTED ELVIS' t-shirt.

in this area, the most notable of which being the Eddie Irvine case against Talksport Ltd, a part of The Wireless Group PLC which is run by ex-tabloid newspaper editor Kelvin MacKenzie. The commercial radio station used a doctored image of the Formula 1 racing driver, apparently listening to the station, in promotional brochures mailed to 1000 prospective advertisers in 1999. Irvine complained about the unauthorized use of his image and won the case, which established an important precedent concerning the principle of the loss of goodwill. In his ruling on 13 March 2003, the high court judge Mr Justice Laddie said: 'Mr Irvine has a property right in his goodwill which he can protect from unlicensed appropriation consisting of a false claim or suggestion of endorsement of a third-party's goods or business.' There was an appeal following the initial ruling on damages, which only awarded Irvine £2000 and left him liable for the costs of the other side. Following the appeal his damages were increased to £25,000 and costs were awarded against Talksport, leaving MacKenzie nursing a bill that was probably the wrong side of £250,000.

However, the finding against Talksport does not completely prohibit the unauthorized use of celebrities in advertising. In order for a celebrity to bring a successful claim of 'passing off' three elements have to be established: loss of goodwill, misrepresentation and damage. Some celebrities, especially those with no merchandising career, and certainly most politicians, will struggle to prove the necessary elements of goodwill and damage. Most importantly, if there is clearly no implication of endorsement of the product advertised then a claim for passing off will not succeed. For example, there were allegations in August 2002 that Ian Botham was intending to sue Diageo, the owners of Guinness, for apparently exploiting his image in a national advertising campaign that featured him in the 1981 Ashes series, but the case was settled out of court. The argument turned on whether or not the advertisement suggested that Botham was endorsing the product and in this case this was clearly a moot point. Thus it is possible for brands to feature celebrities in their advertising as long as there is absolutely no implication that they are endorsing the product or in any way giving it a testimonial. Marketers and their agencies that are considering doing this are strongly advised to take legal advice and also to take advantage of the expertise of the ASA, BACC and the RACC.

Owners of media which are brands in their own right also have to negotiate treacherous waters when it comes to dealing with celebrities. At its most basic, judgements have to be made as to what degree someone who has built their career by being in the public eye and assiduously courting publicity still has a right to privacy in some aspects of their life. Making this judgement is extremely difficult, because it is often the most private and personal aspects of the star's lifestyle and personal relationships that have been exploited in the media at their behest in order to build their newsworthiness. The difficulty is exemplified by the contrasting legal fortunes of Michael Douglas and Catherine Zeta-Jones and Sara Cox compared to Naomi Campbell.

For example, during 2003, the judge found in favour of Michael Douglas and Catherine Zeta-Jones against *Hello!* magazine, which ran paparazzi photos of their wedding, spoiling their exclusive £1 million deal with rival *OK!* and also for Sara Cox, the BBC Radio 1 disc jockey, and the *People* newspaper, which published paparazzi photos of her and her husband Jon Carter sunbathing in the nude on their honeymoon at a private villa in the Seychelles in 2001. Sarah Cox was awarded damages of £50,000 and legal fees of over £200,000. However, Naomi Campbell has so far not been so lucky in the first round of her action against Mirror Group Newspapers, which published photographs of her in 2001 snatched outside a Narcotics Anonymous meeting in Chelsea, thus revealing her as a drug addict (Figure 106).

This is likely to continue to be a contentious area and some stars, such as David Beckham, have registered their names as trademarks in an attempt to afford themselves greater protection, but they can't register their images. Brand owners and their agencies should always check whether a celebrity has applied for and got any such trademarks and it will be interesting to see how effective this is in Beckham's case. During the early summer of 2003 easyJet published some national press ads featuring a photograph of the star in his newly acquired 'cornrow' braided hairstyle with a typically weak pun referring to it and their cheap fare deals in the headline, 'Hair today . . . gone tomorrow'. Beckham's advisers immediately took umbrage at this and threatened to sue easyJet, but perhaps because of the sort of difficulty experienced by Botham, then softened their stance demanding a £10,000

Figure 106 *Celeb.*
Source: Private Eye/Ligger.
© Pressdam Limited 2002. Reproduced by permission.

payment to the NSPCC charity. easyJet's response was to offer to double the donation to £20,000 if Beckham gave permission for them to continue to use the ad. Their latest tactic, following his signing to Real Madrid, was to offer him free flights with an ad using the headline: 'Happy shopping back in Bond Street!'

The fourth major area of pitfalls in the relationship between a celebrity and the brand is where the star undermines the brand by being disloyal to it or by getting involved in some scandal or other which does harm to their reputation and by extension to the corporation, product or service with which they are commercially associated. We have seen how important it is to establish intimacy between the celebrity and the brand and ideally to create something new which they share in common and which adds value to the reputation of both. One of the most damaging pitfalls in this context is a very simple one: this is when the star, for some unaccountable reason, declares in public that they are not really a user of the product or service or worse actually prefer one of its competitors. In a slightly tongue in cheek gesture, which nevertheless signifies the importance of brand loyalty in the star once contracted, Chinese basketball star Yao Ming sought token damages of one yuan from Coca-Cola after they used his photo without permission in 2003. The 7'5" Houston Rockets centre has an endorsement deal with rival brand Pepsi Cola and presumably he wanted to make it very clear where his loyalties lay and gain some extra publicity for his sponsor in the process! In another soft drink glitch Britney Spears, who had a deal with Pepsi Cola, was seen drinking a can of Coke. There's a steady trickle of incidents in which stars are discovered not to be using the brand they endorse: David Beckham shaving his head while in a deal with Brylcreem, 7-Up left wondering what to do with hundreds of thousands of cans bearing the face of Roy Keane, the Irish player sent home in disgrace before the World Cup kicked off, Paul Gascoigne saying that Brut brought him out in a rash, Jamie Oliver admitting his restaurant was not supplied by Sainsbury's and Helena Bonham Carter as the 'face' of Yardley cosmetics declaring she didn't wear makeup. Lloyds TSB dropped 'Cold Feet' star John Thomson from its campaign following reports of drink problems and the number of athletes involved in allegations of performance-enhancing drugs are too numerous to catalogue. Actor Paul Kaye may well have blotted his copybook as far as future brand endorsement deals are concerned when he revealed publicly his bitter regret at having appeared in a Woolworth commercial, using foul language to do so.

Tiger Woods, suffering from a recent lack of form, has switched away from the Nike TW driver back to his Titleist 975. His decision was clearly justified by the statistics: during 2003 Woods was only ranked 128th out of 196 in driving accuracy hitting the fairway only 64% of the time and he lay 24th in terms of distance. However, given that his five-year equipment deal with Nike is reputedly worth £90 million and has been the spearhead for the brand into a market worth £1.25 billion in the USA and $1.5 billion in Europe, this embarrassing volte face must have given his sponsor major cause for concern. These sorts of revelation break the trust in the relationship between the celebrity and the brand and reinforce in the public's mind that 'they're only in it for the money'. Thus it is extremely important that this issue of loyalty is fully covered in the contract.

The case of the celebrity being disloyal to the brand is a pretty straight-forward one to deal with assuming the contract is correctly drawn up, but instances where the star gets into real trouble are much harder to deal with. Whatever the small print says, the marketer has to make a judgement call on whether or not the particular incident is actually damaging to the brand or whether the extra publicity might actually be beneficial. Accusations of murder in 1994 led to O J Simpson losing his contract with Hertz and Michael Jackson, then at the height of his celebrity, was contracted to Pepsi Cola when he was subjected to serious allegations of paedophilia. Pepsi had always positioned itself as slightly more irreverent and rebellious than its main rival Coca-Cola, which has traditionally adopted a more mainstream stance, but even these allegations were too much for Pepsi and they rescinded the contract with Jackson.

In another example in the soft drinks market, the brand owner reacted somewhat differently and used what could have been a very difficult situation to its advantage by being sensitive to the concerns of the celebrity's family and colleagues, and to the attitude of fans. Dr Pepper had made an ad featuring RUN DMC, but before the commercial went on the air, group member Jason Mizell, aka Jam Master Jay, was murdered in New York. After consultations with the surviving members of the group and Mizell's family, Dr Pepper proceeded to run the campaign as a tribute to him. Given the often violent culture which seems to be a part of the appeal of acts like RUN DMC and which builds the mythology of its artists, the brand and the band probably did the right thing.

Another incident which is relatively unusual, but one indicative of the sort of situation that a celebrity can get involved in, and perhaps more easily simply because of their fame, is exemplified by the case of US home style guru, Martha Stewart. Even a star such as Stewart, with a reputation for probity and clean living and who had become a role model for middle America, can stumble and occasionally fall. This has happened to Stewart as a result of allegations of insider trading and it does seem plausible that had she had a much lower profile, the reaction of the markets might not have been so severe. In practice between January and August 2003 the Martha Stewart Living Omnimedia share price has halved with revenues from key areas such as merchandising falling by over 25%, plunging the company into crisis and forcing Stewart to resign as Chairman and CEO.

A more everyday example of something that can happen to anyone, but perhaps is more likely to involve a celebrity, was the arrest in July 2003 of one of America's top basketball stars, Kobe Bryant. Bryant, a member of the US Olympic basketball team and star of the Los Angeles Lakers, lies in third place to Tiger Woods and Michael Jordan in the league table of money received from sponsorship, indeed he signed a five-year $45 million deal with Nike only days before his arrest. He has been charged with raping a hotel desk clerk at an exclusive resort in Colorado and while Bryant admits that he did have sex with the woman, he says it was with her consent. It remains to be seen what the outcome of the Bryant case is, but in others like it, it has sometimes turned out that the celebrity was the victim of a honey trap, either instigated by a newspaper or magazine seeking to create a sensational story or by an individual attempting to make a financial gain by entrapping a famous person and settling out of court. In Bryant's case colleagues have been quick to come forward in his defence, expressing disbelief at the allegations and pointing to his apparently happy marriage and young child as evidence of his being a respectable man and responsible citizen. No doubt an organization as experienced and professional as Nike in managing the relationship with a series of stars over many years will have done their due diligence on Bryant before signing a deal as big as $45 million and probably will have a good level of confidence that their man will turn out to be in the right. A major consideration in all this for a brand like Nike, and indeed for any other company that wishes to have an involvement with celebrities for the long term, is that other stars and their agents will be watching very closely to see how the brand behaves as an indication of its likely actions in future should they get involved with them. If a brand cuts and runs as soon as the going gets even slightly tough, then this sends a bad signal to the celebrity community and will put the brand in a very weak position in any future negotiations.

Any brand owner and their agency that embarks on a campaign using a celebrity must assess the potential downside risk of so doing. It comes back to the basic principle of doing the due diligence about the star and getting the best possible idea of what they're like as a person in the hope of avoiding the high-risk characters. It's also essential to take the best possible legal advice and to negotiate the most comprehensive contract in order to cover all eventualities. But perhaps most important of all, the brand must behave with integrity if and when a controversy arises. In doing this the company must do its utmost to control the PR agenda and preparing crisis management scenarios in advance is a very worthwhile investment. It is also extremely useful to carry out snap market research among key consumer groups in order to gauge their reaction to the scandal as it unfolds. Being in touch with the feelings of the target audience will enable the brand to make the right decisions both for itself and for its customers and, hopefully, for the celebrity too.

The fact that celebrities are subject to human frailty means there will always be a risk in using them to promote brands and this only re-emphasizes the need for a full and proper contract governing the relationship, which takes into account the implications of any illegal or inappropriate behaviour by the star.

PART VI

Ten Successful Ways of Using Celebrities

Introduction

In Part IV, a wide range of possible uses of celebrities to promote brands was discussed and some examples of the effectiveness of these approaches were given. However, there are many factors that can have a bearing on the success of a marketing communications campaign, so how do we know it wasn't some other variable, such as market growth, competitive failure or product improvement, as opposed to the campaign that produced the result?

Fortunately, the IPA Databank now contains in excess of 1000 effectiveness case histories, spawned by the biennial competition inaugurated in 1980 and there are a good number that feature celebrities. In fact, about 10% of the prizewinners have used stars as a key part of their campaign idea and thus we have some excellent examples with which to demonstrate the business contribution and return on investment that this particular creative approach can deliver.

Where possible additional information is provided on the genesis of some of the campaigns that are featured through interviews with the people who were involved in developing them. These conversations give some insight into the thought processes, the accidents and chances that have led to the creation of some of the great campaigns of the recent period.

Clearly, there are almost no limits to the ingenuity with which a celebrity could be used in advertising, and there are a large number of IPA cases to draw on and too few pages available here to cover them all. The appendix contains details of all 27 cases in the IPA Databank that feature stars and from these many lessons can be learned. I've concentrated on what I see as the most obvious and important genres of celebrity usage and narrowed them down to the following ten, which are:

1 **Celebrity as presenter**: e.g. Bob Hoskins for BT; AMV BBDO
2 **Celebrities playing themselves**: e.g. Lennox Lewis et al. for Police Recruitment; M&C Saatchi

3 **Celebrity as brand character**: e.g. Rowan Atkinson for Barclaycard; BMP DDB
4 **Celebrity expertise**: e.g. Jamie Oliver for Sainsbury's; AMV BBDO
5 **Celebrity as role model**: e.g. Kate Moss for Rimmel; JWT
6 **Celebrity cast against type**: e.g. Gary Lineker for Walkers; AMV BBDO
7 **Celebrity acting a part**: e.g. Prunella Scales and Jane Horrocks for Tesco; LOWE
8 **Celebrity revelation**: e.g. Kate Moss et al. for One2One; BBH
9 **Celebrities interacting**: e.g. Ulrika Jonsson et al. for KFC; O&M
10 **Celebrity representations**: e.g. George Best et al. for Dairy Council; BMP DDB

HPI has developed a useful codification of five celebrity campaign types and it is possible to distil these ten approaches into their categories, which are: 'testimonial', 'imported', 'observer', 'invented' and 'harnessed'. However, it's hoped that my longer, more specific list may be more inspiring for creative people and lead to more brand campaigns customers want to 'subscribe' to in terms of the Butterfield model. All would agree that the star vehicle needs to demonstrate the celebrity has 'expertise', is a 'credible source', can be 'trusted' and is 'likeable'.

20

Celebrity as presenter

Just because this is the most straightforward and obvious way of using a celebrity to promote a brand doesn't mean it is ineffective – on the contrary. Indeed BT, through their agency AMV BBDO, used Bob Hoskins as a 'presenter' with such success that their case history won the Grand Prix at the IPA Effectiveness Awards in 1996. This chapter draws on the outstanding entry authored by Max Burt and includes an interview with David Abbott, creative director of the agency at the time and closely involved with the origination of the campaign. His comments give useful insights into the management of celebrity campaigns and specifically the key role of the client as 'brand author' and custodian of their communications.

The BT campaign operated in a market where deregulation was presenting significant challenges to the denationalized quasi-monopolistic incumbent. At this stage in the evolution of the fixed-line telephony market, the strategy adopted by BT was to try and increase the frequency of use of the telephone by a significant number of its existing customers. Their research revealed that one of the barriers to increased usage was the 'gatekeeper' role adopted by males in many households. Their perception was that the telephone was expensive and women in particular indulged themselves in discursive, often purposeless phone calls. This unnecessary putting up of the cost of the bill led many men to take a hostile attitude towards the use of the phone.

Bob Hoskins was chosen to be the celebrity presenter to lead the 'It's Good to Talk' campaign and he was a great piece of casting. At that time Hoskins was riding high on his performances as a gangster in films such as *The Long Good Friday* and had great credibility with the male audience. Thus he was able to take the essentially instructional scripts and educate men as to the benefits of allowing women to talk for longer on the phone and further, how they too might improve their key relationships by doing a little of the same. Trading on his tough guy persona, Hoskins was also able to bring something new to his audience by revealing a more sympathetic side to his character.

Summary of the BT case history

Problem

After its privatization in 1984, BT was faced with several rulings designed to encourage competition and reduce its market share. In response, BT used the power of advertising to stimulate calls. This began with the 'Beattie' campaign starring Maureen Lipman as an extremely talkative housewife.

This campaign ended in 1992, as Beattie and her family had become such famous individuals that the messenger was overwhelming the message.

Beattie had also become a negative stereotype of the 'wasteful' woman chatting 'aimlessly' on the phone.

Beattie and the 'Get Through to Someone' campaign which followed had some success, but BT still needed to change negative attitudes by promoting the positive value of phone communication.

Strategy

BT wanted to prove that: 'You get more out of your life, and your relationships, by communicating [through BT].' This was achieved through AMV BBDO's 'It's Good to Talk' (IGTT) campaign.

Research showed that while women tended to spend time 'chatting' on the phone for the pleasure this gave, men viewed the phone as a functional instrument for delivering rational messages. The agency aimed to persuade people to make more and longer calls by raising the value of female-style calling in men's eyes. This was achieved by comparing its benefits to functional male-style usage and illustrating that individual calls are as low in cost as other everyday purchases. This both legitimized women's phone use and increased male calling levels.

Bob Hoskins was chosen to deliver the message because he was seen as 'one of us' and because he was well loved by both sexes. Women found him endearing and he could tell men to soften up because he himself was perceived as a hard man.

Bob was made more believable by playing the role of a Jiminy Cricket-type conscience figure, sitting unnoticed on people's shoulders and pointing out the benefits of good phone communication.

Results

'IGTT' generated a 1.75% sales uplift for every 100 TVRs spent. This amounted to an incremental value per TVR of £33,000. Overall advertising-generated income over the period amounted to £297 million representing a return on investment of 6 to 1.

In awareness terms, the campaign reached number one in marketing's Adwatch Survey soon after it broke and remained there for 22 of the next 30 weeks.

More importantly, 'It's Good to Talk' changed people's attitudes to telephony and convinced the nation that it really *is* good to talk.

INTERVIEW WITH DAVID ABBOTT

Wendy: Was 'IGTT' the first campaign that AMV did for BT?

David: Yes, it was the pitch. It was the campaign that won the business and, more or less, it ran pretty much as presented.

Wendy: Did you have Bob Hoskins in mind when you presented?

David: Yes, not only in mind but he had more or less agreed to do it. I don't think you can go into a major pitch like that and say this is the idea it would be great if we can get him. You have to go in and say, 'He's agreed to do it.'

Wendy: Why did you choose him?

David: Well, it sprang out of the strategy, which is not always the case but good when it is. BT at the time was still in a situation of being almost a monopoly supplier and so if the market grew, BT did disproportionately well out of it. Stafford Taylor, who was the BT client at the time, and we agreed that growing the market was a smart strategy.

At the time, I believe the average person in the UK spent 10 minutes a week on the telephone, but in the States it was something like

20–25 minutes. If we could get even close to that BT would make a lot more money.

Also, BT at the time was often painted as the bad face of privatization – making too much money and all the rest of it, so there was a dual ambition to warm up the personality.

The two big barriers to the time people spent on the telephone were really to do with men. Men by and large didn't use the telephone for social conversations. Not only were they 'phonophobic', but they were also not very encouraging to the women in their families, because they acted as gatekeepers. They would say 'can't you get off the phone it's too expensive' or 'I can't see what you find to talk about'. They inhibited phone use by being discouraging or disparaging.

We decided to grasp the nettle and to try to convert men in two ways. First, to make them realize that it's all right to be more demonstrative and to have longer phone calls and to chat rather than bark out messages or make arrangements. Second, to try and change their attitudes towards their partner on the phone – the woman on the phone was often the family fixer, the one who kept relationships going and it wasn't sensible to inhibit her.

We were then faced with a greater problem of trying to find a spokesperson to deliver this complicated message. Someone who wouldn't alienate men i.e. come across as a silly 'new man', but who was also sympathetic to women. I quickly thought of Bob Hoskins going back to *Mona Lisa* and *The Long Good Friday*. He was a tough little man and not the sort of Nigel Havers charmer, but women liked him. Another consideration was that he'd never appeared in commercials before. This was the biggest account in the UK and we knew that we had to have a big idea. Because the task was so multifaceted, a spokesperson was a convenient way of doing it but it had to be extraordinary, fresh and new and people had to say 'wow, how did you get him' kind of thing.

Wendy: Was he happy to get involved then?

David: He was initially nervous about it. We were having conversations with Bob before we'd got the account via Alan Cluer, who helped us find talent. I knew Alan as a friend and we'd used him on the Sainsbury's celebrity commercials for years.

So Alan and I talked, and I don't remember if I went to him and said I want to get Hoskins, or if Hoskins came up over lunch in a potential shortlist. Anyhow, I met with Bob Hoskins and Alan and his agent and I gave them some sample scripts. At that time it was quite an altruistic campaign: by communicating, 'It's good to talk', we aimed to make the world a more humane place. Bob was not required to sell any kit; he was just required to sell the telephone habit. He was able, in good conscience to say yes I can do that.

Later in the campaign, when Stafford Taylor died, there was more pressure to use him more extensively on tariffs and all kinds of programmes, which was against the spirit of the campaign and I think was a mistake. It led eventually to overexposure, but in the first two or three years he was kept pure and I think he did an amazing job.

He agreed to do it, subject to us getting the business and subject to some final details about money – it was a very easy sell, really.

I did the presentation alone as Stafford was an ex-sales director and didn't want the usual agency razzmatazz of people jumping up and down – he was from Yorkshire. We knew it went well. We knew that someone would have to be very good to beat us. (Later he was very supportive of the campaign and he let us do some bold things. But he sadly became ill and somebody else took over.)

We tested Bob Hoskins in research and he scored very highly with both women and men. The only bad thing that happened was I got so used to writing with Bob Hoskins voice in my brain that I couldn't present the scripts without doing Bob Hoskins impersonations!

On the set too, when we had to make a change I'd go 'what about this?' and I'd do my 'Bob Hoskins' in front of Bob Hoskins!

Wendy: Did you consider anyone else?

David: Michael Caine was mentioned, but all our research told us that Bob was our person.

Wendy: And it worked.

David: Yes, I think it was a good slogan, and became part of the language and all of that. And Bob was a very good actor too – he wasn't just a personality, he was a first-rate actor so he could do what we wanted. We did one commercial where he sat silently for 30 seconds just looking at the camera. The commercial was about how frustrating it is when people don't get back to you. I don't think there was anything we asked him to do from singing to staying silent that he didn't do extraordinarily well.

Wendy: Did he have his own input?

David: Yes he did, he liked to work with directors he rated. We started with Ridley Scott, then Richard Longcrane did a lot of the commercials. He let you know if he didn't like working with someone and you could tell. He liked directors that had film experience, or knew their way around. Most of the scripts were little scenes from life so that suited him. He was extraordinary but he was a very unstarry, ordinary person. He would say, 'I wouldn't say that'. He didn't like it if you tried to make the scripts too Cockney, he'd spot a false note. It wasn't the writing but his voice, his manner, his delivery that made it peculiarly Hoskins; there was a kind of rhythm to his speech.

Wendy: There was a piece in *Marketing* that said this was more than an ad campaign; it was a piece of 'social engineering'.

David: It was an attempt to do that. I remember Mark Lawson on the 'Late Review' was astounded by the campaign and not in a complimentary way.

In the first script, Bob was a ghostly presence, so he could be in the room but people couldn't see him and he would talk to camera. A chap of about 40 is ringing his mother and he gets on the phone and says something like 'Oh mum, hi, I can't talk for long we're just going out' and Hoskins says 'That's not kind is it? Do you do that, do you ring up and the first thing you say is you won't be on the phone for long' and he said 'There's another way of doing it' and uses the words 'that's kinder isn't it?'

Mark Lawson thought it was inappropriate for a commercial operation or an advertiser to be telling people to be kinder. I don't know why.

I think that was a rather old-fashioned view of what advertising's for and what it does. We were attempting to make men and women realize the value of good communication. It was the Stafford Taylor vision as well as a commercial strategy.

To increase phone usage you had to push social attitudes and I think the push was a good thing. It was a virtuous circle. I certainly felt involved in something worthwhile.

Wendy: How long did the campaign run for?

David: Five or six years, something like that. It ran in its pure form for 2–3 years, I can't remember now.

Wendy: Why did you decide to kill it off?

David: We tried very hard to keep a division between what were the high-ground commercials about social change and the business of selling family packages and other programmes they had. But BT wanted to use the vehicle across the board – that was one of the strengths of Hoskins, you could use him for business and domestic, but I think towards the end, the balance was wrong.

It meant that he was on air too often. However much you might love someone, if you see them on air three or four times a night and they're always popping up you think 'Oh I can't bear that' and of course BT was a big advertiser and took up a lot of airtime.

I think the campaign would've lasted longer with more careful stewardship. Once Stafford Taylor had gone, the subsequent BT execs didn't see why they shouldn't use him across the board.

Wendy: Do you think the public began to trust Bob Hoskins less when he more obviously began to try to sell products?

David: I think he could sell services like 1571 and answerphones and you could do it in the context of 'IGTT' because it's better not to have kids waiting outside school etc. But there were some products I don't think they should have used him to sell – like low rates.

Also, over the years, BT's competitive situation had worsened. The legislator gave other companies more access to BT's lines. They came in and were really caning BT on price, so the strategy of growing the market looked somewhat generous and we had to get back in the market and slug it out on price. The whole game got muddier and dirtier. It was about hanging onto your customers, not about getting them to make more calls. BT thought that 'It's Good to Talk' was less relevant to the situation they found themselves in so it was gradually phased out.

You can argue that they should have kept it going at a high corporate level. I personally supported that view.

It's strange to think that with the mobile, Stafford's dream of getting people to talk more has happened and people now seem to talk for a long time, all the time, with nothing particular to say – they've just got into the habit. In a sense, technology has achieved more than the advertising.

Wendy: Did you use other celebrities after Bob?

David: We used ET, who is a sort of celebrity I suppose. He was the next big idea for that sort of high-level campaign.

Wendy: So why did you choose ET?

David: It was just as I was retiring. Again, BT was looking for a big idea, something that would be famous. ET was a very warm character; there was a kind of 'stay in touch' connection in the movie.

Wendy: Was it easy to get the rights to use ET?

David: That was another one with Alan Cluer. I was retiring but had a year as a consultant. I went to Peter Souter and Michael Baulk and said I've had this thought about ET, which I wanted to stand for 'Extra Technology' but that got lost as the campaign developed.

We approached Spielberg and had several meetings with his staff in the UK. It rather suited their purposes as the film was coming back in 18 months with a new remastered edition so rather to our surprise it looked possible.

We showed them some of the scripts and reassured them that we'd be faithful and honest; that we wouldn't make ET do anything that compromised his role.

Wendy: Had ET been used in ads before?

David: Yes, in other countries, but rather badly. Not in a sustained campaign way, more in a promotional way than a thematic way.

Wendy: Do you think that using a celebrity or famous character such as Bob Hoskins or ET is a short cut or easy way of revitalizing a long-running campaign?

David: It gives you notoriety and visibility but there's no point being visible and being wrong because it makes it worse. The trick is trying to find a spokesperson who is relevant to the needs of the brand, sympathetic to it and who endorses the message rather than becoming a vampire and engulfing it.

As a creative director there's a kind of a reluctance to use celebrities. A lot of creative people think it's a cop out: 'We haven't got a big idea so let's get a big name.' But of course you can have a big idea alongside a big name, and I think that's what IGTT was.

Wendy: So you need a big idea first.

David: Always. Sometimes a famous face can be a hindrance, but it does give you visibility and that's part of the battle so you can see the appeal of it and a great deal of famous advertising has been built around famous people.

From Joan Collins and Leonard Rossiter through to today, it's a huge part of advertising. I mean Eleanor Roosevelt sold margarine so it's one of the oldest tricks in the book!

21

Celebrities playing themselves

Using celebrities to play themselves in a commercial is a very effective technique. By definition the star should be well known to the audience and is thus able to convey instantly an enormous depth of imagery and associations. In effect, the famous person is a form of communication shorthand that accelerates understanding and enhances audience participation.

The IPA Effectiveness Awards database contains several excellent papers detailing the success of campaigns whose objective was to recruit people into various public services. There are cases on recruitment for the army (2000), nursing (1986), the RAF (1996), the navy (1986) the Metropolitan Police (1988) and national police recruitment (2002). Of these, only the last has employed celebrities in its creative approach and it's interesting to note that it has been one of the most successful.

The image of the police has changed considerably over the years and is now in a much weaker position than it was 30 years ago when Sir Robert Mark, the recently retired Commissioner of Police, was recruited to present the new Goodyear tyre in a TV ad. At the time this was seen as a coup, because such powerful and respected figures wouldn't normally lend their names to a commercial enterprise, let alone intone the words which had such impact then: 'I am convinced that the Goodyear Grand Prix S is a major contribution to road safety' (Figure 107).

Sir Mark donated his fee to charity to maintain his integrity, but this example reminds us how different things are now when there is little or no respect for authority, the police have been accused of being 'institutionally racist' and corruption has been exposed at the highest levels in the force.

Persuading people to join the police in this climate of opinion is no easy task and at the turn of the century a recruitment campaign faced a real challenge. The IPA case history describing how success was achieved in this

Figure 107 *Sir Robert Mark.*
Source: Goodyear.

adverse environment was authored by Richard Storey of M&C Saatchi, the
agency which, working with the COI, created the campaign on behalf of
their clients the Home Office and the police. Storey's paper won a Silver
Award and a special prize for 'Best Insight and Innovation' in the national
IPA Effectiveness Awards 2002.

As with other public service jobs, recruiting people for the police is not
an easy task, especially in London. Not only does there need to be a direct
appeal to the right kind of candidates, there also needs to be a climate of
approval for this career choice among the candidate's family and friends. Like
the army recruitment campaign before it, the police campaign strategy was
to issue a challenge that only the right people would respond to, not only in
order to minimize the number of inappropriate applicants who would waste
resources and money during an abortive screening process, but also to create
a heightened sense of esteem around the job. The campaign is an excellent
example of using famous people to exploit their own personas and in this case
their plausibility as police officers. Here were a number of famous people,
known for their personal strengths – integrity, bravery, selflessness etc. – all
revealing their inadequacy as a potential police officer, and admitting that
'I couldn't'. The end title asks the audience the challenging question:
'Could you?'

This admission by each celebrity created something new which was owned
by both the brand, in this case the police, and the stars, and which the

audience became privy to through the advertising, thus gaining an insight, which both rewarded them and redefined the role of a police officer in their minds.

Summary of the police recruitment case history

Problem

M&C Saatchi's national campaign to improve police recruitment to all 43 forces began in August 2000. At this time, the public's perception of the police was poor, morale was low and applications to the police had been falling for ten years, meaning the strength of the force was at an all-time low. In response to this, the Home Office instigated a national campaign to recruit 9000 extra policemen and women over three years.

Strategy

Advertising needed to issue a powerful challenge to:

- actively discourage the vast majority, while inspiring a tiny but committed minority to apply
- drive widespread respect for the police, which would encourage this minority to put themselves forward.

Advertising had to make 999 out of every 1000 people realize they couldn't be a police officer, but respect like hell the one who could.

When interviewing policemen and women about the extremely difficult situations they faced in their work, the agency planner remarked, 'I for one couldn't do that'.

The advertising idea came directly from this realization. The TV campaign features well-known, respected figures (Joan Bakewell, John Barnes, Chris Bisson, Bob Geldof, Lennox Lewis, Patsy Palmer and Simon Weston) using the phrase 'I couldn't' to admit they haven't got the qualities needed to be a police officer (Figure 108).

Scenarios included Lennox Lewis incapable of restraining himself from punching a wife beater and Bob Geldof unable to separate a child from its abusive parents.

In other media additional celebrities were used including Nasser Hussain, Denise Lewis, Michael Nicholson, Raj Persaud, Jon Snow, Gaby Yorath

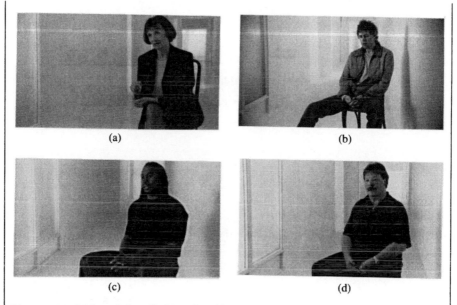

(a)   (b)

(c)   (d)

Figure 108 *(a) Joan Bakewell. (b) Bob Geldof. (c) Lennox Lewis. (d) Simon Weston.*
Source: M&C Saatchi/COI.

and Nina Wadia, thus giving potential recruits the widest possible range of 'access points' to the campaign.

Results

This 'negative', reverse sell approach made the advertising stand out from the media clutter and lodged it in the minds of an unprecedented 98% of the target audience.
The challenge presented has three major effects:

- puts most people off joining the police but in turn increases their respect for the police
- by improving respect it helps boost morale, curtail resignations, reduce fear of crime and influence press reporting
- the challenge encourages an exceptional rate, quality and speed of applications.

Advertising generated 101,795 relevant enquiries up to May 2002, leading to 5998 recruits, an increment of 52%.

This huge increase in inquiries, combined with the exceptional efficiency in numbers of people recruited by this campaign, has saved UK taxpayers more than £30 million.

It has also lifted and sustained much higher levels of respect for the police among those aware of the advertising.

INTERVIEW WITH RICHARD STOREY, ACCOUNT PLANNER AT M&C SAATCHI

Wendy: Your paper showed that compared with previous IPA Effectiveness case histories on recruitment campaign, M&C Saatchi's police recruitment campaign was the most efficient. Why do you think this was?

Richard: The advertising was more challenging, and the advertising issues were more challenging. The nature and strategy of the ads were designed so that people could not just look at it and move on. People were meant to look at it and think: well I wonder if I could do that?

The negativity forces people to question themselves. The case history shows that people have thought about it, many of them rejecting it as a result but they've spent some time thinking 'Well would that be right for me?' So that would be the reason it works, and the celebrities in particular they kind of raise the challenge to a very high level, what they do effectively is to set the bar.

Wendy: Do you think the negative aspect of the campaign would have worked if the ads had shown unknown people instead of celebrities saying, 'I couldn't do that'?

Richard: It may just have worked but not anything like as well. It might have been ok but it wouldn't have been exceptional. It's hard to quantify but what we know is that it's the respect with which those people are held which makes it work. You look at Simon Weston or Lennox Lewis and you think, 'Jesus, that's someone I respect.'

Wendy: So when the original creative idea came about, were celebrities integral to it?

Richard: Integral, yes. Because the whole power of the idea is that you need someone who's right up there on a pedestal saying that they couldn't. That's what gives it the motivational power. In fact we don't actually call them 'celebrities', we refer to them as 'achievers'. They are not just famous personalities – they all well known for having achieved certain things.

We do a lot of work linking the challenge that people talk about with the nature of the celebrity so, to use the latest example, Bob Geldof talks about a subject that is absolutely pertinent to him, being a dad, and everything he's gone through. That's hugely significant and most people know about what he's done for Paula Yates's kid by Michael Hutchence. As we've worked with the campaign, we've learnt to match celebrities increasingly well with the value required by the police work scenario.

As it happens, none of the original celebrities we conceived it with made it through to the actual ads. I think Prince Naseem was the very first incarnation but we ended up with Lennox Lewis who's researched better – he's known for punching and the idea is that he couldn't hold himself back from punching. Plus he would do it and Naseem wouldn't.

Wendy: Who else did you have in mind?

Richard: Kate Adie and various other journalists but there are legal issues about BBC journalists and politicians. We had some people who are 'celebrity' rather than 'achiever', so we had Ben Elton, but in research people didn't think: 'Now there's a man who has survived.'

Wendy: What was the scenario going to be?

Richard: It was relevant, it was about joking, joking and taunting, but it wasn't anything like as powerful as child abuse or wife beating or something like that.

Wendy: I wouldn't have thought that Patsy Palmer was well respected as an achiever either, although her personality does fit perfectly with the scenario in the ad.

Richard: Two things, she comes across very naturally: 'I'm a bit of a talker me.' Secondly, lots of people know that she's a single mum and had a dodgy childhood on a council estate. The scenario was about kids on a council estate and 'shopping' drug dealers. People saw the fit there quite strongly and she was obviously very closely aligned with a young female audience. Joan Bakewell also created empathy.

> **Wendy**: Did you research how a campaign with celebrities would perform versus a campaign without celebrities?
>
> **Richard**: We did a piece of work about a year ago potentially moving the campaign on and we looked at sorts of permutations with or without celebrity and it was very clear. It said that the use of ordinary people, the ordinary Joe Bloggs, was going to reduce the impact and the motivation of the ads.

Using advertising and marketing communications to issue a challenge that only the 'right' people wish to accept seems to be a successful recruitment strategy. When overlaid with celebrity endorsement it becomes even more effective.

22

Celebrity as brand character

It's already been emphasized how important it is for there to be a big idea at the core of the communication for a brand. Once this has been created, then using a famous star to play the part is one of the most effective ways of establishing a long-running brand-building campaign. An excellent example is that of Barclaycard and the comedian Rowan Atkinson, who starred in an outstanding series of commercials featuring the character that has now reappeared in the Hollywood movie *Johnny English*. Atkinson as bungling secret agent Richard Latham and his hapless sidekick Bough produced a whole series of commercials that capitalized on the theme of foreign travel originally built into the brand heritage by the Alan Whicker campaign, but which sought to communicate other benefits of the card such as insurance on purchases made with it. Atkinson retired from the campaign after seven years to take a year off with his new wife and to concentrate on his film career.

Subsequently Angus Deayton was engaged for Barclaycard and produced several commercials, but his series was not as well received as the Atkinson ones and invidious comparisons between the two compounded the problem even before the revelations in the *News of the World* about his use of drugs and prostitutes. Most recently the success of the *Johnny English* movie has no doubt resurrected rosy memories in customer as well as company minds and the agency and brand management at Barclaycard must be regretting ever having had to move away from Atkinson in the first place. Still, it was the right call for Rowan, who is now one of Hollywood's wealthiest stars, with a fortune built on the *Mr Bean* movie, which took $280 million at box office and sold 600,000 units at video.

Illustrating how effective a strategy the 'celebrity brand character' can be is the Barclaycard case history by Paul Feldwick, Louise Cook and Sarah Carter of BMP DDB, which built on the previous entry by Sarah Carter in 1992, and won a Gold Award and the Charles Channon Award in 1996 for campaigns that benefited a business by maintaining or strengthening a brand over a long period. This case history is amplified by an interview with Chris Cowpe, Joint Chief Executive of BMP DDB, who worked on the brand at the time. The Rowan Atkinson campaign for Barclaycard is a classic of its kind and illustrates how powerful a great actor in a role invented for a brand can be.

Summary of the Barclaycard case history

Problem

In 1990 important changes were taking place in the UK credit card market threatening the position of the two dominant brands, Barclaycard and Access. At this time card penetration levelled at around 32% and there were more than 30 cards available so profitability became harder to achieve. As a result in 1990 Barclaycard's card-issuing operation was in danger of making a loss.

In reaction to this a fee was introduced as one element in a major product relaunch and Barclaycard lost about a million 'dormant' customers – who are a source of cost, not revenue – and a much smaller number of active customers than expected. But more was needed.

Strategy

BMP DDB (now known as DDB London) were set three goals for advertising: customer retention, increasing turnover and increasing share of new cardholders.

Research showed that most people saw all credit cards as very similar and in response Rowan Atkinson's character Richard Latham was created. The bungling secret agent was always dismissive about his Barclaycard, which allowed Bough, his assistant, to demonstrate the benefits of Barclaycard usage and provided a mouthpiece for information about it.

Between 1991 and 1995, the period covered by the case, 14 films were made featuring eight different benefits (Figure 109).

Results

Awareness of Barclaycard TV advertising grew steadily from 28% at the beginning of 1991 throughout 1992 and 1993 and, since then, has remained high at around 50%. Furthermore it is a considerable achievement for Barclaycard to have increased its share of cards from 29% just after the launch to 32% in 1996.

Figure 109 *Rowan Atkinson.*
Source: BMP DDB.

In the short term the £110 million spent on Barclaycard advertising between 1991 and 1995 increased turnover per Barclaycard Visa card by an average of 3% in each of those years.

INTERVIEW WITH CHRIS COWPE, JOINT CHIEF EXECUTIVE OF DDB LONDON

Wendy: What was the original idea? How did the campaign originate?

Chris: Barclaycard and we were looking to relaunch the brand with a range of new products and services. Alan Whicker had been the long-standing and hugely successful brand spokesperson: urbane, international and popular. But a change of direction strongly suggested a change of presentation.

Initially, we thought we might replace Alan with an alternative globetrotter; Rowan Atkinson's name was mentioned as a possible candidate. But then a creative team suggested creating the 'next' Blackadder: a James Bond character whose self-confidence and self-worth far exceeded his abilities, supported by a more pragmatic and practical number 2. This was the origin of the Latham and Bough duet.

Wendy: Did you have anyone else in mind and was he happy to do it?

Chris: Not really – the idea was largely created for Rowan as another 'Blackadder'. His initial response was 'yes-ish'. He was probably more concerned that the quality of the campaign would match his own high standards of scripting, performance and so forth.

Wendy: Why was it so successful?

Chris: Inevitably there are many success ingredients: sufficient media weight, relevant products, outstanding scripts, great direction by John Lloyd, but perhaps the key magic ingredient was the sheer brilliance of Rowan's performances. Even today, ten or more years later, people can remember scenes, storylines and even dialogue. It's difficult to imagine this campaign without Rowan; after all it was designed around his previous Blackadder personas

Wendy: Why did you 'kill' him off?

Chris: Basically because Rowan wanted to concentrate on making his movie *Mr Bean*. He and his advisors felt that he worked best when he was totally focused and that more Barclaycard commercials would be an unwelcome distraction. We were both incredibly sad to end such a productive partnership: it's not often that someone like Rowan gets so involved even to the point of attending a research tracking study debrief!

Wendy: Did you know Rowan Atkinson was planning the *Johnny English* film?

Chris: Yes, in the sense that Rowan had asked and got our and Barclaycard's permission to use the character at some later date in a film. And of course we knew about the film at an early stage when he and his agents contacted us to discuss the actual script and so forth.

Wendy: In summary, what makes a good celebrity ad/campaign?

Chris: Apart from all the various practical issues – availability, cost, willingness to do commercials and so on – it really boils down to a few simple principles.

If they are being used as a spokesperson in their own right (e.g. Alan Whicker) ensure that they are relevant to the brand, its personality and the audience.

If they are being used to play a character (e.g. Rowan Atkinson) ensure that the character they play resonates with the actor's 'persona', and that the character is then suited to the brand and the audience. And make sure they can perform in front of the camera!

One of the greatest dangers of using a celebrity is that they are seen to be doing it 'just for the money'. They need to retain a real sense of integrity and credibility in their relationship with the brand and the advertising campaign.

23

Celebrity expertise

Many celebrities have become famous because they're very good at something. This is particularly true in the world of sport and the use of stars as role models to promote particular brands of footwear, clothing or other equipment is one of the longest standing applications of celebrity to brands. But the same approach can be very effective in all sorts of markets where there are star performers who have particular skills that the public admires, seeks to learn from or emulate.

The use of expertise can go much further than employment in commercials as we have seen and Sainsbury's involvement with Jamie Oliver is a very good example of this. Beyond advertising, the supermarket retailer has also harnessed Oliver's expertise as a food consultant to build its business. With his input their herb, bread and meat ranges have been relaunched, the last with '21-day meat' sourced from suppliers he had visited and helped select (Figure 110).

The IPA Effectiveness Awards case for Sainsbury's was authored by Bridget Angear and Rebecca Moody of agency Abbott Mead Vickers BBDO and won a Silver Award in 2002. Leading econometrics consultancy OHAL is reported as saying that it's the best campaign they've ever evaluated. The paper shows how effective it can be to build on a celebrity's existing persona, in this case created by Jamie Oliver in his own 'Naked Chef' and 'Jamie's Kitchen' TV series, and enable him to do more of the same in about 100 TV commercials so far. The casting of Oliver also works really well for Sainsbury's, which has always been perceived as somewhat middle class and perhaps a little aloof. Jamie Oliver's enthusiasm, directness and common touch, plus his altruism and suffering in TV show 'Jamie's Kitchen', diffuses all that and makes Sainsbury's much more contemporary and approachable.

Figure 110 *Jamie Oliver 1.*
Source: AMV.

Summary of the Sainsbury's case history

Problem

After being Britain's biggest supermarket for many years, Sainsbury's had lost the number one slot to Tesco in 1995. Over the next five years, Sainsbury's like-for-like sales steadily declined and finally dropped into negative figures in 1999.

In that year, Sainsbury's was losing customer spend to Tesco, Asda and Morrison's to the tune of £299 million.

When Peter Davis returned as Sainsbury's Chief Executive in March 2000 he set about reinvigorating the business.

Strategy

Abbott Mead Vickers needed to devise new advertising to inspire people to want to shop at Sainsbury's again. It had to stop any more consumers leaving the brand and to encourage existing shoppers to shop differently. The advertising idea had to emphasize Sainsbury's core strength of good-quality food and innovation. AMV wanted to use a chef as an advocate for Sainsbury's as this would be someone who would demand high standards from the supermarket in which they shopped.

Figure 111 *Jamie Oliver 2.*
Source: AMV.

Jamie Oliver, a 24-year-old, moped-driving chef, already famous through his 'Naked Chef' series was the perfect choice for this. He was a living embodiment of the personality and values Sainsbury's was looking for. He was well known for his passion for food and genuine about his mission to get everyone enjoying better food. He was also seen as down to earth, accessible, youthful and dynamic (Figure 111).

Results

Sales of products featured in ads leapt hugely:

310,000 Thai prawn curries were made in the six weeks after launch
4-weekly sales of 'Be Good to Yourself' balti sauce increased by 1040%
49,000 packs of 'Blue Parrot Café Fish Fingers' were sold in the first week of TV airing.

Since 2000, the Jamie Oliver campaign has helped turn around Sainsbury's business fortunes delivering £1.12 billion in incremental revenue and a ROI of £27.25 for every advertising pound spent.
In reinvigorating the brand mission of 'Pioneering better quality everyday food', Jamie has given customers new food ideas that have encouraged them to shop, cook and eat differently.
This has helped halt defection and enticed loyalists to spend more at Sainsbury's, ultimately helping to improve shareholder value – potentially to the tune of £1.76 billion.

INTERVIEW WITH PETER SOUTER, CREATIVE DIRECTOR
OF AGENCY AMV BBDO

Wendy: We have the IPA Effectiveness Case History for Sainsbury's, which shows how successful the campaign has been. What we'd like to find out is how the idea originated.

Peter: Sainsbury's had a very clever marketer called Sara Weller who had come up with a positioning statement for Sainsbury's: 'pioneering everyday quality'. It's kind of 'marketing speak', and not for consumers, but quite a good way of saying what they're about. So I sat down and thought about a way of getting that into people's heads quickly and obviously you can't use those particular words!

So the basic thing with celebrities in ads is it's fast, it's the quickest way to get something done. Commercials are very short and they're very expensive to run: you don't want to spend time establishing who the character is, the characteristics they have, what they're for. A celebrity is the quickest way of saying this person stands for that kind of attitude or this is the obvious person to use for that product because of X.

So with Jamie, if you take 'pioneering everyday quality', you know he's pioneering, he's an inventive new chef, he's everyday because he's a cockney rather than a posh Delia Smith kind of chef and quality: he's interested in good ingredients. So it was quite easy to say to Sainsbury's, we think we should have one thing that ties all your ads together.

David Abbott had a lovely phrase, which was having an army rather than having a series of individual foot soldiers, so making the thing stick. I went to Sara and talked to her about Jamie and we showed her some very rough scripts. The idea is basically that he's the personification of what Sainsbury's are good at. They're not the cheapest supermarket in the world but they're a good way of lots of people getting good food.

Wendy: Lots of people had already seen him do the same thing with the Naked Chef.

Peter: Yes that's right. I looked at the 'Naked Chef' and liked the energy. I think we have the most energetic supermarket campaign and that's because of what Jamie's like. And then we were very lucky that he turned out to be a great performer, which is cool too.

The lady who's really clever is the one who found him as the vegetable chef at the River Café! So it's not the biggest creative leap in the world, you know he just seemed somebody who'd be a good representative for them.

Wendy: So would you have considered using another chef?

Peter: I felt not. Most of our artists are booked by Alan Cluer who's a very good, very clever agent and he said 'I could get you all sorts of different people' but I felt very strongly that it shouldn't be an Anthony Worral-Thompson. There are lots of other people around but I looked at the things that Jamie was good at and I liked the fact that he was so young and energetic and he was what Sainsbury's needed.

Wendy: So it was not a case of simply having a celebrity, the celebrity has to fit really well with the brand and the message?

Peter: It's still casting, it's like anybody else you put in an ad. I'm very interested that clients very rarely research casting but it makes a huge difference as to whether people actually like an ad. So the fact that he was famous was helpful but his character and the way that he performed was what makes him good in the commercials.

Wendy: So do you think that Jamie has been vital to the success of this campaign? Do you think it would have been successful without him?

Peter: No, oddly I think that we could have maybe even have made the campaign without Jamie being famous. I think that the campaign could work with him in it if we'd have been clever enough to spot him before. It would have been slower and harder to sell to Sainsbury's but no I don't think the campaign works without him. I think it's just a mirror to what he's like but I think it's appropriate to Sainsbury's. I think it works because there's a good link between the two of them. I don't think he'd be very good at selling Asda for example. I think he is vital to the success.

Wendy: We've been thinking about older Sainsbury's ads and they used people like Catherine Zeta-Jones in the 90s in the recipe ads. Were the Jamie ads a way of refreshing the same idea of 'good quality food'?

Peter: All the Jamie ads are a more energetic and more single-minded version of the recipe ads. They were a brilliant campaign. The only downside of them is that they were quite posh and they kind of emphasized Sainsbury's problem with price. Whereas what's good about Jamie is that he's very much more approachable. But it's very much a development of those things. I mean we did some very bad ads in between: the John Cleese ads, 'prices to shout about . . .'.

Wendy: That message fitted John Cleese perfectly, it was just wrong for Sainsbury's. We know that the truth is celebrities both do and do not work, but here you've got the same brand using celebrities but very differently and one fits perfectly and one was disastrous.

Peter: Yes it was just for the wrong client, it didn't fit Sainsbury's and I learnt a real lesson, it was very upsetting for the staff. So John Cleese as he's done many times is very good in some ads for some products but that message didn't ring true.

Wendy: One idea we've got is that celebrities are great for achieving brand awareness or brand fame, and that very high levels of awareness are achieved very quickly with celebrity ads, but we haven't managed to prove it yet. Do you believe this?

Figure 112 *Jamie Oliver 3.*
Source: AMV.

Peter: That's what they're for. Here you go, the conclusive proof that advertising works is that £11 billion gets spent on it each year. I like talking in very large, general terms ok, so if it didn't work, clients who are as hard as nails wouldn't spend £11 billion on it. My guess is that £4 billion of that is spent on celebrity advertising. The proof that celebrity advertising works is that clients come back for it again and again (Figure 112).

Wendy Tanner was also able to talk with David Abbott, who with art director Ron Brown originated the very first 'brand' as opposed to 'price' advertising for a UK supermarket, with work for Sainsbury's using double-page spreads and headlines such as 'If we don't sell our meat in a day, we don't sell it.' The brave client then was Marketing Director Peter Davis, now Sir Peter and Chairman of Sainsbury's!

Abbott's print campaign for Sainsbury's evolved to use celebrities in TV ads and it's interesting to get his viewpoint on the 'Jamie' campaign in this context.

INTERVIEW WITH DAVID ABBOTT

Wendy: Sainsbury's have returned to the use of celebrities over the years with great success. We have Jamie Oliver at the moment, and there were the celebrity recipe ads. Has this been a successful way for them to revitalize their message of 'Good quality food'?

David: Yes, I think it has. Recipes and celebrities are part of the brand's history and it's smart to go on using them. Back in the eighties we'd been running print ads for Sainsbury's that really defined the brand at the time. They were all about food and food ideas, which was innovative then because supermarket advertising was usually all about price. We then had the chance to pitch for the TV ads against Saatchi's and wanted to take this new positioning on to television. (Easier said than done as it turned out.) We got the account, but a year or so later were under the cosh trying to get the right TV idea. I'd talked to Sainsbury's about recipes from time to time and they had always felt recipes were boring. But I was persistent because out there in the marketplace, the biggest selling books were recipe books.

We knew our customers liked food because they read about food in our print ads. (We knew they read them because sales of the products featured in the print ads always shot up.) I wondered whether or not we could give a complete recipe on TV in 60 seconds with absolutely luscious photography. Nobody had done that before.

To make the idea more interesting, I decided we'd have a celebrity voice and reveal their identity on camera only at the end of the film with the line, 'Sainsbury's. Everyone's favourite ingredient.'

We wanted the films to be about the pleasure of cooking as well as a source of ideas, which was a difficult idea to explain – so we shot a test commercial with Selina Scott. I found the recipe, Alan Cluer helped persuade Selina to do it and my friend John Clarke shot it for us.

We showed the pilot to the client and they loved it. The Selina commercial ran pretty much as it was and I got a new career talking to food writers!

The films were enormously successful both in image terms and sales. The country sold out of mozzarella cheese because of one ad and filo pastry another time. It did change the eating habits of the nation.

Wendy: Do you think it could have worked without the celebrities?

David: We could have done it without the celebrities but it wouldn't have been as interesting, we wouldn't have got the publicity and they wouldn't have provoked the same involvement.

Wendy: Which celebrities did you use?

David: Catherine Zeta-Jones, Dennis Healey, Sue Lawley, Ernie Wise, Lauren Bacall, Kiri Te Kanawa – all kinds of people. We shot 20 or so. It was easy for them to do it. They weren't flogging Sainsbury's products directly and so felt comfortable.

Wendy: Why did you choose these particular celebrities?

David: I chose them for variety – male, female, young, old – it kept the campaign alive and surprising.

We found we could get the most unexpected people. It became a club that people wanted to join. It was so easy for them to do – an hour in a recording studio and half an hour in front of the camera. In the end we had agents ringing up saying 'Any chance of doing a recipe?'

My own view is that even in that format the campaign could be running today. It had become an institution, and it would have been simple to make it younger, etc. It never stopped working and they dropped it far too soon.

Wendy: It still works now with Jamie Oliver. I think around 300,000 people made his Thai prawn curry after it appeared in his first ad for Sainsbury's.

David: Yes, getting Jamie was a triumph for Peter and the agency but

I think Sainsbury's should think about slowing Jamie down a bit. He's running around too much and they've got him flogging too many lines, too directly. The great thing about a recipe campaign is that it appears to be very generous advertising – the company taking 60 seconds of valuable airtime just to give people ideas. I think that impression is worth preserving. Sometimes the less you seem to sell, the more you do.

24

Celebrity as role model

In a way every use of a celebrity in a brand campaign has an aspect of role modelling to it. However, there are some market sectors where the technique is used in such a way that it encourages customers to project themselves into the persona of the celebrity and to use the fantasy involved as their own R&D. This was indicated earlier in the data from mruk Research, which suggested that some markets are more amenable to the use of celebrities than others. Personal products and services were some of those where famous people seem to be at their most effective in promoting brands.

Makeup is one of these key market categories and the industry has been built around the iconography of famous movie stars and models. Nearly all the leading brands in the personal care arena have a famous 'face' to represent them and it does seem that people use these celebrities in a pretty direct way as role models. It is relatively rare for the stars to actually speak for cosmetics brands in a literal sense and their role is to enable the customer to infer from their appearance what their own might be, with the assistance of that particular brand's alchemy.

In this category of 'celebrity as role model' there is a case history on the campaign for the UK cosmetics brand Rimmel featuring supermodel Kate Moss (Figure 113). Rimmel signed London-born Moss, who had been using their brand since she was a teenager, in September 2001 as their first ever sole representative 'face'. This paper was authored by Joanna Bartholomew of agency J Walter Thompson and won a Bronze Award in the IPA Effectiveness Awards 2002. Perhaps one of the reasons for the success of the campaign is that Kate Moss has a face that is capable of wearing many different looks. So she appeals to a very wide spectrum of customers who can identify with her and extrapolate from her case to their own. The summary is supported by an interview with Kenny Hill, Account Director, Rimmel at J Walter Thompson.

Figure 113 *Kate Moss – London Eye.*
Source: Rimmel/JWT.

Summary of the Rimmel case history

Problems

In recent years the Rimmel brand had lost its shine and its image values had declined. In 1998 29% of Rimmel users were under 25, only one year later this dropped to 20%. At the same time the brand and its products were perceived as cheap and of low quality. The cosmetics market had grown enormously. There were more brands and more product innovation. In this new world Rimmel's positioning looked increasingly tired and out of touch.

Objectives

There were three main objectives set. First, to close the pricing gap between Rimmel and the mass market average without loss of volume, second, to position Rimmel as the provider of a new kind of beauty and lastly to re-engage the interest of younger women.

Strategy

J Walter Thompson discovered two important facts: that young women were bored of fake and perfect beauty and that brands needed to be experienced and be implicitly recommended from a trusted source.
The phrase Rimmel = Beauty made in London seemed to summarize perfectly all the ideas that were needed to make Rimmel stand out. Kate Moss completed the image, epitomizing cool London values without defining beauty as impossible perfection. She was seen as approachable and likeable (Figures 114, 115 and 116).

Figure 114 *Rimmel double act DPS layout.*
Source: Rimmel/JWT.

Figure 115 *Rimmel autumn 2003.*
Source: Rimmel/JWT.

Figure 116 *Sheer temptation.*
Source: Rimmel/JWT.

Results

In October 2001 Rimmel increased their prices by an average of 14% from the previous year and up 29% from the previous two years. Remarkably, volume did not decrease and there was in fact a small increase of 1.8% across the board and a significant increase in sales of the particular products that had been advertised on TV.

In the year ending March 2002 Rimmel had a net sales increase of +21% and a profit increase of +25%. In six months they increased their profitability by 25%. In re-engaging younger users Rimmel was also successful: sales at Superdrug, which has a young consumer profile, increased by 40%.

Thus £1000 of advertising sold at least £1439 worth of product. Accounting for gross margins, Rimmel actually therefore made at least £1079 from each £1000 of advertising spend.

The six-month journey to reposition the brand from 'Beauty on a Budget' to 'Beauty Made in London' has been a phenomenal success. Kate Moss was a credible celebrity to use, also providing implicit recommendation of the brand. From being a brand with little street cred, Rimmel has been transformed into a cool leading edge London brand.

INTERVIEW WITH KENNY HILL, ACCOUNT DIRECTOR AT AGENCY J WALTER THOMPSON

Wendy: How did the Rimmel campaign featuring Kate Moss originate?

Kenny: Our strategy was to re-engage a large group of girls who had become cynical about beauty advertising and its portrayal of an unachievable perfection. We wanted to play up the quality and credibility of Rimmel combined with its experimental, fashionable side. The 'Rimmel London' campaign featuring Kate Moss was perfect to do that for the brand.

Wendy: Did you always have Kate Moss in mind; did you want to use a celebrity?

Kenny: No, we set out to create the Rimmel London idea, that's what came first and that could've been done with more than one model so it wasn't specifically, 'Let's find a celebrity.' In fact that came towards the end of the process. We thought 'Who could bring this whole idea of Rimmel London to life the best?' Really it's obvious, you could get a room full of people to agree that Kate Moss is the ultimate London girl: cool, experimental and edgy and a bit of a chameleon as well, which fits perfectly with the experimental fun side of Rimmel.

Wendy: Lots of people I've spoken to about successful examples of celebrity advertising have said the same thing: the idea has to come first but it's great if you can find a famous face to completely fit with your brand and your idea.

Kenny: Yes because I think the danger is if the advertising is purely about the celebrity, what happens if the celebrity is no longer right? Then you're stuck. You also can't let the celebrity overshadow the brand. This is not Kate Moss makeup but Rimmel makeup and Kate Moss wears it.

Kate is unique in the model world and she does her own thing and she does it her way and isn't the 'perfect beauty' but she has got a look that people love.

Kate has never sold out. She's done a lot of advertising for Chanel, Burberry and others but she's never done anything naff or cheesy and that's also reflected in the covers she does, such as British and American *Vogue* and style magazines like I-D or W with the world's top photographers.

Equally, Kate's got that slightly enigmatic air about her because she's quite a private person who doesn't go around doing interviews and selling herself out. That actually makes her more attractive to girls because she's still one of them (Figure 117).

Wendy: Do you think it could have succeeded without her?

Figure 117 *Rimmel Double Act.*
Source: Rimmel/JWT.

Kenny: Yes, I think it would have succeeded without Kate Moss but we would've had to work harder. It still would've been 'Rimmel London' but it wouldn't have had the stature that it has or the 'talkability'. That's the other thing she brings, she helps to take it out of pure advertising and make Rimmel a cool brand for people talk about and that's been crucial to the success of the 'Rimmel London' campaign.

You see Kate Moss in the Rimmel ad, you think she's a girl that does things her own way, that's beautiful, successful but still has her feet on the ground, likes to experiment with fashion but in everything she wears, everything she does she looks amazing. Kate Moss is the ultimate arbiter of style. If she wears something then it's guaranteed to be instantly cool (Figure 118).

Wendy: Did you pre-test to see if Kate Moss was going to be right?

Kenny: We did pre-test our finished ads but we already knew from earlier research that she was well liked and fitted with the 'Rimmel London' campaign and the 'punk princess' idea. Girls mentioned her spontaneously as a good example of that and of who they looked up to and admired so we were very confident that she was right.

Figure 118 *Rimmel London.*
Source: Rimmel/JWT.

It's interesting to note that some of the most successful supermodels, such as Kate Moss, are those whose faces, while distinctive, represent an archetypal shape and colour and are also able to adapt to many different interpretations in terms of hair and colour cosmetics, making them accessible to a wide range of women.

25

Celebrity cast against type

When the partnership between a brand and the celebrity in advertising campaign create something new, it adds significant value. One way of doing this is for the core idea to give an insight, real or imagined, into the star's personality that enhances the entertainment value and thus involvement of the audience. Hence the creative technique of 'casting against type' in which the campaign idea plays off the received view of the celebrity's personality.

The advertising campaign for Walkers, starring Gary Lineker in the UK's longest running ad featuring a celebrity, is perhaps one of the best examples where, through consistency and controlled evolution, a genuine brand property has been created, which has benefited both the company and the star. In fact there are two IPA effectiveness case histories on the campaign: Gavin MacDonald and Jeff Lush of agency BMP DDB (now known as DDB London), where the Lineker idea was originated, authored the 1996 paper and it won a Silver Award. The 2002 paper was written by Bridget Angear at AMV BBDO, the agency to whom the account was awarded as a part of an international realignment, which also won a Silver Award.

The Walkers' campaign operates in a market where impulse purchase, based on appetite appeal and instant gratification, are key dynamics. Kids are big consumers of snack products, but adults are too as a big proportion of all purchases are made by mums in supermarkets. Thus using Gary Lineker was a good idea to start with since he has a strong appeal to men and boys as a football star, plus good looks and a 'Mr Nice Guy' persona, which were equally attractive to women. As Chris Cowpe of agency DDB London says:

The original creative brief was one word: 'irresistibility' and at the time there was a wonderful set of coincidences: Gary Lineker was strongly associated with Leicester, Walkers' home town, and he was returning from Japan where he had ended his playing career, with the talent and dignity he had shown throughout it. Once we'd begun developing the idea of Gary as 'No more Mr Nice Guy', it's difficult to imagine anyone else playing this role. Gary's association with Leicester, his impeccable on and off the field character and his appeal to all ages made him a virtually unique choice.

But even with all the back-up research and the gut feeling that this was indeed a big idea, Cowpe confirms a truth about the advertising business: it's an art as much as a science and it's very hard to predict with absolute certainty how a concept will 'play' when it's out in the media. Having a famous celebrity on board does often seem to increase the odds, as in this case:

> We all hoped he'd be a long-term campaign, partly because Walkers had never had a long-running campaign that reflected their reality as being one of the biggest and fastest growing brands. But as with many campaigns, we could not be sure exactly how big this was going to be. But within days we were all convinced that we'd got a really major break-through that could indeed run and run – as it has done.

Getting Lineker to behave out of character in a series of TV commercials in which the professional footballer, who had never got a single yellow card throughout his whole career, was seen stealing crisps from defenceless kids, was the core of the 'big idea' for the brand that has continued ever since: the crisps were so nice they made him nasty. As his confidence has grown through his new career as television pundit and presenter, so has Lineker's acting ability in the Walkers' commercials improved. Whereas in the beginning he had few if any words to say, now he takes a full part in the action with lots of dialogue. Other celebrities such as Paul Gascoigne and Michael Owen have been introduced to good effect, but perhaps the cleverest move of all has been for Walkers to actually name product variants after their star. Walkers' 'Salt and Lineker' is a real demonstration of intimacy between a brand and a celebrity and the coup was repeated with their 'Cheese 'n' Owen' variety (Figure 119).

Executed with a lot of charm and tongue firmly in cheek, this series of ads has created an image asset of enormous value. It's also to the credit of agency AMD BBDO, and their client, that they chose to continue with this big idea, which was originated by a rival firm, BMP DDB.

Figure 119 *Michael Owen enjoying his 'Cheese 'n' Owen' crisps.*
Source: AMV.

Summary of Walkers Crisps case histories

Problem

By 1995 Walkers Snack Foods were the biggest salty snack company in Britain.
Despite this, Walkers was facing many difficult challenges:

- Distribution-fuelled growth was coming to an end, meaning Walkers needed to find another way to generate growth.
- In the highly competitive snack foods market, the launch of Pringles was a huge threat to Walkers.
- Walkers needed to remain central in people's snack food repertoire, while defending itself against competitive threats.

Strategy

Advertising had to devise strongly branded motivating 'news' to increase brand awareness and ensure the brand was front of mind, to make news work both in the short term and the long term.

Figure 120 *Gary Salt 'n' Shake.*
Source: AMV.

Advertising also had to ensure that the news cut through and was clearly communicated. The advertising also had to appeal to both kids and adults (Figure 120).

Walkers Crisps introduced the 'No More Mr Nice Guy' campaign featuring Gary Lineker in 1995. Gary Lineker was originally chosen as brand spokesman by BMP DDB for his reputation of being the 'Mr Clean' of English football. The campaign launch also coincided with his well-publicized return from playing in Japan, offering unique PR opportunities. The advertising poked fund at his 'nice guy' image showing that Walkers are so irresistible they turn even the nicest guy nasty.

The Walkers account was inherited by AMV BBDO in 1997. In order to keep the campaign fresh, Gary's role developed and other celebrities have been introduced to introduce brand extensions. These have included Steven Redgrave (Figure 121), Vinnie Jones (to promote the bigger, stronger 'Walkers Max'), Michael Owen for the 'Cheese 'n' Owen' flavour and most recently, Tara Palmer-Tomkinson for the 'posh' 'Walkers Sensations' (Figure 122).

Results

The campaign's ability to retain consumer loyalty helped double Walkers' sales in a mature market.

Figure 121 *Steve Redgrave and Gary Lineker in training.*
Source: AMV.

Figure 122 *Tara Palmer-Tomkinson gets 'chauffeured'.*
Source: AMV.

Between 1995 and 2002, Walkers' sales grew from 1.34 billion to 2.75 billion packs per year – an uplift of 105%. Their market share rose 6% in grocery and 3% in impulse, while that of their competitors' declined.

Immediate ROI of £1.70 compares to an average ROI for TV advertising of £0.52. Walkers' parent company Frito Lay works on the assumption that long-term effects will be three times those of short-term ones, meaning advertising ROI will build to £5.10 in the future.

The 'No More Mr Nice Guy' campaign concept is a success around the world. Gary Lineker ads are used in the UK and Ireland, while local stars are used by other Frito Lay brands around the world. In Holland PepsiCo adapted the idea using a mainstream heartthrob pop-star Marco Borsata, in South Africa it was François Piennar, in Poland an Olympic boxer and in Iberia they used Antonio Banderas.

In each case, the campaign took an almost 'saintly' famous personality and turned him into a comedic 'devil'.

INTERVIEW WITH JOHN WEBSTER, CREATIVE DIRECTOR AT BMP DDB AT THE TIME THE CAMPAIGN WAS ORIGINATED

Wendy: How did the Walkers' campaign featuring Gary Lineker originate?

John: I was the creative director on the campaign at the time and Malcolm Green and Gary Betts were the creative team. They wrote a campaign including Gary Lineker who at that time was in the news as he was about to come back from Japan and end his football career.

He was a big hero; he'd scored a lot of goals for England and was famous for having never been booked. He was 'Mr Nice Guy'.

So it was a very current thing at that moment and when I saw their work, I thought the idea of using Gary Lineker was great because he was so popular. He also had a connection with Walkers through his father who was a greengrocer and supplied Walkers with potatoes.

Gary is from Leicester and Walkers' factories are in Leicester too – they both originated there so it seemed like a great idea. The concept at that time was that Gary's coming back to England and the real reason he's coming back is because he loves Walkers Crisps.

But the campaign they'd actually written was, in my opinion, wrong, they'd made Gary a buffoon and had him trying to get a job in a theatrical agency dressing up as a chicken and I turned the work down. But I loved Gary and suggested that they rewrite him in another form. They found it hard to do the rewrite and so in the end I did a new campaign for Lineker based on their idea. I came up with the notion that because he was so famous for being nice, he was Mr Clean. I thought it would be fun that though he was such a nice guy, he couldn't resist pinching a kid's crisps. I didn't know how Gary would react to that but he actually saw the joke immediately and was all for it.

Walkers was American owned and the Americans said when we shot the first film, 'You can't do this to a national sports hero: call him a thief!' We said everyone will get that it's a joke but they said no they won't get it – you're calling him a thief. They insisted we shoot two endings, one where he gives the crisps back and one where he didn't.

Wendy: Did you test both endings?

John: Yes we did and of course people got the joke and that made it. So the first commercial showed Gary Lineker pinching the crisps and running away from the child who wanted his crisps back.

[Behind the scenes, Martin Glenn, now President, Walkers Group, but then UK Marketing Director and the client, was working hard on his boss, Peter Thompson, who has dual UK and US citizenship and therefore empathy with both cultures. Thompson did initially request an alternative end shot in which Gary would give the crisps back, but then agreed with Glenn's local market rationale that the UK consumer would react more positively to the irony of the original. Thompson then went on to back the adoption of the idea in many other countries.]

Wendy: And that was the welcome home ad?

John: Yes, the song was Peters and Lee's, 'Welcome Home', which was a pretty corny song but it fitted really well.

Wendy: Did you originally plan a long-running campaign with Gary or were you only thinking of using him for the one commercial?

John: We always thought it would be an extended campaign but the ad itself was fantastically popular. It was in the newspapers, got a lot of coverage and was immediately famous.

Wendy: How much of the success of the campaign do you think is down to Gary?

John: Oh he's essential. Because of the timing of it, he was a national hero and funnily enough he acts really well ... he's essential. He's so popular. In fact when we did that commercial in Leicester people were coming out of their houses going 'Hello Gary' – they all knew him!

Wendy: What made you introduce other famous people, like Gazza?

John: That was the idea of another creative team here. Really, we wanted to show how much mileage there was in it and including other famous personalities was part of that mileage. But Gary's sense of fun was such a help – we were always dressing him up, he enjoyed it.

Wendy: And the campaign moved to AMV in 1998?

John: Yes, it was a political decision. Walkers was part of an empire, Frito Lay, which was American owned and Britain was only a little piece of that. Funnily enough, the idea of the campaign was used around the world, the nice guy idea. Other heroes, not only sports heroes, were used. They cast a famous comedian in Holland and it was so successful here that even though it changed agencies they continued with the same campaign.

Wendy: Yes, and in their 2000 case history they say that Gary has signed up for another five years. That's a very long-running campaign! Did you have any idea that it could have carried on for this long?

John: No, usually I'd give a campaign three to five years until it runs out of steam but this has gone on a lot longer than that. He's developed as the campaign has gone on. I think it's brought out a side of him that people had never seen before.

Wendy: Do you think the campaign could have worked using Gary giving a straight testimonial?

John: Absolutely not. The important thing about personalities in advertising is that if it stinks of insincerity, you know, 'Give me the money and I'll say anything', people can see through that. I think that clever use of personalities integrated into an idea that's bigger than them is the way to do it. You know, Gareth Hunt and his coffee beans is the way not to do it.

Wendy Tanner also talked to Peter Souter about the campaign and how agency AMV BBDO took BMP DDB's original idea and developed the role of Gary Lineker within it. Souter gives a good deal of credit to director Paul Weiland for bringing out Lineker's acting abilities and this is an excellent example of where using a top directing talent has paid dividends.

INTERVIEW WITH PETER SOUTER, CREATIVE DIRECTOR OF AGENCY AMV BBDO

Wendy: When you inherited the 'Gary Lineker' campaign was there any question that you'd replace him?

Peter: No, but I wanted to do something slightly different with him, which is I wanted him to lose more. The best analogy of that is 'Wile E Coyote' from Roadrunner: what we've done to Gary is blown his head off and shot him. That's the only thing that we've really changed and we've made him not the guy that gets the crisps, but the guy that *nearly* gets the crisps, plus we've got a lot more jokes in.

Wendy: Also in the original ads he didn't do much at all.

Peter: No he didn't and I think that we've got much more adventurous. He's got one of these fantastic symbiotic relationships because after a footballer retires, usually not much happens to them, so it was great for him to start the campaign. Then he got really good at doing the ads and I think Paul Weiland, the director, should take credit for this as he's taught Gary to act. Then Gary's career as a presenter took off and he's now famous to kids who don't even know that he used to play football.

Wendy: Kids now can't know that he ever had the 'nice guy' image either.

Peter: I know, but after a while he's become a branding device to Walkers.

Wendy: What do you think you've achieved with the campaign?

Peter: Look at the case study; we've sold a shit load of crisps! The bit I really like, and I respect BMP immensely for starting the campaign, is that since we've carried it on, they've got far higher sales now than they ever did. I always think that agencies get bored first, then clients get bored and then years after that the consumer gets bored. What's great about Walkers is that this is the longest running celebrity campaign in British advertising.

Wendy: I think choice of celebrities for the brand extensions have also worked really well. Like Vinnie Jones, the hard man for 'Walkers Max'.

Peter: It's that thing of renewal: we try to pair him up with different people for the sub-brands. With the 'Sensations' we started with Posh but she wouldn't do another one so we got another posh person. She agreed to do her first Walkers' commercial because apparently her and David were in bed and they saw the David Seaman one which they thought was really funny so when we rang up they were well disposed towards it!

26

Celebrity acting a part

The key thing to remember with any brand campaign is that a great core idea must come first and that the casting comes afterwards. As Alan Cluer points out: 'Stars are merely actors that people like better than other actors.' So having got a big brand idea, using a famous person to act the part can make it even bigger.

The Tesco campaign originally started with commercials featuring the comic star Dudley Moore who was seen memorably searching the length and breadth of France for free range chickens (Figure 123). Lowe soon moved

Figure 123 *Dudley Moore.*
Source: Tesco

onto the campaign that is still running, which is an excellent example of the use of famous actors and actresses in roles which could theoretically have been played by unknowns. The long-running theme of Tesco's brand positioning is 'Every Little Helps' and the structure of the television campaign is to provide a series of self-contained vignettes from a heightened version of everyday life, that demonstrate some aspect or other of the Tesco product or service offer which fulfils this brand promise.

The continuity of the three characters ensures campaignability and their characterization creates empathy with three major chunks of the target audience. Prunella Scales as 'Dotty', the fanatical shopper, appeals more to the older woman of a more traditional type who sees her skill as a housewife and shopper as being important to her and her family. While Jane Horrocks, as 'Kate', her long-suffering daughter, is on the wavelength of the younger more independent woman who has got lots of better things to do than go to the supermarket, but if she has to wants to go somewhere offering excellent produce, efficient service and good value. The introduction of John Gordon Sinclair as Kate's husband allowed Tesco to draw in the third vital part of the targeted audience, as well as playing on the ever popular 'mother-in-law' card. Using three outstanding actors in this way creates a depth of characterization that is wholly convincing, exudes quality and works very well for Tesco.

The case for Tesco was authored by Ashleye Sharpe and Joanna Bamford of agency Lowe Lintas and won the IPA Effectiveness Awards Grand Prix in 2000, ironically when Sir George Bull was Chairman of the Judges and also Chairman of Sainsbury's!

Summary of the Tesco case history

Problem

In the early 1980s Tesco was still 'piling it high, and selling it cheap'. Consumers saw no comparison with the sophisticated lines that the market leader, Sainsbury's, stocked. Yet Tesco had set their sights on market leadership. They initiated a major programme to counteract their key weakness – quality.

From around 1983, Tesco had upgraded stores and the quality and range of what they sold. Yet even by 1990, they had failed to dent Sainsbury's dominance.

Tesco's brief to Lowe Lintas was 'We are looking to smash away pre-conceptions about our business with advertising . . . to develop an image campaign which will lift us out of the mould in our particular sector.'
Advertising had to persuade non-shoppers to think again about Tesco by presenting it as a credible alternative to Sainsbury's: everything they could find at Sainsbury's they could buy at Tesco – and it would be just as good quality.

Strategy

Lowe's first campaign, the 'Quest for Quality', ran from 1990 to 1992. In total 18 executions ran, with 400 ratings being the typical burst weight.
The campaign concentrated on product quality and featured Dudley Moore as a Tesco buyer who scoured the world in pursuit of an elusive flock of French free-range chickens, en route discovering other surprisingly high-quality products to add to Tesco's range. The campaign was very impactful, generating 89% awareness.
In 1993 Tesco embarked on a newer and bigger strategy. Because the Dudley Moore campaign had focused so closely on products, new advertising was needed to highlight the whole Tesco experience.
The advertising idea was that while not everything in life goes perfectly, Tesco were doing their best to make shopping easier. Although each of the 25 commercials that were made focused on one particular initiative, a new line, 'Every Little Helps', was used across all executions to capture Tesco's new consumer-orientated philosophy of always 'doing right by the customer'.
The new campaign starred 'the mother of all shoppers', Dotty Turnbull, who regards each of Tesco's initiatives as an opportunity to put the store to the test. Dotty is played by Prunella Scales while Jane Horrocks plays her long-suffering daughter Kate and John Gordon Sinclair plays her husband who finds himself frequently tested to his limits by Dotty. In testing Tesco to the limit, Dotty gives it and its staff the opportunity to shine.

Results

Through its effect on Tesco's image, advertising has encouraged more people to shop at Tesco and, latterly, to stay loyal to it.
From 1990 Tesco's turnover increased from £8 billion to £17.4 billion and its share rose from 9.1% to 15.4%, overtaking Sainsbury's to become

market leader in 1995. The 'Dotty' campaign has consolidated Tesco leadership. As well as customers, campaign has had good effects on staff morale and has directly affected the share price.

The 'Dotty' campaign has delivered an incremental £2.206 billion of turnover (excluding VAT) across fiscal years 1995–1999.

Using Tesco's average operating margin over that same period of 5.9% it has been calculated that the campaign delivered an incremental operating profit of £130 million.

So every £1 spent on advertising generated an incremental £38 of turnover and £2.25 of operating profit. Thus the campaign paid for itself more than twice over, delivering a 225% return on investment.

INTERVIEW WITH RUSS LIDSTONE, DEPUTY PLANNING DIRECTOR AT LOWE

Wendy: How did the idea for the 'Every Little Helps'/'Dotty' campaign originate?

Russ: 'Dotty' followed on from the successful vignette campaign that launched the idea of Tesco's commitment to customer service and the slogan 'Every Little Helps'. This campaign ran from 1992 to 1995 and focused on the new initiatives that Tesco had developed to demonstrate its commitment to customers.

Whilst it was very successful at talking about Tesco's initiatives like their milk-warming service, the brief for a new campaign came about because we wanted to give Tesco advertising more of a unique and identifiable campaign feel. The brief was to show Tesco's commitment to making shopping a bit easier and bring to life the fantastic initiatives that Tesco had developed.

Wendy: Why did you choose Prunella Scales and Jane Horrocks to play 'Dotty' and her daughter 'Kate'?

Russ: The creative idea developed was to highlight Tesco initiatives through giving them a 'torture test' from the worst kind of shopper.

Prunella with her well-known heritage as Basil Fawlty's wife in the legendary hit series 'Fawlty Towers' and her ability as a terrific actress, was perfect casting and she was the only real contender for the role. Jane was an up-and-coming actress that we felt our target audience would be able to empathize with as the harassed daughter.

Wendy: Did you have anyone else in mind?

Russ: Not really.

Wendy: Why do you think the 'Dotty' campaign has been so successful for Tesco?

Russ: Because we can all relate to the universal truth of the 'shopper from hell' whether they're our Mum, a relative or a friend. We feel for the Tesco staff but moreover we admire and respect their ability to respond to the challenges laid down by Dotty.

Wendy: How much of this success has been down to the Dotty character?

Russ: It's difficult to imagine this advertising without Prunella and Jane and there is no doubt that the success of the campaign is in some way due to them. However, there are many factors that have made it so successful: the brilliance of the scripts, a good media spend, but moreover the ability of Tesco to generate initiatives that make it easy to write advertising around.

Wendy: Do you think that the character could have worked or would have been as effective if played by an unknown actress?

Russ: It's clearly hard to say, but what we had with Prunella was a shortcut to consumer understanding of 'the woman from hell'. Whilst it is possible that an unknown actress could have delivered this, it is unlikely that we would have created that understanding so quickly and powerfully or in such a humorous way.

As this outstanding Tesco case history shows, casting is crucial. The right choice of star for an ad can really bring a role to life, as in any movie or stage show. And there's always the tantalizing 'what if?' question to answer. It's rumoured that Maggie Smith was an initial idea for the part of 'Dottie' – how might that have turned out? In the end great creativity is part art, part science. This unpredictable alchemy is how agencies build brands.

27

Celebrity revelation

In a sense every time a celebrity does anything they reveal something of themselves and appearing in an advertising campaign is no different. Part of the effectiveness of the celebrities in the police recruitment campaign was the way they surprised us by revealing they 'couldn't do it', but there are some executions that focus primarily on creating a sense of revelation. In so doing they are interesting and involving for the audience and give credit to the brand that enabled this to happen. A carefully constructed creative idea with the right stars cast in the action can use 'revelations' to communicate key messages about the brand in a more powerful and engaging way. A good example of how this can be done to great effect is documented in the IPA case on One2One. Authored by Nick Barham of agency Bartle Bogle Hegarty it won a Four Star Award and a special prize, the ISBA Award for the 'Best New Client Entrant', at the IPA Effectiveness Awards in 1998.

The core of the One2One campaign idea was 'Who would you like to have a one to one with?' and was expressed by asking a series of celebrities who they would most like to have a mobile phone call with. Kate Moss chose Elvis Presley, John McCarthy chose Yuri Gagarin and Ian Wright chose Martin Luther King. This campaign is an outstanding example of using famous stars to reveal something very personal and human about themselves, which is almost certainly news to their fans, and thus makes for a very engaging series of commercial, while creating 'intimacy' between brand and celebrity and adding value to both reputations. It also works in terms of celebrity interactions, albeit of a posthumous kind! John Hegarty, creative founder of BBH, has given an interview on the use of celebrities in this campaign, which has sadly ended as a result of the takeover and rebranding of One2One by Germany's T-Mobile.

The One2One campaign operated in a market where there was already very stiff competition from the likes of Vodafone, Cellnet and Orange, and thus the challenge for the brand was to develop a distinctive persona and market positioning. The route chosen by One2One was to try to move the brand away from the relatively functional positionings of Vodafone and Cellnet and use a more involving and emotional one than that of Orange, which was seen as a relatively cool and futuristic brand.

Summary of the One2One case history

Problem

Before the advertising campaign began in 1996, Mercury One2One was seen as the weakest of the four mobile phone operators in the UK (others: Vodafone, Cellnet and Orange), consumer confidence was low and this had negative impact on staff morale. BBH's brief was to rectify these problems.

Strategy

It was clear that any solution needed to restore confidence and to build a bond with consumers. In Mercury One2One's history of free calls and social usage, there were some positive associations in customers' minds. Here, they had an advantage. BBH recognized the opportunity to build on Mercury One2One's existing human roots and differentiate the brand from its competitors. They decided to position Mercury One2One as the human face of mobile telephony. The brand would help people find a way through intimidating technology.

The creative team were asked to devise an idea in which brand fame and humanity took precedence. At the same time, the brand name was liberated from the Mercury prefix and simply became One2One.

The relaunch advertising, based on the question 'who would you most like to have a One2One with?', was born out of the newly liberated brand name. It suggested exploration via an intimate conversation. This was initially between famous people in order to capture interest and improve brand status.

One2One was relaunched in October 1996. The ads showed Kate Moss, Ian Wright and John McCarthy imagining conversations with Elvis Presley, Martin Luther King and Yuri Gagarin. Later, 'Derek2Tanya' explained the new prepayment option, and 'Mum' communicated One2One's expanded coverage.

Ian2Martin script: Ian Wright and Martin Luther King

[Open on a casually dressed Ian Wright in the Highbury changing rooms. Hanging up his Arsenal shirt.]

Ian: Who would I most like to have a One2One with? . . . A man who inspired a generation.

[Cue to period footage of a large crowd.]

Ian: Martin Luther King.

[Cut to a closeup of Martin Luther King.]

MLK: I just wanna do God's will.

[We now see a very grubby drinking fountain next to a far more salubrious one. Above one is the word 'coloreds'; above the other the word 'whites'.]

Ian: I'd ask him how he coped with being seen as second class just because of the colour of his skin.. . . .

[We see a closeup of someone drinking. Through the water we see Ian.]

MLK: . . . and I've seen the Promised Land.

Ian: . . . and if there was one incident. . .

[Cut to inside a packed bus where we see an old black woman immediately stand and give her seat to a white guy who's just got on.]

Ian: . . . that drove him to become part of the civil rights movement.

[As they drive off we see a rueful Ian Wright watching from the back of the bus. Cut to footage of marching protestors.]

Ian: Was he ever frightened of those who opposed him?

[Cut to unsympathetic state patrol waiting for them.]

Ian: . . . And did he realize how much he frightened them?

[Cut to a group of shouting rednecks.]

Ian: Most of all I'd ask if I could have a One2One with him?

[Cut to a closeup of Ian's face.]

Ian: . . . I'd ask him how he maintained his principle of peaceful protest.. . . .

[Cut to a black man being ejected from a public building.]

MLK: We've got some difficult days ahead.

Ian: . . . in the face of such provocation.

[Cut to footage of the demonstration being broken up by a jet of water. Cut to Dr King giving his final 'Promised Land' speech.]

MLK: But it really doesn't matter with me now. I may not get there with you . . .

[Cut to a pensive Ian.]

MLK: But I want you to know tonight that we as a people will get to the Promised Land.

[Cut to present day and Ian Wright signing autographs. The screen divides into two with a smiling Ian giving the autograph in the top-left hand corner and Martin Luther King in front of a bank of microphones in the bottom right.]

FVO: Who would you most like to have a One2One with? Our mobile phone service gets people talking.

Results

The idea of having a One2One had captured the public's imagination. The campaign worked primarily by helping the customer to believe in One2One's capability as a company. It made One2One famous.

Within London, by 1998, brand awareness had shot up, returning to the heights of the original launch and recapturing first place from Orange. Outside London, One2One witnessed spectacular growth in all regions. In the majority of them it leapt into second place behind the longer established Orange.

By March 1998 customer satisfaction surveys showed that One2One customers were happier than the customers on any other network.

In terms of staff morale, the number of employees agreeing with the statement 'I am proud to work for One2One' saw an increase from 69% in 1996 to 87% in 1997.

In 1997 One2One's customer base grew by more than any other network's. One2One's advertising spend was £36.7 million between October 1996 and January 1998. During this time, the total number of customer connections attributable to advertising was 167,944. The value of these additional 167,944 customers comes out as £115.9 million.

The effect of the advertising did not end in January 1998. To the end of December 1999, a further 120,851 gross customer additions can be attributed to the advertising, resulting in a further value of £83.4 million. Therefore the total payback from a £36.7 million advertising spend was £199.3 million.

INTERVIEW WITH JOHN HEGARTY, CHAIRMAN AND WORLDWIDE CREATIVE DIRECTOR OF BBH

Wendy: What were the origins of the One2One campaign?

John: Well, a bit of the marketing background. The mobile phone companies had all launched and within a short period of time, there was tremendous distrust of them. Consumers thought they were all just selling them deals, overcharging them, getting them to sign up to packages that were very expensive and felt they were being conned. For instance, they were rounding up the minutes, so if you spoke for 3 minutes 38 seconds, they rounded up to 4 minutes. Orange, of course, launched on the back of this by saying it wouldn't do this. There were lots of these things, they gave you the phone cheap but would sell you a package of calls that were very expensive. Basically, they were all distrusted, all of them were.

So, we got to work with Mercury One2One as they were called then and we said to them that the biggest thing they had to do is gain the customer's trust. Be the mobile company that people really felt they could have a relationship with.

We convinced them that they should drop the name Mercury and focus on One2One. At the time, they were also trying to compete with BT. Mercury had landlines that were particularly unsuccessful and they were pulling out all of their telephone kiosks, so the name was a bit sullied. We said, just concentrate on calling it One2One, and actually, One2One is the most honest relationship you can have with somebody or even the most honest conversation you can have with somebody. Make your advertising about that.

Now the great way to execute 'Who would you rather have a One2One with?' is to get famous people talking about who they'd like to have a One2One with, not only as a way of bringing the thought alive, but also by getting a different view of that famous person, getting a view of a world that you're not totally aware of. Giving you an insight into that person's personality and their relationship with celebrity and fame.

So with Kate Moss, the model, we reveal that actually the one person she would've loved to have a conversation with was Elvis. And the reason she wanted to have a conversation with Elvis? She wanted to have a conversation with him because he was very lonely and she understands that, because in what she does as a model, there is an element of loneliness.

We were creating an insight into that person's world, and also an insight into how they would've related to somebody else and so it stirred your imagination into thinking well who would I like to have a One2One with and what is it about me that would relate to somebody else?

So with each person we took, we tried to take some element of what they were about, who they would've had a conversation with and illustrate through that how they would've dealt with their shortcomings and the other person's shortcomings. So we gave it substance.

Wendy: I think there's something voyeuristic about it – people like to see celebrities doing something they don't normally see them do or see them in a different light.

John: Absolutely, that's why *Hello!* works so brilliantly. Here they are at home, here they are with their hair down, here they are in Waitrose. But I think you've got to put a lot more into it than that – you're creating a slightly more intense insight. We went from Kate Moss, then we had John McCarthy. John wanted to have a conversation with Yuri Gagarin, the first man in space. With John, it was about what it's like to be suddenly famous. No preparation for it at all: one minute you're the world's most unknown man and the next minute, you're famous all over the world.

And of course, that's what he had to deal with. McCarthy was an unknown journalist, who during the five years he was held hostage, wasn't aware of what was going on and he came back into the UK the most famous man in the country.

Wendy: Did you pick very different celebrities on purpose?

John: Yes, we wanted it to have breadth as well as depth: Kate Moss was a famous model, John McCarthy was a man who'd been through tremendous stress and strain and trauma, and we also then had a great comic, Vic Reeves, who wanted to talk to Terry Thomas. What was interesting in the campaign is that it worked incredibly well and people said, try and give us something with even more substance, try and push it further. We were very encouraged, and so we then did Ian Wright and Martin Luther King. Ian Wright had a very explosive personality and would always be getting booked and losing it on the pitch. The reason he wanted to talk with Martin Luther King was to understand how, under extreme provocation, did Martin Luther King keep his cool? How did he resist losing it, and that was the thing he most admired in him, and by implication 'that's been my failing, but I've recognized it and I look to this man and think how does he do it?'

So it had a really powerful tension in it. You were expressing and exposing something in the personality and there were different lessons in all of them.

Wendy: Do you think the campaign could have succeeded without these celebrities?

John: No. What created the attention value was we were looking at somebody that we all knew and therefore, there was a communal insight into them. You needed that insight into the person to understand why they were having a conversation with the third party. We did try it with non-famous people, of course the client wanted non-famous people, it would be cheaper! But it didn't have the impact a celebrity gave it.

Wendy: Do you think that's why celebrities work so well, with a celebrity, you don't need to take time explaining to the viewer who this person is, and what values they have?

John: I think they work on a number of levels. I mean obviously you have to cast them correctly, they have to be right for your brand, right for what you're saying and they have to carry with them values your brand either embodies or wants to adopt.

What it gives you is instant recognition and in a short space of time it accelerates your brand forward in the consumer's mind. Which is why we use personalities, the media uses them and that's why Hollywood uses them. It works in exactly the same way.

I'm always surprised when people ask 'do personalities work in advertising?' Personalities work because personalities work! That is why the entertainment industry uses them. They work everywhere. What you've got to do is cast them correctly. Which is what Hollywood understands. You must cast somebody people have a relationship with and which makes the right connections for the role they're playing.

A creative idea that reveals something new about the celebrity and delivers a key customer benefit adds enormous value to both star and brand: it's clearly a powerful way to build business. The 'celebrity revelation' approach demands imagination and the successful negotiation of a high degree of intimacy between brand and famous personality. Having done this deal and then portrayed it with the cinematic expertise used by BBH in the One2One campaign, the results can be in the £100 millions.

28

Celebrities interacting

There's a scene in the film *Help!* where the four Beatles live in a street and they go home through separate gates, enter separate front doors and then travel up inside. Then we go inside with them and realize that behind the terrace façade it's one big house and they all live together. In the same way we might imagine that there is a celebrity world where famous stars from all parts of the galaxy live together. There's something rather intriguing about the idea of stars with no connection in their professional showbiz lives being put together in a campaign for a brand. Blending these different personalities and juxtaposing the imagery can produce a potent new cocktail. Fast food chain KFC is an example of a brand that has used several celebrities in a mix to good effect. Interesting rival Pizza Hut has taken a similar 'celebrity interaction' approach.

There are several ways in which celebrity interaction works for KFC and Pizza Hut. First of all the appearance of more than one star in the commercials gives a powerful endorsement and reassures people as to the calibre of the eating experience. Seeing famous people really tucking into the same sort of food that you and your family might eat when out at the weekend significantly increases its appetite appeal. Second, and this is less easy to explain, there is a sense in which celebrities enjoying themselves in an ad for a restaurant is a fantasy version of seeing a real famous star at the table next to you. It means it's a popular restaurant and patronized by people in the know and whom you know and trust.

In the UK, KFC has a high percentage of franchisee-owned outlets and perhaps the 'glue' that a famous campaign provides was a particular motivator for the organization. Another noteworthy point is the amount of free publicity that celebrity interaction can generate in a media environment in which journalists and hard-bitten sub-editors are quick to remove brand names from stories. When there's in-demand celebrities involved and the brand is giving the media access to a good story, then the chances of a brand name mention are significantly higher. The 'Success by the bucketload: Advertising's contribution to building the KFC brand' case history was authored by Nick Jones, Simeon Duckworth and Christian Cocker of agency Ogilvy & Mather.

Summary of the O&M KFC Success by the Bucketload case history

Problems

The UK market for quick serve food is both fragmented and highly competitive. In 1994 although both KFC sales and numbers of stores had been increasing, each store appeared to be serving fewer customers. KFC's own data showed a reduction of over 25% in average transactions per store between 1990 and 1993. KFC needed to be a bigger player in the UK fast food market. At the same time it needed to gain confidence among its franchisees that made up over 70% of all stores.

Strategy

Ogilvy & Mather Ltd won the KFC account in 1994 and there has been a marked increase in sales since that time. Core store growth rose by 6% in 1995, year on year. In 1997 it was decided that the brand needed a more coherent and higher profile image. To this end Ryan Stiles from 'Whose Line is it Anyway?' was chosen to represent the brand. Other celebrities included Ulrika Jonsson (Figure 124), Ivana Trump, Tara Palmer-Tomkinson and Tamara Beckwith.

Results

In all the total amount of sales generated by 'Ryan' advertising was £64 million. At the same time the proportion of franchisees rating the parent company as outstanding in terms of its support for the franchise community rose from 21% in 1996 to 33% in 1997 – a level twice that of the international average.

Figure 124 *Ulrika Jonsson KFC.*
Source: Ogilvy & Mather.

Wendy Tanner's interview with Alun Howell, Copywriter at Ogilvy & Mather, gives some of the inside story on the development of the campaign and how public relations played a significant part in the success.

Wendy: How did the KFC Campaign originate?

Alun: In this case it was unusual because the client specifically requested British female celebrities to be included in an international campaign that was already going into production. The campaign was based around 'craving', featuring Ryan Stiles who was only really known by people who watched 'Whose Line is it Anyway?'

The client wanted what they called 'water cooler advertising', something that people would talk about, so they said they needed celebrities.

KFC already worked with Freuds (a leading UK public relations agency) so we worked with them to come up with and secure the celebrities. They suggested the ones they knew would get the most PR. They've got real power with the media so we got loads of free media coverage which made people talk about it.

So we rewrote the first set of ads to include the celebrities, which was not easy. The first one had Dani Behr and she was only in it for about two seconds – but they still got enormous press in the tabloids.

For the subsequent ads we were able to tailor the ideas to the celebrities so for the 'Tower Burger' spot we came up with Ivana Trump mistakenly thinking she was getting a tower like the Trump Tower rather than a Tower Burger.

The spot with Ulrika in the sauna was made up on the shoot after the original idea was snowed off.

At one point Ulrika tweaked Ryan's nipple, which the client was a bit worried about. We reassured them we would never use the shot but of course in the end we did and *The Sun* printed a photo of them with 'Ultweeka' as their front-page headline! It's definitely true in British tabloids: the sexier the ad the more coverage.

The spot with Tara Palmer-Tomkinson and Tamara Beckwith was quite an amazing shoot as three film crews turned up just to document the occasion and numerous paparazzi. They looked quite hilarious wearing the KFC uniforms. Tara was having a laugh about it but Tamara didn't like wearing it at all. We were filming at Shepperton and Sean Connery and Ralph Fiennes were there. Tara and Tamara were trying to act like stars but they were wearing their KFC uniforms!

In the final ad, KFC didn't want a celebrity but wanted the Colonel's Face to feature heavily. So we decided to use the KFC bucket in front of the face of a mystery celebrity, with the music 'Who's That Lady'. There was no celebrity this time but ironically it probably got the most publicity. Certain papers ran betting odds as to who it was, thinking we would reveal it at the end but it was just an unknown model. So by then we didn't need a celebrity, the ad still generated publicity.

In fact there was an article in a Sunday supplement about the fact that loads of posh people had been in ads and they rang me up and asked me who it was in the ad and I said 'I can't tell you but she's definitely posh' and they printed a story about it!

Wendy: Could it have worked without the celebrities?

Alun: It could have worked and had already researched positively but it might not have done so well because people simply wouldn't have been aware of it or talked about it as much.

Wendy: What do you think celebrities bring to an ad campaign in general?

Alun: Awareness first and foremost. If it normally costs £70,000 to buy a full page in a paper you get a lot of free publicity for your money. I think the other thing they bring is acceptance – if they use it why shouldn't I? In the best examples there's a positive association with the values of the brand and the character of the personality.

Wendy: A few creative directors I've spoken to say that people are usually reluctant to use a celebrity because it's seen as a copout. Do you agree with that?

Alun: People do think that the industry is snobby about celebrities. When we used Tara Palmer-Tomkinson and Tara a tabloid ran it as their 'Turkey of the Week' before we had even shot it or they had seen the script.

I think it is seen as a copout, which it is, unless you do it well and the celebrity is right for the spot.

I think it's more acceptable now and also celebrities used to think they'd lose credibility from being in ads but I don't think they think that so much now.

Wendy: Why did you stop the campaign?

Alun: The client changed and the new client wanted to introduce an international campaign featuring an animated Colonel Sanders that had been successful in Australia.

The public imagines a world in which celebrities live together. And of course they're right: stars feel more comfortable with others stars, and not just for mutually reinforcing ego-bound reasons. They're in the same goldfish bowl and have lots in common even if it's just insecurity, paranoia, the same agents, invites to the same 'openings', and parts in reality TV shows. Occasionally brands crystallize this world to their benefit by clever multi-celeb casting as KFC, Pizza Hut and indeed Walkers have done. However, the all-too-costly Christmas ad featuring a 'personality parade' usually lacks an idea and has all the impact of a country town panto.

29

Celebrity representations

This creative approach is a fascinating use of celebrities in that it employs cartoon or 3-D model versions of them as opposed to real live ones. The technique has been used effectively by Hollywood in both directions: some cartoon characters such as Superman, Batman and Spiderman have been portrayed in movies by real live actors, while some stars have been turned into animated characters such as the Cameron Diaz princess and the Eddie Murphy donkey in *Shrek*.

This does something very interesting to the personalities of the stars. Their media personas are clearly evident, but the fact that they are treated in a modern animation style seems to detach their characters from reality and make them timeless. Thus the celebrities chosen for the UK Dairy Council's 'The White Stuff' campaign, many of whom are in late middle age, are re-presented to the audience as if they were perennial Peter Pans. This makes their appeal to teenagers and young kids much greater because the barrier of age is removed, while reminding their parents of much loved stars. Perhaps there is even a sense in which adults viewing celebrities who are their own age, but who appear more contemporary, is flattering to them too.

Another great executional benefit of creating cartoons out of celebrities is that they can be made to do whatever the script requires, assuming their basic agreement to the concept, and this means that the creative possibilities are infinite. It also means that the star need not be tied up in a studio or on location, which is a major benefit to them as they can be earning without turning up.

A similar approach has been taken by agency Delaney Lund Knox Warren in developing its IPA Effectiveness Award-winning campaign for Halifax. Having established Howard Brown as the star, he has now been rendered in a 'plastimation' version and thus has turned into an ageless icon, which will forever capture his personality at the peak of its appeal and then go on to build it in an entirely imaginary world built around the brand. Given the complexities of dealing with live actors and celebrities in particular, as detailed elsewhere, it will be interesting to see whether increasing numbers of famous stars reach agreements with brands to use their likenesses and personas in this way.

Certainly this creative technique has delivered great results for the Dairy Council, as set out in the case on their 'The White Stuff' campaign, authored by Andrew Perkins, Myriam Vander Elst and Sarah Donoghugh, of agency BMP DDB (now known as DDB London), which won an IPA Effectiveness Silver Award in 2002.

Summary of the Dairy Council case history

Problem

When BMP DDB and OMD UK won the Dairy Council account, milk was a product going downhill fast. It had a poor image, it was a victim of changing demographic and social trends and it was being squeezed out by increasingly competitive and sophisticated soft drinks marketing.

The total consumption of milk had been in almost continuous year-on-year decline since the mid-1970s.

Research showed that people's relationship with the drink had soured. It was so familiar that it went almost unnoticed and lacked any sort of strong personality. In other words, it was a commodity. Any personality it did have was fairly abysmal – bland, boring, babyish. Milk drinkers were seen as dull.

BMP DDB and OMD UK's objective was to turn milk from a bland commodity into a credible brand and to reverse the decline in sales.

Strategy

Advertising had to achieve four image shifts for milk:

- from dull and boring to heroic
- from old fashioned to modern
- from private to public
- from anonymous to ubiquitous.

Figure 125 *(a) Prince Naseem and Chris Eubank. (b) George Best. (c) Rolf Harris.*
Source: BMP DDB.

The ads showed milk-fortified celebrity animated characters performing acts of everyday heroism. These included Prince Naseem, Rolf Harris and George Best. They had gumption and they had backbone.

And each of the ads was signed off with a classic piece of British pluck: the theme tune to *The Great Escape*.

The ads took place in a cool, animated world that made milk feel contemporary. In this 'White Stuff World' celebrities live side by side with ordinary folk – a world where George Best pops into the local sports shop and Rolf Harris is your next-door neighbour. The advertising had broad appeal, speaking to parents, but without being 'mumsy' and alienating non-parents or children (Figure 125).

Results

In 18 months milk underwent a metamorphosis. The sales decline that had gone on for 25 years was reversed; the campaign had increased the market by 82 million litres and the campaign generated over £1.5 million worth of media coverage.

Each household in the UK had purchased an extra six and a half pints of milk in the last 18 months and twice as many consumers knew the true fat content of milk. Furthermore, recognition of the phrase 'The White

Stuff. Are you made of it?' and the campaign was at 90% among parents and the campaign had been successfully used to promote school milk bars. The campaign has also been voted 'Best Dairy Marketing Campaign in the World'.

INTERVIEW WITH TED HEATH AND PAUL ANGUS, THE CREATIVE TEAM ON 'THE WHITE STUFF'

Wendy: How did this idea for the Dairy Council originate?

Paul: It came out of the line 'The White Stuff. Are you made of it?' The idea is based around characters who show resourcefulness as a result of drinking milk and the 'Great Escape' is a theme we all know and love.

Wendy: Why did you choose Rolf Harris, George Best, Chris Eubank and Prince Naseem?

Ted: The characters were picked as a result of the scenarios on the script and just seemed to fit in well with the action. They also had wide appeal and were well known to young and old.

Wendy: Did you have anyone else in mind?

Ted: Actually any popular celebs were considered. From Michael Flatley to Oprah, Eric Cantona and even the Red Hot Chilli Peppers.

Wendy: Were the celebrities happy to be used in the campaign?

Paul: On the whole, they were fine about it, although Prince Naseem wasn't too keen on appearing 'wimpy'!

Wendy: Why do you think the campaign has been so successful?

Paul: Because the cartoon format appeals to both parents and children alike and operates on two levels with different things in it for kids and adults. Also the fact that the scripts were so irreverent added to the appeal.

Wendy: Is it down to the celebrities you used?

Ted: In part, especially as we all like to see a celeb that doesn't mind being set up. It makes it more fun and them more human.

Wendy: Do you think that the campaign could have worked or would have been as effective if played by unknowns?

Paul: No famous people were used because of the way people like to see them in cartoon form as in 'The Simpsons' or when animation movies use famous stars as the basis of the characters or even their voices. There's a fascination in seeing different versions of a famous star – it's another way of looking at them.

Wendy: What were the pros and cons of using representations of celebrities as opposed to live celebrities?

Ted: The pros were that you can accentuate their character traits and physical shape. Also they can be made to perform any act, so you've got a lot more creative flexibility. And they behave!

The cons were that sometimes voiceover artists sound more like them than they do!

Where Hollywood leads, so often Adland follows. The idea of reinterpreting a live action character as a cartoon, or vice-versa, adds another dimension to a famous person. The medium of animation, whether in cartoon or modelling, seems to be intrinsically childish, and locks an image in youth but can still allow adult characteristics to come through. This is the charm of Tony Blair guesting in The Simpsons, and many people enjoy this two-level communication. If a brand does this in its advertising, it produces a clever new take on the star's persona, which works especially well for dual target audiences of adults and kids.

PART VII

The Future of Celebrity

30

Ten predictions on future trends

I hope I've established that one of the fastest and most effective ways of giving a brand lift-off is to harness the power of an established star. Celebrity does sell in so many ways.

But what of the future trends in celebrity and in the use of famous personalities? I have the following ten predictions:

1 There will be more of it.
2 Charismatic stars of minority sports or leisure pursuits will be brought to the fore and into the mainstream.
3 There will be more cross-over between cultures and continents with stars from one geography or nationality being used in another.
4 Celebrities will continue their key role in leading social behaviour and pushing back the boundaries of acceptability.
5 There will be increased use of celebrities in the more personal product fields.
6 There will more campaigns in which the 'confessional' potential of celebrities will be used.
7 Fears over invasion of privacy and the threat of stalkers will lead to stars becoming more litigious and security conscious.
8 There will be more involvement of celebrities in 'higher order' issues of a political, charitable or spiritual nature.
9 The blurring of the lines between 'real' and 'ersatz' celebrities will continue as people play the fame game in ever more sophisticated ways.
10 New technologies that increase interactivity will enable fans to get even closer to their idols and star images will populate these new media platforms.

The public's fascination with famous people will continue unabated because of its role in society as entertainment and R&D. Thus there will be an increased use of celebrities in advertising. Further, the return on investment will be more clearly understood as agents and advertisers and their agencies become more professional in the use of the technique and in evaluating campaigns. As celebrities get more comfortable with the idea of an involvement with brands, their agents will see it as a standard income stream and move from a passive to a more proactive approach to securing deals. The era of permission marketing will force brands to ensure they are wanted ones and an association with a desired celebrity will create the necessary customer 'pull'.

For some time now sector celebrities have 'crossed over' and promoted brands in markets beyond their own. This will happen more in future as the voracious media appetite for stars discovers them in ever smaller niches and then globalizes them. Whether it be archery or astrophysics nearly every activity seems to generate competition among its participants. Thus outstanding practitioners rise to the top of the heap, become conspicuous to their peer group and are the sector's celebrities. Their expertise and talent in their chosen field gives them heritage and credentials, which, if combined with media friendliness, can enable them to work for brands far away from their starting point. In the future might we not succumb to a photogenic champion fisherman?

As the media globalizes and the 'village' becomes smaller, the potential for a celebrity to cross borders increases. This has happened for years via movies and music, much of it generated in the USA, but as the Indian and Chinese behemoths accelerate in economic terms we can expect cultural traffic to start coming the other way. This offers brands interesting opportunities to find new slants on their market where people of foreign origin are now living. For example, in the USA, the Hispanic community is going into numerical majority in many key states and this means roles for major stars from Spain or Spanish-speaking South American countries. The British Indian population is also very large and 'Bollywood' is already big in the UK, with the links and salience of Indian stars likely to grow as access to the subcontinent via the internet increases. We're all victims of national stereotypes and in this future scenario these will become more diverse as we become acquainted with the characteristics of more nations. This offers brands the chance to use these archetypes and their values to their advantage as British Airways has done in casting Irish American P J O'Rourke in its commercials. In them he talks about the foibles of the British while he's soft selling the national airline in his charming transatlantic brogue (Figure 126).

Figure 126 *PJ O'Rourke for BA.*
Source: British Airways.
Reproduced by permission of M&C Saatchi.

Figure 127 *Newcastle Brown spoof of Opium ad.*
Source: Circus.

Stars have always led the way in social mores, most obviously in the sexual arena. An actress in the 1960s appears naked on stage for the first time in *Hair!* and we're not so shocked by nudity any more. By 2002 even megastar Nicole Kidman goes nude in *The Blue Room*, but context is increasingly important – even for a celebrity. Steven Meisel, who also shoots pictures for Dolce e Gabbana, Valentino, Prada and Escada, produced Sophie Dahl's stunning nude photo for YSL's Opium fragrance (Figure 127). But the poster campaign was too public and provoked so many complaints to the Advertising Standards Authority (ASA) that it had to be taken down. From one point of view this was a shame as Sophie Dahl has probably done more than any other person to show women of a 'plus' dress size that they too can

Figure 128 *Celeb 'Pregnant'.*
Source: Private Eye/Ligger.
© Pressdram Limited 2002. Reproduced by permission.

be beautiful and sexually attractive: this iconic photograph will have done wonders for the self-image of those who can never attain the waif-like form of the other supermodels.

Despite the ban, or perhaps because of it, the Opium ad has still been widely distributed by dozens of articles featuring the image in magazines and newspapers and in the celebrity age another brand, Newcastle Brown, can run a spoof poster and everybody gets the joke! Elton John, George Michael, Boy George and a host of others have rendered gay men mainstream. Sting and Trudie Styler have alerted us to the wonders of tantric sex, Madonna kisses Britney Spears and Christina Aguilera on TV and suddenly a lesbian fling may be a little more acceptable. Sharon Tate, Demi Moore and Nicole Appleton bare their swollen tummies and suddenly it becomes chic to expose your pregnancy rather than cover it up (Figure 128).

A host of female stars take on toy boy partners and the 'Mrs Robinson' syndrome becomes okay for every Mrs. A star's baby can have a test tube father – so can your neighbour's. The influence of celebrities on ordinary people's lives will continue to increase as they push the boundaries of acceptable behaviour and no doubt they'll lead the way back to puritanism if there's a backlash. In the meantime it's likely that stars will continue to push back the boundaries of sexual behaviour and be used for related products and services. Rafael Corrales Palmeiro, the $9,000,000 a year Texas Rangers baseball star, is one of only 19 players ever to have hit 500 or more home runs, but he may end up being as famous for endorsing Viagra. Not only that, he has released a single, 'Blue', that features vocals by Palmeiro and a cameo appearance by Kylie Minogue, who sings the chorus of 'Git it up, Git it up till you can't git it up no mo' (Figure 129).

Many of the celebrity reality TV shows such as 'The Osbournes', which quickly became the highest grossing MTV syndication property

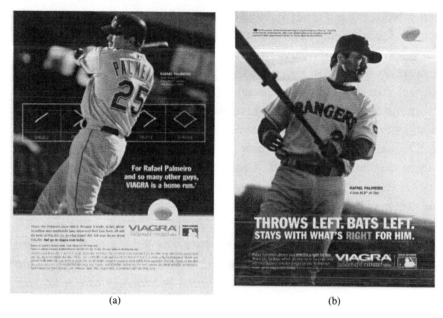

Figure 129 (a) *Rafael Corrales Palmeiro and Viagra 1*. (b) *Rafael Corrales Palmeiro and Viagra 2*. *Source: Pfizer.*

internationally, have a powerful 'confessional' dimension in which the protagonists are encouraged to talk about their feelings apparently in private but in fact in front of an audience of millions. Like the religious version these confessions bring about a sense of absolution and release and this cathartic process occurs by proxy for the viewer – they can mentally confess to the same sorts of guilt, shortcoming or weakness. When the stars do this the effect is even more powerful. Brands can also take advantage of this propensity among stars. Mercedes did this brilliantly when confronted with the disastrous instability test results on their wonderful new baby, the A-Class car. In a courageous move, another famous German brand, Boris Becker, who was also widely known to have transgressed in life, was recruited to the defence. He was able to admit that he had made mistakes, but had learned from them and put things right – a perfect parable for Mercedes, whose key A-Class model recovered quickly after reengineering work and has gone on to be a huge seller in the key home market and worldwide.

It seems that we spend a lifetime trying to self-identify and 'find ourselves'. As we have become wealthier and more prosperous in material terms, preoccupations have moved on from the basic subsistence needs of life. We've ascended Maslow's hierarchy of needs to the higher order considerations of self-esteem and self-realization. Stars can have a significant impact in these 'higher order' areas and many have used their celebrity to become powerful advocates of good causes and campaign against social injustices. Celebrities such as John Travolta or Madonna 'get' religion and this provokes people to think more about spiritual issues.

Michael Buerk's BBC documentary in October 1984 brought home the true horror of the famine in Ethiopia to people in the UK. Provoked by this, Bob Geldof created 'Band Aid', the name of the group which recorded the single 'Do They Know It's Christmas?/Feed The World'. It went on to sell over three million copies in the UK and to raise over £8 million worldwide. Eventually the 'Live Aid' concert mushroomed into 16 hours of music from around the world, featuring many of the biggest stars of the time and raised over $100 million for Ethiopian famine relief.

Diana, Princess of Wales put the landmines issue on the map, Sting has campaigned for years on deforestation and environmental damage, Bono has raised the concept of paying off the Third World debt at the highest levels of government and Coldplay's Chris Martin is now campaigning on Oxfam's behalf for 'fair trade'. Charities are fully aware that the engagement of celebrities in these causes gives them invaluable publicity and raises the profile of these issues with their fan bases. It also reveals new depths to the stars' personalities and increases their appeal, so we can expect to see many more of these charity/celebrity liaisons in future which will avoid the pitfall of superficiality by being sincere and long-term relationships (Figure 130).

Something very powerful is driving vast numbers of people in Westernized democracies towards an increasing fascination with celebrity and celebrities. Some even become obsessed with the star of their affections and there are many anecdotes of fans who will go to enormous lengths in their adulation of their favourite star, manifested by extraordinary attendance at live performances or the amassing of hugely expensive collections of

Figure 130 *Celeb 'No Smoking Day'.*
Source: Private Eye/Ligger.
Pressdram Limited 2002. Reproduced by permission.

associated memorabilia. The natural extension of actually seeing a celebrity and perhaps shaking their hand or even talking with them briefly is the desire we have for souvenirs. In the same way as the early Christians kept relics as the Turin Shroud which still evoke powerful feelings today, we seek contemporary relics from our own stars. There are millions of autograph hunters, wearers of T-shirts and collectors of celebrity memorabilia. All these items have been touched by stars and therefore acquire a kind of luminosity and value for their owner. Andy Warhol observed that one of the unifying things between stars and real people is that they consume the same Coca-Cola and yet a bottle of Coke that was known to have been drunk by Marilyn Monroe would definitely have a far greater value than one drunk by the girl next door. In making this observation Warhol was illustrating the difference between stardom and everyday life: after all he made the most prosaic of packaged goods, Campbell soup and household cleaners, into stars in the art world. The value of these star artefacts will continue to rise, especially as the current generation passes on, increasing their scarcity value. Meanwhile, the threat of the stalker is likely to increase, thus driving stars to insulate themselves even more from the real world with large entourages and security people.

Over and over again in the reporting of celebrities and their lifestyles we read that stars make a very strong distinction between their public and private lives. Indeed much of the tension in the relationship between these famous people and the media on which they feed, and which feed on them, arises from the desire of the stars to preserve significant parts of their lives into which journalists and photographers may not intrude. To what degree do people who put themselves in the public domain for personal gain have the right to retain any significant degree of privacy? It's clear that in concept celebrities do have both private and public lives, but where does real life end and media life begin? This debate is likely to intensify and stars will get more litigious in protecting themselves.

As the cost of using top stars continues to be high, it's likely that more brands will develop their own brand properties and make them into celebrities. An example of this is 'Michael Power' who, through starring in Guinness commercials in Africa, not only became one of the most famous of *all* personalities in the continent but also transformed the fortunes of the Guinness brand there. As a result of the campaign by Saatchi & Saatchi, Africa has gone from being the third largest region in the world for Guinness to number one. Michael Power has now gone on to star in his own feature film *Critical Assignment*, with crowds of fans mobbing him at the premiere. This line between 'true' celebrity and a 'manufactured' one will become progressively more blurred.

Figure 131 *Alison Jackson Beckham.*
Source: Alison Jackson.

As is so often the case, artists have the gift for showing us new ways of seeing and considering knotty questions such as these. The art of Alison Jackson is doing this for us in the realm of celebrity. Her work does what people do – it plays with the concept and explores new aspects of this perceptual game. Her art events in which look-alikes are planted in a public place and instantly cause a feeding frenzy are very revealing: even when the public realizes that the setup is a hoax, they still want the autographs of the 'stars' (Figure 131).

Jackson has used her innovative technique to create scenes we'd like to see and visualizes them for us. This produces provocative images that have the aura of the paparazzi about them and raise fascinating questions about our own attitudes to the incident portrayed. For example, her photo of the Queen having a drink with Camilla, forces us to address our true feelings about the Prince of Wales and his mistress – do we really care or is this the end of the royal family as we know it (Figure 132)?

The advertising world feeds off the media and arts worlds in equal measure and agency Mother picked up early on Jackson's work and spotted the opportunity for their client Schweppes. One of the assets in this brand's heritage is the famous 'Secret of Sch...' campaign featuring William Franklin and so there was an excellent fit with the mystery scenarios portrayed in Jackson's pictures. The collaboration between artist and agency produced some intriguing advertising that was the most awarded in the UK industry in 2002 (Figure 133).

As the technology advances it's inevitable that artists, the media and creative people in agencies will be able to play with the inter-relationship

Figure 132 *Alison Jackson Queen–Camilla.*
Source: Alison Jackson.

Figure 133 *Alison Jackson Sven.*
Source: Alison Jackson.

between celebrity image and reality and engage customers in the process. The internet and advanced software have enormous untapped potential in this area and as the bandwidth increases, stars, or their doppelgängers, will be able to interact with their fans in ever more exciting and intimate ways.

As always, these new developments will bring opportunities for commercial communications and celebrity in all its forms – real or manufactured, genuine or everyday, live or animated – will continue to offer customer benefits as they act as 'entertainers' adding lustre to life, 'educators' bringing new ideas, 'editors' helping us choose, 'endorsers' giving us confidence and of course 'enhancers' in our usage of brands.

Webography

Advertising regulations

ASA (Advertising Standards Authority)
http://www.asa.org.uk
BBC codes
www.bbc.co.uk/info/policies/producer_guides/text/section5.shtml)
Programme sponsorship and TV codes
www.itc.org.uk

Artists' agents

Agents Association of Great Britain
http://www.agents-uk.com/main.asp
Association of Talent Agents Actors Agent Search
http://www.agentassociation.com/frontdoor/actors_agent_search.cfm
Association of Talent Agents Members List
http://www.agentassociation.com/frontdoor/membership_directory.cfm

Market research companies

AC Nielsen
www.acnielson.com
HPI
www.hpiresearch.com
Millward Brown
www.millwardbrown.com
mruk Research
www.mruk.co.uk

NTC Research
www.ntc-research.com
TGI
http://www.bmrb-tgi.co.uk/gateway.asp

Publishers

Brand Republic
http://www.brandrepublic.com
Butterworth-Heinemann
www.bh.com
John Wiley & Sons
www.wiley.com
Mad
http://www.mad.co.uk
WARC.com
http://www.warc.com/

Sources

Adforum
http://www.adforum.com
American Society of Plastic Surgery
http://www.plasticsurgery.org/
Babies' names
http://www.statistics.gov.uk
'Blue Plaques'
http://www.english-heritage.org.uk
BMW films
http://intl.bmwfilms.com
Brand names in music
www.americanbrandstand.com
Celebdaq
http://www.bbc.co.uk/celebdaq/
Celebrities who appear in Japanese commercials
http://www.japander.com
English Heritage
http://www.English-heritage.org.uk
Entertainment Resources & Marketing Association (ERMA) – Product Placement
www.erma.org
Elvisly Yours
www.elvisly-yours.com
Forbes Celebrity 100
www.forbes.com/celebrity100/
Hollywood Reporter/Star Power
http://www.hollywoodreporter.com/thr/starpower/index.jsp

International Modeling and Talent Association
http://www.imta.com/links.php
Martha Stewart
http://www.marthastewart.com/home.jhtml
Movie rankings
http://www.imdb.com
MTV Cribs
http://www.mtv.com/onair/cribs/
Propeller Communications for 'Ads That Make News' survey
http://www.propellercom.com
SG 100 Index for Autographs
http://www.frasersautographs.com/100index.html
Spotlight
www.spotlightcd.com
Sunday Times Pay List 2002
http://www.timesonline.co.uk/section/0,,4221,00.html
Update@CAP News Stories: 'Minority Report'
http://www.cap.org.uk
Word Advertising Research Centre
www.warc.com

Trade bodies

Advertising Association
www.adassoc.org.uk
Communications Agencies Federation
http://cafonline.org.uk
D&AD (British Design & Art Direction)
http://www.dandad.org
Direct Marketing Association
www.dma
IPA for the Institute of Practitioners in Advertising and an extensive links directory
www.ipa.co.uk
ISBA (Incorporated Society of British Advertisers)
http://isba.org.uk

Appendix

IPA Effectiveness Awards Databank: 'Celebrity' cases

This appendix contains the complete list and summary information on all 27 winning cases from the IPA Effectiveness Awards published in *Advertising Works* books 1980 to 2002.

Please subscribe to www.warc.com in order to download the full cases or refer to the IPA Databank at www.ipa.co.uk for the management summaries and full list of cases. Volumes 9, 10, 11 and 12 of the books themselves can be ordered from the IPA or direct from www.warc.com.

There are no standardized measures of success that apply across the spectrum of the winning cases in the IPA Effectiveness Awards. However, Roger Ingham of Data Alive Ltd has read and reclassified all the published papers as part of a project to make the IPA Databank much more accessible to users from April 2004 onwards.

In the process, he has extracted the key measures from the cases that feature celebrities and these are summarized below. As can be seen, the degree of sophistication has increased considerably since the inception of the IPA competition in 1980 as best practice has been disseminated through publication of the winning cases to the benefit of marketing.

There has been a slight increase in the percentage of winning papers about campaigns that feature celebrities up to the current level of 14%.

Year	Cases in Adworks	Featuring celebrity	%	4-year trend		
				Cases in Adworks	Featuring celebrity	%
1980	18	1	5.6			
1982	18	1	5.6			
1984	19	3	15.8			
1986	20	0	0.0	75	5	6
1988	21	1	4.8	78	5	6
1990	20	1	5.0	80	5	6
1992	21	1	4.8	82	3	3
1994	20	2	10.0	82	5	6
1996	20	4	20.0	81	8	9
1998	30	3	10.0	91	10	11
2000	33	4	12.1	103	13	12
2002	36	6	16.7	119	17	14
TOTAL	**276**	**27**	**9.4**			

Including summaries for 1/2 star winners

2002 – Advertising Works 12

Title	**Police recruitment: how thinking negatively ended the negative thinking**
Celebrities	Joan Bakewell, John Barnes, Chris Bisson, Lennox Lewis, Patsy Palmer
Author/Agency/Client	Richard Storey M&C Saatchi for the Home Office
Award gained	Four Star
Key results	• The campaign drove a 73% increase in recruits, reversing a 7-year decline in recruits • Cost per response rates 10% better value than that achieved by previous campaigns • The national campaign cost £15 m but:

Title	Police recruitment: how thinking negatively ended the negative thinking
	○ The cost of outsourcing to external recruitment consultants would have been £43 m ○ Simply paying the police more to attract more recruits would have cost the taxpayer an initial £428 m (assuming a £2000 per head increase) with ongoing costs of £260 m ○ Using the police themselves to recruit by talking up the job would, if they allocated 1% of their time to this exercise, cost £124 m in lost police resources Reducing entry standards to boost entry was not considered an option as a 10% decrease in recruits' efficiency was estimated to cost £52 m a year in police resources

Title	From bland to brand: how the Dairy Council showed it was made of 'The White Stuff'
Celebrities	George Best, Chris Eubank, Rolf Harris, Prince Naseem
Author/Agency/Client	Andrew Perkins, Myriam van der Elst, Sara Donaghugh BMP DDB for the Dairy Council
Award gained	Four Star

Title	From bland to brand: how the Dairy Council showed it was made of 'The White Stuff'
Key results	• Original target for the campaign to generate sales of 35 m litres after 12 months and 63 m litres after 18 months. Actual additional sales generated 12 m litres after 12 months and 266 m litres after 18 months • Dairies received a £9.9 m return for their £4.1 m investment while farmers received a £10.9 m return on their £4.1 m investment • Campaign created an environment where retailers were able to increase the retail price of milk and improve their own margins

Title	Walkers Crisps: staying loyal to Lineker
Celebrities	Gary Lineker
Author/Agency/Client	John McDonald, Bridget Angear AMV BBDO for Walkers Snack Foods
Award gained	Four Star
Key results	• Over the course of the campaign Walkers Crisps sales have more than doubled in a market felt to be mature • In two years, advertising responsible for selling 114 million packs • £1 invested in advertising estimated to deliver £1.70 in revenue ROI, building to £5.10 in the long term through repeat sales, an ROI 7 times higher than the category average

Title	Domino's Pizza
Celebrities	The Simpsons
Author/Agency/Client	Charlie Makin
	BLM Media for Domino's Pizza
Award gained	Four Star
Key results	• An investment of £2.4 m in sponsorship using The Simpsons generated incremental sales in excess of £12.7 m

Title	Sainsbury's: a recipe for success
Celebrities	Jamie Oliver
Author/Agency/Client	Bridget Angear, Rebecca Moody
	AMV BBDO for J Sainsbury plc
Award gained	Four Star
Key results	• The campaign running from 2000 generated £1.2 bn incremental revenue and a return in investment of £27.25 for every advertising pound spend based on media expenditure of £28 m
	• Applying a marginal profit figure of 20% the advertising generated £5.45 for every £1 spent, equating to £153 m a year or £2.9 m profit a week to the bottom line
	• Modelling indicates that each TVR employed was responsible for £69,000 in revenue − 65% more efficient than any previous Sainsbury's advertising modelled

Title	Rimmel: reclaiming the streets of London
Celebrities	Kate Moss
Author/Agency/Client	Joanna Bartholmew J Walter Thompson for Rimmel
Award gained	Bronze
Key results	• The accumulated growth at 31 March 2002 was 6.3% in Boots and 15.1% in Superdrug, with greater peaks immediately after the campaign launched • In six months the campaign had an impact on profit. In the year ending March 2002 Rimmel had a net sales increase of +21% and a profit increase of +25% • From a value position Rimmel has begun successfully to close the price gap without any loss of volume and with a small increase across the brand • Estimated using modelling that £1000 of advertising sells at least £1439 worth of product. Accounting for gross margins, Rimmel actually therefore makes at 75% £1079 for each £1000 of advertising. Therefore, on the basis of short-term returns alone, the communication has a return of more than 108%

2000 – Advertising Works 11

Title	Tesco: 'Every Little Helps'
Celebrities	Jane Horrocks, Prunella Scales
Author/Agency/Client	Ashleye Sharpe, Joanna Bamford Lowe Lintas for Tesco plc

Title	Tesco: 'Every Little Helps'
Award gained	Five Star and Grand Prix
Key results	<ul><li>Turnover more than doubled from £8 bn to £17 bn</li><li>Market share increased from 9.1% to 15.4% to become market leader</li><li>Each £1 spent on advertising generated an additional £38 of turnover and £130 m extra profit to Tesco business</li></ul>

Title	Surf's up!: how likeable advertising in the laundry category washed up dazzling results
Celebrities	Pauline Quirke, Linda Robson
Author/Agency/Client	Lowe Lintas for Lever Brothers UK
Award gained	Four Star
Key results	<ul><li>Increased share of the market by over 40%</li><li>Over 2 years the size of the brand more than doubled and returned it to profit</li><li>Advertising, conservatively, paid for itself more than two times over</li></ul>

Title	Terry's Chocolate Orange: a big bright, orange future
Celebrities	Dawn French
Author/Agency/Client	Matt Willifer, Andrew Deykin, Richard Reynolds BMP DDB for Kraft Foods UK

Title	Terry's Chocolate Orange: a big bright, orange future
Award gained	Three Star
Key results	• Econometric modelling proved that advertising created additional sales of 5.7 m chocolate bars and the equivalent of 1.6 m chocolate orange 'balls' • Significant effects beyond sales in respect of distribution – reversing a steady decline and potential de-listing • In the short–medium term the brand recouped 61% of spend before increased distribution and the lack of de-listing are taken into consideration

Title	Chicken Tonight Sizzle & Stir: the golden turkey
Celebrities	Ian Wright
Author/Agency/Client	Eleni Papadakis J Walter Thompson for Van den Bergh Foods
Award gained	Two Star
Key results	• Produced a £20 m brand in less than 2 years • Growth at a significantly higher level than another brand owner (Van den Burgh) launch • Brand leader in the ethnic sauce market and the lead variant of the UK's biggest selling curry sauce

1998 – *Advertising Works* 10

Title	Pizza Hut: turning around the way you look at Pizza Hut
Celebrities	Caprice, Martin Clunes, Jonah Lomu, Caroline Quentin, Jonathan Ross
Author/Agency/Client	Jeremy Poole AMV BBDO for Pizza Hut UK Ltd
Award gained	Three Star
Key results	• Advertising created an upturn in brand saliency and achieved the communication objectives of increased frequency of restaurant visits and a decline in the number of lapsed users • Econometric modelling calculated a 3:1 payback on advertising investment • Incremental revenue of £54.9 m from a total investment in advertising, including media and production of £17.8 m • Increase in average revenue per restaurant of over 21%

Title	One2Many: how advertising affected a brand's stakeholders
Celebrities	John McCarthy, Kate Moss, Ian Wright
Author/Agency/Client	Nick Barham Bartle Bogle Hegarty for One2One
Award gained	Four Star and ISBA Prize for Best New Entrant

Title	One2Many: how advertising affected a brand's stakeholders
Key results	• Total payback of £199.3 m generated from a total advertising investment of £36.7 m • Increased credibility of the brand as a contender in the mobile telecoms sector and a fundamental change in the attitudes of the City enabling £1.6 bn to be raised to fund future investment

Title	First Direct: advertising as a communications magnifier
Celebrities	Bob Mortimer, Vic Reeves
Author/Agency/Client	George Bryant, Bryan Birkhead WCRS for First Direct
Award gained	Five Star
Key results	• Re-launch increased dramatically consumer understanding of First Direct. The number of people aware that the brand was a bank more than doubled over a 2-year period • The bank obtained a 25% share of customers switching banks from a base share of 2% of accounts • Estimated payback of £223 m from an original investment of £8 m

1996 – *Advertising Works 9*

Title	BT: 'It's Good to Talk'
Celebrities	Bob Hoskins
Author/Agency/Client	Max Burt
	AMV BBDO for British Telecom
Award gained	Gold
Key results	• Estimated payback in the domestic market of 6:1 in the short–medium term – likely to be considerably higher as international business generated is excluded from the figures
	• 1.75% sales uplift for every 100 TVRs employed
	• High level of awareness for the campaign. The brand remained No.1 of *Marketing*'s Adwatch Survey for 22 out of 30 weeks

Title	Reebok: using advertising to improve Reebok's performance in the football market – or from relegation zone to championship contention
Celebrities	Ryan Giggs
Author/Agency/Client	Jon Howard
	Lowe Howard Spink for Reebok
Award gained	Bronze
Key results	• Rate of sale doubled year on year
	• Volume increased by 282% in a market where competitors grew by 73%

Title	Reebok: using advertising to improve Reebok's performance in the football market – or from relegation zone to championship contention
	• Market share increased from 5% to 10% and rank position from 7th to 4th • Increase of incremental profit of between £2.2 m and £2.8 m from an additional investment of £2 m

Title	Barclaycard: 'Put it Away, Bough!'
Celebrities	Rowan Atkinson
Author/Agency/Client	Paul Feldwick, Sarah Carter, Louise Cook BMP DDB for Barclaycard
Award gained	Gold
Key results	• £40 m of advertising from 1991 to 1995 stimulated an additional 3% of turnover per card per year. More than sufficient to pay for the cost of the advertising • Barclaycard Visa's share of new card issued increased from 15% to 25%, with advertising partly but not solely responsible for this • Share of cards held by consumers stable in an increasingly competitive market

Title	Walkers Crisps – Garymania!: how an already successful brand benefited from famous advertising
Celebrities	Gary Lineker
Author/Agency/Client	Gavin MacDonald, Jeff Lush

Title	Walkers Crisps – Garymania!: how an already successful brand benefited from famous advertising
	BMP DDB for Walkers Snack Foods
Award gained	Silver
Key results	• Econometric modelling indicated that the advertising contributed to the sale of an additional 2.76 million packs over the advertised period equivalent to 20% of total sale with a profit margin in excess of 2p a pack • Growth of volume of 44% in the grocery sector between September 1994 and February 1996 • Average rate of sale 23% higher in the first 12 months of the campaign compared with that seen in the previous year

1994 – Advertising Works 8

Title	Cadbury's Boost: why work and rest when you can play?
Celebrities	Bob Mortimer, Vic Reeves
Author/Agency/Client	Derek Robson Bartle Bogle Hegarty for Cadbury
Award gained	Silver
Key results	• Uplift in sales of 55% over the 3-year period of the advertising with advertising more than paying for itself over this period

Title	Cadbury's Boost: why work and rest when you can play?
	• Significant penetration and frequency of purchase among the core audience of 16–24-year-old adults changing the demographic profile of the brand in line with the strategy adopted for the campaign

Title	John Smith's – 'A Widget We Have Got': how advertising helped John Smith's Bitter break into an established market
Celebrities	Jack Dee
Author/Agency/Client	Dean Webb, Richard Butterworth BMP DDB Needham for Courage Limited
Award gained	Bronze
Key results	• Off-trade sales increase of 42% year on year over the 1993 Christmas period • Rate of sale and volume share growth significantly outperformed that of other draught bitter-in-a-can launches

1992 – Advertising Works 7

Title	Alliance & Leicester Building Society: advertising effectiveness, 1987–1991
Celebrities	Stephen Fry, Hugh Laurie
Author/Agency/Client	Will Collin BMP DDB Needham for Alliance and Leicester

Title	Alliance & Leicester Building Society: advertising effectiveness, 1987–1991
Award gained	Second
Key results	• In the short term, advertising generated an additional £656 m in net receipts and £554 m in the longer term from an advertising investment of £22 m • The £1.2 bn loaned to home buyers estimated to produce an additional £93 m of gross profit

1990 – Advertising Works 6

Title	Alliance & Leicester: first-time buyer mortgages
Celebrities	Stephen Fry, Hugh Laurie
Author/Agency/Client	Anthony Buck BMP DDB Needham for Alliance & Leicester
Award gained	First Prize
Key results	• Additional first year profit of between £3.2 m and £8.8 m and of between £4.3 m and £28.2 m over a 5-year period (with the mid-points the best estimates of the advertising effect based on an investment in advertising of £3 m)

1988 – Advertising Works 5

Title	Alliance & Leicester Building Society
Celebrities	Stephen Fry, Hugh Laurie
Author/Agency/Client	Yvonne McClean BMP Davidson Pearce for Alliance & Leicester
Award gained	Second Prize
Key results	• During the advertised period the campaign contributed 28% of Alliance & Leicester's net receipts with the campaign almost paying for itself over this period with the prospect of generating additional profits over the following 2 years • Over the two bursts of the campaign the £2.6 m advertising budget generated an extra £2.18 m gross margin

1986 – Advertising Works 4

No cases identified

1984 – Advertising Works 3

Title	Paul Masson California carafes: 'They're Really Good'
Celebrities	Ian Carmichael
Author/Agency/Client	Leslie Butterfield Abbot Mead Vickers/SMS for Seagram

Title	**Paul Masson California carafes: 'They're Really Good'**
Award gained	Certificate of Commendation
Key results	• Advertising to sales ratio of 9.7% cost effective when compared to that for competitive brand • In the year to March 1984 £614 k advertising expenditure generated £6.34 m in sales • Over the life of the brand between 1980 and 1984 sales were achieved with an advertising support of 7–8p a bottle, less than 21/2% of retail value

Title	**Breaking the bran barrier: Kellogg's Bran Flakes**
Celebrities	Gordon Kaye
Author/Agency/Client	Jeremy Elliot J Walter Thompson for The Kellogg Company
Award gained	First Prize
Key results	• Increase in sales of 73% over the advertised period versus competitive growth of 35% worth an additional £3 m in incremental sales revenue

Title	**Repositioning Hellmann's Mayonnaise**
Celebrities	Bob Carolgees
Author/Agency/Client	Paul Feldwick

Title	Repositioning Hellmann's Mayonnaise
	The Boase Massimi Pollitt Partnership for CPC (UK)
Award gained	Second Prize
Key results	• The campaign produced accelerated increases in volume of 33% in 1982 and a further 30% in 1983 against 22% in 1980 and 18% in 1981 • Research showed a broadening of uses for the product in line with the overall strategy for the campaign

1984 – Advertising Works 2

Title	Advertising: key to the success of Kellogg's Super Noodles
Celebrities	The Flintstones
Author/Agency/Client	Peter Croome, Jocelyn Horsfall Leo Burnett for the Kellogg Company
Award gained	First Prize
Key results	• Achieved the 3-year target of £3 m turnover set for the brand by the end of year 2 • Ex-factory sales in year 2 significantly ahead of those forecast (index of 141 against a forecast of 126) • Sales gain of 26% over the period of the advertising campaign

1980 – *Advertising Works*

Title	**Whitegates: a regional success story**
Celebrities	Raymond Baxter
Author/Agency/Client	David Blythe
	Bowden Dyble & Hayes for Whitegates Estate Agency
Award gained	Second Prize
Key results	• Within the first year of trading Whitegates quadrupled the number of branches that it had from 2 to 8
	• By the end of 2 years of advertising Whitegates was the biggest estate agent in Yorkshire

Index

About the Author

Hamish Pringle graduated from Trinity College, Oxford with a degree in PPE in 1973 and joined Ogilvy & Mather as a trainee. There followed spells at McCormick Richards, BMP, Publicis, AMV, his own agency Madell Wilmot Pringle, and Leagas Delaney. In 1992 he joined KHBB and became Chairman & CEO in 1995. Following the merger in 1997, he became Vice-Chairman, and Director of Marketing of Saatchi & Saatchi. In 1999 he founded his brand and marketing consultancy, Brand Beliefs Limited, and worked with clients such as The Virtual Office, TriSystems, Mirror Group Newspapers, The Lord's Taverners, Music3w.com, DLA and the IPA.

In August 2001 Hamish became Director General of the IPA, the trade body and professional institute representing advertising, media and marketing communications agencies (www.ipa.co.uk). He represents the IPA on a number of UK industry bodies including the Advertising Association (AA), the Audit Bureau of Circulations (ABC), the Advertising Standards Board of Finance (ASBOF), the Broadcasters Audience Research Board (BARD), Radio Joint Audience Research (RAJAR), and the Communications Agencies Federation (CAF). He is also a Director of the European Association of Communication Agencies (EACA) and Vice-Chairman of its National Associations Council.

Hamish is a member of the Marketing Society, the Marketing Group of Great Britain, D&AD, the Solus Club and Soho House. He became a Fellow of the IPA in 1992, won a D&AD Silver Art Direction Award for Pentax in 1996 and received the NABS' (National Advertising Benevolent Society) Ron Miller Award for services to the charity in 1999.

Hamish has co-authored two best-selling business books, both published by John Wiley & Sons, Ltd:

Brand Spirit: *how cause related marketing builds brands*, with Marjorie Thompson
Brand Manners: *how to create the self-confident organisation to live the brand*, with William Gordon.

For further information about *Celebrity Sells* and other Wiley publications please visit www.wiley.co.uk.

www.celebritysells.co.uk